ESSENTIALS OF POLITICAL IDEAS

Essentials of Political Ideas

For A-Level

Andrew Heywood

 macmillan education palgrave

First published 2018 by
PALGRAVE

Palgrave in the UK is an imprint of Macmillan Publishers Limited, registered in England, company number 785998, of 4 Crinan Street, London, N1 9XW.

Palgrave® and Macmillan® are registered trademarks in the United States, the United Kingdom, Europe and other countries.

ISBN 978–1–137–61167–3 paperback

This book is printed on paper suitable for recycling and made from fully managed and sustained forest sources. Logging, pulping and manufacturing processes are expected to conform to the environmental regulations of the country of origin.

A catalogue record for this book is available from the British Library.

A catalog record for this book is available from the Library of Congress.

Printed and bound in Great Britain by Bell and Bain Ltd, Glasgow

For Jean, Mark, Rob, Helen, Jessie, Oliver,
Freya, Dominic and Toby

Brief Contents

Contents

Contents

List of Illustrative Material

KEY CONCEPTS

KEY FIGURES

PERSPECTIVES ON ...

DIFFERENCES BETWEEN ...

FIGURES

Using this Book

This book is a companion volume to *Essentials of UK Politics*, 4th edition. Together they cover two of the three parts of the new AQA and Edexcel A-Level Politics specifications (for examination from 2019 onwards) – 'Government and politics in the UK' and 'Political ideas'. Where helpful, references are made in the current volume to extension material that can be found in *Essentials of UK Politics*.

In line with the specifications, the book is organised on the basis of the major political ideologies. Part 1 considers the political ideas that have emerged in connection with the 'traditional' or 'core' political ideologies – liberalism, conservatism and socialism (Chapters 2–4). These are the ideologies that have dominated political theory and political practice since the late eighteenth century, each representing a distinctive attempt to shape or reshape industrial society. Part 2 examines the political ideas that have emerged in connection with a range of other ideological traditions – anarchism, nationalism, feminism, ecologism and multiculturalism (Chapters 5–9). These other traditions have extended ideological thinking either by using liberal, conservative or socialist ideas to explore new or more specific areas of political debate (national identity, gender relations, cultural diversity and so on), or by challenging and seeking to go 'beyond' liberalism, conservatism and socialism.

Chapter 1 offers an introduction to the role of political ideas and the nature of political ideologies, but the material in this chapter will not form part of any assessment. Chapters 2–9 have a common three-part structure:

1. A 'Historical overview' reflects on the origins and development of the ideology in question.

2. The 'Core ideas and principles' of the ideology are then discussed. In Part 1, this is done through an examination of the ideology's distinctive approach to 'Human nature', 'Society', 'The state' and 'The economy'. This reflects the fact that traditional ideologies are comprehensive in scope and address all major aspects of human existence. However, in view of the narrower focus of the other ideological traditions, in Part 2 this section is organised around concepts and beliefs that are specific to the ideology in question (although reference is made to human nature, society, the state and the economy, as relevant).

3. The remainder of the chapter explores differing views and tensions within the ideology in question, recognising that disagreements between supporters of the same ideology are sometimes more passionate than disagreements between supporters of rival ideologies. This is done by an analysis of the ideology's major types or sub-traditions.

FEATURES OF THE BOOK

'Preview'. Provides a summary of the broad themes and key issues to be considered in each chapter. ──

On-page definitions. These provide single-sentence definitions of key terms at appropriate points in each chapter. (You can search for defined terms by looking for bold entries in the index. They also appear on the website; see Online support.) ──

2 Liberalism

PREVIEW

The term 'liberal' has been in use since the fourteenth century but has had a wide variety of meanings. The Latin *liber* referred to a class of free men; in other words, men who were neither serfs nor slaves. It has meant generous, as in 'liberal' helpings of food and drink; or, in reference to social attitudes, it has implied openness or open-mindedness. It also came to be associated increasingly with the ideas of freedom and choice. The term 'liberalism', to denote a political allegiance, made its appearance much later: it was not used until the early part of the nineteenth century, being first employed in Spain in 1812. By the 1840s, the term was widely recognised throughout Europe as a reference to a distinctive set of political ideas. However, it was taken up more slowly in the UK: though the Whigs started to call themselves Liberals during the 1830s, the first distinctly Liberal government was not formed until Gladstone took office in 1868.

The central theme of liberal ideology is a commitment to the individual and the desire to construct a society in which people can satisfy their interests and achieve fulfilment. Liberals believe that human beings are, first and foremost, individuals, endowed with reason. This implies that each individual should enjoy the maximum possible freedom consistent with a like freedom for all. However, although individuals are entitled to equal legal and political rights, they should be rewarded in line with their talents and their willingness to work. Liberal societies are organised politically around the twin principles of constitutionalism and consent, designed to protect citizens from the danger of government tyranny. Nevertheless, there are significant differences between classical liberalism and modern liberalism. Classical liberalism is characterised by a belief in a 'minimal' state, whose function is limited to the maintenance of domestic order and personal security. Modern liberalism, in contrast, accepts that the state should help people to help themselves.

---

moral worth, an idea sometimes referred to as 'foundational equality'. Such thinking not only provided inspiration for the writing of documents such as the US Declaration of Independence (1776), the French Declaration of the Rights of Man and the Citizen (1789) and, more recently, the UN's Universal Declaration of Human Rights, but it has also meant that liberalism has provided fertile ground for the growth of feminist thinking. Liberal feminism (discussed in greater detail in Chapter 7) has been articulated by thinkers ranging from Mary Wollstonecraft (see below) to Betty Friedan (see p. 14).

A further component of the liberal view of **human nature** is the belief that humans are reason-guided creatures, capable of personal self-development and of bringing about wider social and political development. In this sense, liberalism is, and remains, very much part of the **Enlightenment** project. The central theme of the Enlightenment was the desire to release humankind from its bondage to superstition and ignorance, and unleash an 'age of reason'. Enlightenment rationalism (see below) has influenced liberalism in a number of ways. For example, it strengthened its faith in both the individual and **freedom**. To the extent that human beings are rational, thinking creatures, they are capable of

Human nature: The essential and innate character of all human beings; what the individual owes to nature rather than to society.

Enlightenment: An intellectual movement that reached its height in the eighteenth century which challenged traditional beliefs in religion, politics and learning in general in the name of reason and progress.

Freedom (or liberty): The ability to think and act as one wishes, a capacity that can be associated with the individual, a social group or a nation.

KEY FIGURE

Mary Wollstonecraft (1759–97)

 A British philosopher and novelist, Wollstonecraft developed the first systematic feminist critique some 50 years before the emergence of the female suffrage movement. Her *A Vindication of the Rights of Men* (1790) was a response to Burke's (see p. 40) views on the French Revolution. Wollstonecraft's most famous work, *A Vindication of the Rights of Women* (1792), advanced an agenda for women's emancipation based on the assertion that, as human beings, women are rational creatures. As such, they are entitled to the same rights of liberty and self-determination as male rational creatures claim for themselves. Wollstonecraft placed a particular emphasis on the capacity of education to develop women's talents and character. Wollstonecraft's writings are widely seen to have established the basis for the tradition of liberal feminism, characterised as it is by a commitment to formal equality; that is, an equal distribution of both legal and political rights, and civil liberties, including the right to a career. For more on Wollstonecraft, see pp. 138 and 147.

Key concept ... RATIONALISM

Rationalism is the belief that the world has a rational structure, and that this can be disclosed through the exercise of human reason and critical enquiry. As a philosophical theory, rationalism is the belief that knowledge flows from reason rather than experience, and thus contrasts with empiricism. As a general principle, however, rationalism places a heavy emphasis on the capacity of human beings to understand and explain their world, and to find solutions to problems. While rationalism does not dictate the ends of human conduct, it certainly suggests how these ends should be pursued. It is associated with an emphasis on principle and reason-governed behaviour, as opposed to a reliance on custom or tradition, or on non-rational drives and impulses.

'Key figure' boxes. These consider the key ideas and contribution to the ideology of a range of stipulated thinkers related to each political ideology.

'Key concept' boxes. These provide fuller explanations of significant political ideas and concepts.

'Perspectives on' boxes. These highlight contrasting approaches to key political ideas and concepts, from the perspective of rival ideologies.

Modern liberals defend welfarism on the basis of equality of opportunity. If particular individuals or groups are disadvantaged by their social circumstances, then the state possesses a social responsibility to reduce or remove these disadvantages to create equal, or at least more equal, life chances. Citizens have thus acquired a range of welfare or social rights, such as the right to work, the right to education and the right to decent housing. Welfare rights are positive rights because they can only be satisfied by the positive actions of government, through the provision of state pensions, benefits and, perhaps, publicly funded health and education services. During the twentieth century, liberal parties and liberal governments were therefore converted to the cause of social welfare. For example, the expanded welfare state in the UK was based on the Beveridge Report (1942), which set out to attack the so-called 'five giants' – want, disease, ignorance, squalor and idleness. It memorably promised to protect citizens 'from the cradle to the grave'. In the USA, liberal welfarism developed in the 1930s during the administration of F. D. Roosevelt, but reached its height in the 1960s with the 'New Frontier' policies of John F. Kennedy, and Lyndon Johnson's 'Great Society' programme.

Social liberalism was further developed in the second half of the twentieth century with the emergence of so-called social-democratic liberalism, especially in the writings of John Rawls. Social-democratic liberalism is distinguished by its support for relative social equality, usually seen as the defining value of socialism. In *A Theory of Justice* (1970), Rawls developed a defence of redistribution and welfare based on the idea of 'equality as fairness'. He argued that if people were unaware of their social position and circumstances, they would view an egalitarian society as 'fairer' than an inegalitarian one, on the grounds that the desire to avoid poverty is greater than the attraction of riches. He therefore proposed the 'difference principle': that social and economic inequalities should be arranged so as to benefit the least well-off, recognising the need for some

Differences between ...
CLASSICAL AND MODERN LIBERALISM

CLASSICAL LIBERALISM	MODERN LIBERALISM
economic liberalism	social liberalism
egoistical individualism	developmental individualism
maximise utility	personal growth
negative freedom	positive freedom
minimal state	enabling state
free-market economy	managed economy
rights-based justice	justice as fairness
strict meritocracy	concern for the poor
individual responsibility	social responsibility
safety-net welfare	cradle-to-grave welfare

'Differences between' boxes. These draw attention to points of tension within an ideology by highlighting differences between the thinking of key sub-traditions.

Questions. These questions are designed to consolidate learning by provoking discussion and debate. They are accompanied by suggestions for **further reading**.

Online support. The website associated with this book provides, amongst other things, a searchable glossary of all on-page definitions. See: **www.macmillanihe.com/heywood-essentials-of-political-ideas**

Reproduced book page (2 Liberalism, p.15):

PERSPECTIVES ON ... FREEDOM

LIBERALS give priority to freedom as the supreme individualist value. While classical liberals support negative freedom, understood as the absence of constraints – or freedom of choice – modern liberals advocate positive freedom in the sense of personal development and human flourishing.

CONSERVATIVES have traditionally endorsed a weak view of freedom as the willing recognition of duties and responsibilities, negative freedom posing a threat to the fabric of society. The New Right, however, endorses negative freedom in the economic sphere, freedom of choice in the marketplace.

SOCIALISTS have generally understood freedom in positive terms to refer to self-fulfilment achieved through either free creative labour or cooperative social interaction. Social democrats have drawn close to modern liberalism in treating freedom as the realisation of individual potential.

ANARCHISTS regard freedom as an absolute value, believing it to be irreconcilable with any form of political authority. Freedom is understood to mean the achievement of personal autonomy, not merely being 'left alone' but being rationally self-willed and self-directed.

NATIONALISTS view freedom as national self-determination, the right of a nation to shape its own destiny by achieving independence from foreign control and establishing itself as a sovereign entity through constructing a nation-state.

FEMINISTS have understood freedom both in terms of women's emancipation, focusing on the acquisition of legal and political rights, and in terms of women's liberation, focusing on the overthrow of the patriarch, possibly also implying sexual fulfilment as subjects, not as objects.

ECOLOGISTS, particularly deep ecologists, treat freedom as the achievement of oneness, self-realisation through the absorption of the personal ego into the ecosphere or universe. In contrast with political freedom, this is sometimes seen as 'inner' freedom, freedom as self-actualisation.

exercised over any member of a civilised community, against his will, is to prevent harm to others'. Mill's position is libertarian in that it accepts only the most minimal restrictions on individual freedom, and then only in order to prevent 'harm to others'. This idea is sometimes described as the 'harm principle'. An alternative way in which liberals have highlighted legitimate constraints on freedom is through the notion of an equal right to liberty. This has been expressed by John Rawls (see p. 30) in the principle that everyone is entitled to the widest possible liberty consistent with a like liberty for all.

However, although liberals have agreed that individuals should enjoy the greatest possible freedom, they have not always agreed about what it means for an individual to be 'free'. In 'Two Concepts of Liberty' ([1958] 1969), Isaiah Berlin (see p. 196) distinguished between a 'negative' theory of liberty and a 'positive' one. Early or classical liberals have believed in **negative freedom**, in that freedom consists in each person being left alone, free from interference and able to act in whatever way he or she may choose. This conception of freedom is 'negative' in that it is based on the absence of external restrictions or

Negative freedom: The absence of external restrictions or constraints on the individual, allowing freedom of choice.

15

QUESTIONS FOR DISCUSSION

- Does individualism necessarily imply egoism?
- In what sense is liberalism linked to the Enlightenment project?
- How, within liberalism, is freedom linked to rationalism?
- Why do liberals reject unlimited freedom?
- How convincing is the liberal notion that human beings are reason-guided creatures?
- What are the key implications of social contract theory?
- How do classical liberals defend unregulated capitalism?
- How far are modern liberals willing to go in endorsing social and economic intervention?
- Do modern liberals have a coherent view of the state?
- Is liberal democracy the final solution to the problem of political organisation?
- To what extent is cosmopolitanism based on liberal assumptions?
- Are liberal principles universally valid?

FURTHER READING

Bellamy, R., *Liberalism and Modern Society: An Historical Argument* (1992). An analysis of the development of liberalism that focuses on the adaptations necessary to apply liberal values to new social realities.

Fawcett, E., *Liberalism: The Life of an Idea* (2015). A fluent and stimulating history of liberal thinking from the early nineteenth century to the present day.

Gray, J., *Liberalism*, 2nd edn (1995). A short and not uncritical introduction to liberalism as the political theory of modernity; contains a discussion of post-liberalism.

Kelly, P., *Liberalism* (2005). An engagingly written defence of liberalism as a normative political theory, which particularly examines its link to equality.

TRADITIONAL POLITICAL IDEAS

32

MAXIMISING PERFORMANCE

How can you ensure that your performance in Government and Politics is as good as it can be? How can you ensure exam success? Below are some helpful hints on how you can maximise your performance as you study the subject and as you prepare for the examination.

STUDYING THE SUBJECT

- **Keep up to date with current affairs.** This will both make the subject more interesting to study (politics never stands still) and give you useful ammunition to use in the examination. Your knowledge needs to be as up-to-date as possible, and examiners are particularly looking to reward contemporary knowledge and understanding. Use websites, read a 'quality' newspaper (many of which can be accessed online) and articles in journals such as *Politics Review*, and watch the news and current affairs programmes on television.

- **Understand key terms and concepts.** Much of political understanding is based on a grasp of major terms and concepts – democracy, representation, authority, freedom, justice, and so on. Make sure you have a thorough grasp of these terms, and be sure that you can define and explain them reliably in the examination itself.

- **Be aware of competing viewpoints.** Just about every issue in politics is the subject of debate and discussion. You need to show an awareness of the different sides of an argument – almost every statement you make in politics could be followed by 'However...'. But you also need to develop your own views, which means being able to support a particular viewpoint on the basis of evidence – make a point and prove it.

PREPARING FOR THE EXAMINATIONS

- **Draw up a revision plan.** Revision is seldom done effectively if it is left until 'the mood takes you'. Draw up a plan of which topics you are going to revise and when – and then stick to it!

- **Know your specification inside out.** You have an outline above of the main topics covered in each unit. But the specification itself, as well as supporting materials provided by the awarding body for students, provides you with greater detail, including the identification of key concepts and an outline of the content.

- **Be familiar with past papers, marking schemes and examiners' reports.** These are all provided by awarding bodies, and they contain invaluable information about the kinds of questions that will come up and the level of performance that will be expected.

- **Have as much exam practice as possible.** In the run-up to the examination, frequently practise answering examination questions in examination conditions and within examination timescales. If nothing else, this will ensure that your do not get your timings wrong – the silliest of all reasons for poor exam performance.

- **Pay attention to 'command words' and key terms in questions.** These are words such as 'define', 'explain', analyse', 'assess' or 'evaluate'. You need to know what each of these words means to ensure that you carry out the 'right' task in answering each question. For example:
  - *Define* – say what a word or phrase means
  - *Features* – the parts that define what a thing is
  - *Functions* – the roles that highlight what a thing does
  - *Explain* – show how something works, often by identifying causes and effects
  - *Analyse* – break something into its component parts and show how they relate to one another

- *Evaluate* – make judgements about something's value, its strengths and weaknesses
- *Assess* – 'weigh up' a statement, showing an awareness of arguments in favour and against.

- **Be aware of what you get marks for.** This is spelled out in the three assessment objectives (AOs) that are relevant to Politics. These are:

  - AO1: Demonstrate knowledge and understanding of political institutions, processes, concepts, theories and issues.
  - AO2: Analyse aspects of politics and political information, including in relation to parallels, connections, similarities and differences.
  - AO3: Evaluate aspects of politics and political information, including construct arguments, make substantiated judgements and draw conclusions.

- **Answer the *precise* question set.** The most common reason for exam underperformance is a failure to 'target' the question set. Common mistakes include providing a pre-prepared answer to a question from a previous examination, or writing generally about the topic of the question, rather than addressing the particular question itself. To help avoid these mistakes, get in the habit of regularly using the terms from the question in your answers.

Preface

This book is an adapted version of *Political Ideologies: An Introduction*, sixth edition. It has been designed to meet the needs of students studying for the 'new' A-Level Politics, and fully covers the relevant parts of both the Edexcel and AQA specifications. In addition to ensuring that material is clearly organised and presented in line with the themes and topics that appear on the A-Level specifications, material that goes beyond the requirements of A-Level study has been removed. *Essentials of Political Ideas* thus does not include a discussion of matters such as the importance and changing nature of political ideologies, the 'end of ideology' debate ('endism'), the extent to which major political events have been shaped by either ideological or practical forces, and the impact on political ideologies of globalisation and related developments. Limited reference is also made in this book to ideological traditions that fall outside the A-Level specifications, notably fascism and Islamism.

I would like to thank all those at Palgrave who contributed to the production of this book, particularly Lloyd Langham, Chloe Osborne, Tuur Driesser and Amy Brownbridge. This book is dedicated to my wife, Jean, my sons and daughters-in-law, and my grandchildren – truly, the very best of inventions!

ANDREW HEYWOOD

Acknowledgements

The author and publishers would like to thank the following, who have kindly given permission for the use of pictorial copyright material (names in brackets indicate the subjects of photographs):

Press Association, pp. 13 (Mary Wollstonecraft), 14 (Betty Friedan), 27 (John Stuart Mill), 36 (Thomas Hobbes), 40 (Edmund Burke), 67 (Karl Marx), 102 (Pierre-Joseph Proudhon), 113 (Jean-Jacques Rousseau), 121 (Johann Gottfried Herder), 142 (Kate Millett), 151 (Simone de Beauvoir), 196 (Isaiah Berlin); Getty Images, pp. 30 (John Rawls), 54 (Robert Nozick), 72 (Friedrich Engels), 131 (Charles Maurras), 150 (Sheila Rowbotham), 154 (bell hooks), 178 (Aldo Leopold); Alamy, pp. 17 (John Locke), 52 (Ayn Rand), 68 (Beatrice Webb), 76 (Rosa Luxemburg), 84 (Anthony Crosland), 96 (Emma Goldman), 97 (Mikhail Bakunin), 104 (Peter Kropotkin), 107 (Max Stirner), 125 (Giuseppe Mazzini), 149 (Charlotte Perkins Gilman), 159 (Rachel Carson), 167 (Ernst Friedrich Schumacher), 191 (Charles Taylor); LSE Archive, p. 37 (Michael Oakeshott); LSE/Nigel Stead, p. 87 (Anthony Giddens); Library of Congress, p. 122 (Marcus Garvey); Janet Biehl, p. 175 (Murray Bookchin); Peg Scorpinski, p. 176 (Caroline Merchant); Will Kymlicka, p. 190; Tariq Modood, p. 194; Bhiku Parekh, p. 197.

Every effort has been made to contact all copyright holders, but if any have inadvertently been omitted the publishers will be pleased to make the necessary arrangement at the earliest opportunity.

1 Introducing Political Ideas

PREVIEW

All people are political thinkers. Whether they know it or not, people use political ideas and concepts whenever they express their opinion or speak their mind. Everyday language is littered with terms such as 'freedom', 'fairness', 'equality', 'justice' and 'rights'. In the same way, words such as 'conservative', 'liberal', 'socialist', 'communist' and 'fascist' are regularly employed by people to describe either their own views, or those of others. However, even though such terms are familiar, even commonplace, they are seldom used with any precision or a clear grasp of their meaning. What, for instance, is 'equality'? What does it mean to say that all people are equal? Are people born equal; should they be treated by society as if they are equal? Should people have equal rights, equal opportunities, equal political influence, equal wages? Similarly, words such as 'socialist', 'nationalist' and 'feminist' are commonly misused. What does it mean to call someone a 'nationalist'? What values or beliefs do nationalists hold, and why do they hold them? How do socialist views differ from those of, say, liberals, conservatives or anarchists?

This introductory chapter examines, first, the role of political ideas, together with rival views about the relationship in political life between, on the one hand, values, doctrines and beliefs and, on the other hand, the material world and the quest for power. Do political ideas 'make' the world in which we live, or are they merely a reflection of that world? Second, it considers the nature of the ideological traditions that have done so much to shape political thinking in general and, most specifically, to determine the meaning (and, all too frequently, the meanings) of political ideas. What are political ideologies and why do they matter? Third, it examines the significance and implications of the distinction between left-wing ideas and right-wing ideas. Do the notions of left and right sharpen political thinking, or do they simply cause confusion?

CONTENTS

- Role of political ideas
- Understanding political ideologies
- Left- and right-wing ideas

ROLE OF POLITICAL IDEAS

This book examines political ideas from the perspective of the key ideological traditions. It focuses, in particular, on the 'traditional', or 'core', ideologies (liberalism, conservatism and socialism, which are examined in Part 1), but it also considers a range of other ideological traditions, which have arisen either out of, or in opposition to, the traditional ones (anarchism, nationalism, feminism, ecologism and multiculturalism, which are examined in Part 2).

However, not all political thinkers have accepted that ideas and ideologies are of much importance. Politics has sometimes been thought to be little more than a naked struggle for power. If this is true, political ideas are mere propaganda, a form of words or collection of slogans designed to win votes or attract popular support. Ideas and ideologies are therefore simply 'window dressing', used to conceal the deeper realities of political life. The opposite argument has also been put, however. The UK economist John Maynard Keynes (1883–1946), for example, argued that the world is ruled by little other than the ideas of economic theorists and political philosophers. As he put it in the closing pages of his *General Theory*:

> Practical men, who believe themselves to be quite exempt from any intellectual influences, are usually the slaves of some defunct economist. Madmen in authority, who hear voices in the air, are distilling their frenzy from some academic scribbler of a few years back. (Keynes, [1936] 1963)

This position highlights the degree to which beliefs and theories provide the wellspring of human action. The world is ultimately ruled by 'academic scribblers'. Such a view suggests, for instance, that modern capitalism (see p. 62) developed, in important respects, out of the classical economics of Adam Smith (1723–90) and David Ricardo (1772–1823), that Soviet communism was shaped significantly by the writing of Karl Marx (see p. 67) and V. I. Lenin (1870–1924), and that the history of Nazi Germany can only be understood by reference to the doctrines advanced in Adolf Hitler's *Mein Kampf* (1925).

In reality, both of these accounts of political life are one-sided and inadequate. Political ideas are not merely a passive reflection of vested interests or personal ambition, but have the capacity to inspire and guide political action itself and so to shape material life. At the same time, political ideas do not emerge in a vacuum: they do not drop from the sky like rain. All political ideas are moulded by the social and historical circumstances in which they develop and by the political ambitions they serve. Quite simply, political thought and political practice are inseparably linked. Any balanced and persuasive account of political life must therefore acknowledge the constant interplay between ideas and ideologies on the one hand, and historical and social forces on the other.

Ideas and ideologies influence political life in a number of ways. They:

▶ structure political understanding and so set goals and inspire activism

▶ shape the nature of political systems

▶ act as a form of social cement.

In the first place, ideologies provide a perspective, or 'lens', through which the world is understood and explained. People do not see the world as it is, but only as they expect it to be: in other words, they see it through a veil of ingrained beliefs, opinions and assumptions. Whether consciously or subconsciously, everyone subscribes to a set of political beliefs and values that guide their behaviour and influence their conduct. Political ideas and ideologies thus set goals that inspire political activism. In this respect, politicians are subject to two very different influences. Without doubt, all politicians want power. This forces them to be pragmatic, to adopt those policies and ideas that are electorally popular or win favour with powerful groups, such as business or the military. However, politicians seldom seek power simply for its own sake. They also possess beliefs, values and convictions (if to different degrees) about what to do with power when it is achieved.

Second, political ideologies help to shape the nature of political systems. Systems of government vary considerably throughout the world and are always associated with particular values or principles. Absolute monarchies were based on deeply established religious ideas, notably the divine right of kings. The political systems in most contemporary western countries are founded on a set of liberal-democratic principles. Western states are typically founded on a commitment to limited and constitutional government, as well as the belief that government should be representative, in the sense that it is based on regular and competitive elections. In the same way, traditional communist political systems conformed to the principles of Marxism–Leninism. Even the fact that the world is divided into a collection of nation-states and that government power is usually located at the national level reflects the impact of political ideas, in this case of nationalism and, more specifically, the principle of national self-determination.

Finally, political ideas and ideologies can act as a form of social cement, providing social groups, and indeed whole societies, with a set of unifying beliefs and values. Political ideologies have commonly been associated with particular social classes – for example, liberalism with the middle classes, conservatism with the landed aristocracy, socialism with the working class, and so on. These ideas reflect the life experiences, interests and aspirations of a social class, and therefore help to foster a sense of belonging and solidarity. However, ideas and ideologies can also succeed in binding together divergent groups and classes within a society. For instance, there is a unifying bedrock of liberal-democratic values in most western states, while in Muslim countries Islam has established a common set of moral principles and beliefs. In providing society with a unified political culture, political ideas help to promote order and social stability. Nevertheless, a unifying set of political ideas and values can develop naturally within a society, or it can be enforced from above in an attempt to manufacture obedience and exercise control. The clearest examples of such 'official' ideologies have been found in fascist, communist and religious fundamentalist regimes.

UNDERSTANDING POLITICAL IDEOLOGIES

Ideology is one of those controversial concepts encountered in political analysis. Although the term now tends to be used in a neutral sense, to refer to a developed social philosophy or 'world-view', it has in the past had heavily negative or pejorative connotations. During its sometimes tortuous career, the concept of ideology has commonly been used as a political weapon with which to condemn or criticise rival creeds or doctrines.

The term 'ideology' was coined in 1796 by the French philosopher Destutt de Tracy (1754–1836). He used it to refer to a new science of ideas (literally, an idea-ology) that set out to uncover the origins of conscious thought and ideas. De Tracy's hope was that ideology would eventually achieve the same status as established sciences such as zoology and biology. However, a more enduring meaning was assigned the term in the nineteenth century in the writings of Karl Marx and Friedrich Engels (see p. 72). For Marx and Engels, ideology amounted to the ideas of the ruling class, ideas that therefore uphold the class system and perpetuate exploitation. In their early work, *The German Ideology*, Marx and Engels wrote the following:

> The ideas of the ruling class are in every epoch the ruling ideas, i.e. the class which is the ruling material force in society is, at the same time, the ruling intellectual force. The class which has the means of mental production at its disposal, has control at the same time over the means of production. (Marx and Engels, [1846] 1970)

The defining feature of ideology in the Marxist sense is that it is false: it mystifies and confuses subordinate classes by concealing from them the contradictions on which all class societies are based. As far as capitalism is concerned, the ideology of the property-owning bourgeoisie (bourgeois ideology) fosters delusion or 'false consciousness' among the exploited proletariat, preventing them from recognising the fact of their own exploitation. Nevertheless, Marx and Engels did not believe all political views had an ideological character. They held that their work, which attempted to uncover the process of exploitation and oppression, was scientific. In this view, a clear distinction could be drawn between science and ideology, between truth and falsehood. This distinction

Key concept ... **IDEOLOGY**

From a social-scientific viewpoint, an ideology is a more or less coherent set of ideas that provides a basis for organised political action, whether this is intended to preserve, modify or overthrow the existing system of power relationships. All ideologies therefore (1) offer an account of the existing order, usually in the form of a 'world-view', (2) provide a model of a desired future, a vision of the 'good life', and (3) outline how political change can and should be brought about. Ideologies are not, however, hermetically sealed systems of thought; rather, they are fluid sets of ideas that overlap with one another at a number of points.

tended, however, to be blurred in the writings of later Marxists such as the Bolshevik leader V. I. Lenin (1870–1924) and the Italian revolutionary and political theorist Antonio Gramsci (1891–1937). These referred not only to 'bourgeois ideology', but also to 'socialist ideology' or 'proletarian ideology', terms that Marx and Engels would have considered absurd.

Alternative uses of the term have been developed by liberals and conservatives. The emergence of totalitarian dictatorships in the inter-war period encouraged writers such as Karl Popper (1902–94), J. L. Talmon (1916–80) and Hannah Arendt (1906–75) to view ideology as an instrument of social control designed to bring about compliance and subordination. Relying heavily on the examples of fascism and communism, this Cold War liberal use of the term treated ideology as a 'closed' system of thought, which, by claiming a monopoly of truth, refuses to tolerate opposing ideas and rival beliefs. In contrast, liberalism, based as it is on a fundamental commitment to individual freedom, and doctrines such as conservatism and democratic socialism that broadly subscribe to liberal principles, are clearly not ideologies. These doctrines are 'open' in the sense that they permit, and even insist on, free debate, opposition and criticism. A distinctively conservative use of the term ideology has been developed by thinkers such as Michael Oakeshott (see p. 37). This view reflects a characteristically conservative scepticism about the value of rationalism (see p. 13), born out of the belief that the world is largely beyond the capacity of the human mind to fathom.

LEFT- AND RIGHT-WING IDEAS

The origins of the terms 'left' and 'right' in politics date back to the French Revolution and the seating arrangements of radicals and aristocrats at the first meeting of the Estates General in 1789. The left/right divide therefore originally reflected the stark choice between revolution and reaction. The terms have subsequently been used to highlight a divide that supposedly runs throughout the world of political thought and action, helping both to provide insight into the nature of particular ideologies and to uncover relationships between political ideologies more generally. Left and right are usually understood as the poles of a political spectrum, enabling people to talk about the 'centre-left', the 'far right' and so on. This is in line with a linear political spectrum that travels from left-wing to right-wing, as shown in Figure 1.1. However, the terms left and right have been used to draw attention to a variety of distinctions.

Stemming from their original meanings, left and right have been used to sum up contrasting attitudes to political change in general, left-wing thinking welcoming change, usually based on a belief in **progress**, while right-wing thinking resists change and seeks to defend the **status quo**. Inspired by works such as Theodor Adorno et al.'s *The Authoritarian Personality* (1950), attempts have been made to explain ideological differences, and especially rival attitudes to change, in terms of people's psychological needs, motives and desires (Jost et al., 2003). In this light, conservative ideology, to take one example, is shaped by a deep psychological aversion to uncertainty and instability (an idea examined in

Progress: Moving forward; the belief that history is characterised by human advancement underpinned by the accumulation of knowledge and wisdom.

Status quo: The existing state of affairs.

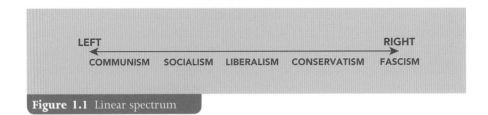

Figure 1.1 Linear spectrum

Chapter 3). An alternative construction of the left/right divide focuses on different attitudes to economic organisation and the role of the state. Left-wing views thus support intervention and collectivism (see p. 64), while right-wing views favour the market and individualism (see p. 12). Bobbio (1996), by contrast, argued that the fundamental basis for the distinction between left and right lies in differing attitudes to equality, left-wingers advocating greater equality while right-wingers treat equality as either impossible or undesirable. This may also help to explain the continuing relevance of the left/right divide, as the 'great problem of inequality' remains unresolved at both national and global levels.

As a means of providing insight into the character of political ideas and ideologies and how they relate to one another, the traditional linear political spectrum nevertheless has a range of drawbacks. For example, the ideologies that are traditionally placed at the extreme wings of the linear spectrum may have more in common with one another than they do with their 'centrist' neighbours. During the Cold War period in particular, it was widely claimed that communism and fascism resembled one another by virtue of a shared tendency towards **totalitarianism**. Such a view led to the idea that the political spectrum should be horseshoe-shaped, not linear (see Figure 1.2).

Moreover, as political ideologies are fluid entities, capable, some would argue, of almost constant re-invention, our notions of left and right must be regularly updated. This fluidity can be seen in the case of reformist socialist parties in many parts of the world, which, since the 1980s, have tended to distance themselves from a belief in nationalisation and welfare and, instead, embrace market economics. The implication of this for the left/right divide is either that reformist socialism has shifted to the right, moving from the centre-left to

Totalitarianism: An all-encompassing system of political rule, typically established by pervasive ideological manipulation and open terror.

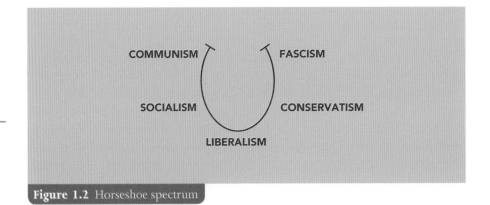

Figure 1.2 Horseshoe spectrum

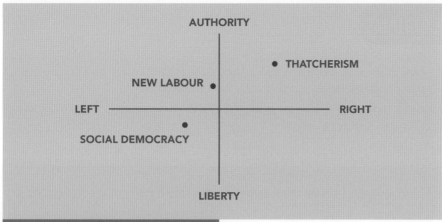

Figure 1.3 Two-dimensional spectrum

the centre-right, or that the spectrum itself has shifted to the right, redefining reformist socialism, and therefore leftism, in the process.

Finally, as ideological debate has developed and broadened over the years, the linear spectrum has seemed increasingly simplistic and generalised, the left/right divide only capturing one dimension of a more complex series of political interactions. This has given rise to the idea of the two-dimensional spectrum, with, as pioneered by Hans Eysenck (1964), a liberty/authority vertical axis being added to the established left/right horizontal axis (see Figure 1.3).

 FURTHER READING

Festenstein, M. and Kenny, M. (eds), *Political Ideologies: A Reader and Guide* (2005). A very useful collection of extracts from key texts on ideology and ideologies, supported by lucid commentaries.

Freeden, M., *Ideology: A Very Short Introduction* (2004). An accessible and lively introduction to the concept: an excellent starting place.

Freeden, M. et al., *The Oxford Handbook of Political Ideologies* (2015). A wide-ranging, up-to-date and authoritative account of debates about the nature of ideology and the shape of the various ideological traditions.

McLellan, D., *Ideology* (1995). A clear and short yet comprehensive introduction to the concept of ideology.

PART 1

TRADITIONAL POLITICAL IDEAS

These political ideas are associated with ideological traditions that developed from the late nineteenth century onwards, and offered contrasting ways of shaping emergent industrial society. Each of these ideologies is characterised by a distinctive view of human nature, society, the state and the economy.

2 Liberalism

PREVIEW

The term 'liberal' has been in use since the fourteenth century but has had a wide variety of meanings. The Latin *liber* referred to a class of free men; in other words, men who were neither serfs nor slaves. It has meant generous, as in 'liberal' helpings of food and drink; or, in reference to social attitudes, it has implied openness or open-mindedness. It also came to be associated increasingly with the ideas of freedom and choice. The term 'liberalism', to denote a political allegiance, made its appearance much later: it was not used until the early part of the nineteenth century, being first employed in Spain in 1812. By the 1840s, the term was widely recognised throughout Europe as a reference to a distinctive set of political ideas. However, it was taken up more slowly in the UK: though the Whigs started to call themselves Liberals during the 1830s, the first distinctly Liberal government was not formed until Gladstone took office in 1868.

The central theme of liberal ideology is a commitment to the individual and the desire to construct a society in which people can satisfy their interests and achieve fulfilment. Liberals believe that human beings are, first and foremost, individuals, endowed with reason. This implies that each individual should enjoy the maximum possible freedom consistent with a like freedom for all. However, although individuals are entitled to equal legal and political rights, they should be rewarded in line with their talents and their willingness to work. Liberal societies are organised politically around the twin principles of constitutionalism and consent, designed to protect citizens from the danger of government tyranny. Nevertheless, there are significant differences between classical liberalism and modern liberalism. Classical liberalism is characterised by a belief in a 'minimal' state, whose function is limited to the maintenance of domestic order and personal security. Modern liberalism, in contrast, accepts that the state should help people to help themselves.

CONTENTS

HISTORICAL OVERVIEW

As a systematic political creed, liberalism may not have existed before the nineteenth century, but it was based on ideas and theories that had developed during the previous 300 years. Liberalism as a developed ideology was a product of the breakdown of **feudalism** in Europe, and the growth, in its place, of a market or capitalist society. In many respects, liberalism reflected the aspirations of the rising middle classes, whose interests conflicted with the established power of absolute monarchs and the landed aristocracy. Liberal ideas were radical: they sought fundamental reform and even, at times, revolutionary change. The English Revolution of the seventeenth century, and the American Revolution of 1776 and French Revolution of 1789 each embodied elements that were distinctively liberal, even though the word 'liberal' was not at the time used in a political sense. Liberals challenged the absolute power of the monarchy, supposedly based on the doctrine of the '**divine right** of kings'. In place of **absolutism**, they advocated constitutional and, later, representative **government**. Liberals criticised the political and economic privileges of the landed aristocracy and the unfairness of a feudal system in which social position was determined by the 'accident of birth'. They also supported the movement towards freedom of conscience in religion and questioned the authority of the established church.

The nineteenth century was in many ways the liberal century. As industrialisation spread throughout western countries, liberal ideas triumphed. Liberals advocated an industrialised and market economic order 'free' from government interference, in which businesses would be allowed to pursue profit and states encouraged to trade freely with one another. Such a system of industrial capitalism developed first in the UK, from the mid-eighteenth century onwards, and subsequently spread to North America and throughout Europe, initially into western Europe and then, more gradually, into eastern Europe. From the twentieth century onwards industrial capitalism exerted a powerful appeal for developing states in Africa, Asia and Latin America, especially when social and political development was defined in essentially western terms. However, developing-world states have sometimes been resistant to the attractions of liberal capitalism because their political cultures have emphasised community rather than the individual. In such cases, they have provided more fertile ground for the growth of socialism, nationalism or religious fundamentalism (see p. 135), rather than western liberalism.

Liberalism has undoubtedly been the most powerful ideological force shaping the western political tradition. Nevertheless, historical developments since the nineteenth century have clearly influenced the nature and substance of liberal ideology. The character of liberalism changed as the 'rising middle classes' succeeded in establishing their economic and political dominance. The radical, even revolutionary, edge of liberalism faded with each liberal success. Liberalism thus became increasingly conservative, standing less for change and reform, and more for the maintenance of existing – largely liberal – institutions. Liberal ideas, too, could not stand still. From the late nineteenth century onwards,

Feudalism: A system of agrarian-based production that is characterised by fixed social hierarchies and a rigid pattern of obligations.

Divine right: The doctrine that earthly rulers are chosen by God and thus wield unchallengeable authority; divine right is a defence for monarchical absolutism.

Absolutism: A form of government in which political power is concentrated in the hands of a single individual or small group, in particular, an absolute monarchy.

Government: The machinery through which collective decisions are made on behalf of the state, usually comprising a legislature, an executive and a judiciary.

the progress of industrialisation led liberals to question, and in some ways to revise, the ideas of early liberalism. Whereas early or **classical liberalism** had been defined by the desire to minimise government interference in the lives of its citizens, **modern liberalism** came to be associated with welfare provision and economic management. As a result, some commentators have argued that liberalism is an incoherent ideology, embracing contradictory beliefs, notably about the desirable role of the **state**.

CORE IDEAS AND PRINCIPLES

HUMAN NATURE

The central idea of liberalism is that human beings should be understood as individuals. Individualism (see below) is thus the basic principle of liberalism. Just about every aspect of liberal thinking can be traced back to assumptions about the primacy of the individual. But what does it mean to view human beings as 'individuals'? Thinking of people as individuals has two contrasting implications. The first is that each human being is a separate and unique entity, defined by inner qualities and attributes that are specific to themselves. To be an individual, in this sense, is to be different. This implication of individualism is captured in the idea of **individuality**. The second implication is that, as individuals, each of us shares the same status. Our identity is not defined by social categories such as gender, social class, ethnicity, religion, nationality and so on, but by the fact that we are individuals. To be an individual, in this sense, is to be the same. Liberals, in this light, are often portrayed as being 'difference-blind'.

Perhaps the clearest expression of ethical individualism lies in the doctrine of **rights**, the belief that the basic condition for **justice** is that rights are upheld and respected. For liberals, rights belong strictly to the individual, ideas such as group rights or minority rights being looked on with much suspicion. Human beings should therefore be treated as 'rights-holders'. In the form of **natural rights** or, in their modern guise, **human rights**, these rights reflect the fact that human beings are 'born' equal in the sense that each individual is of equal

Classical liberalism: A tradition within liberalism that seeks to maximise the realm of unconstrained individual action, typically by establishing a minimal state and a reliance on market economics.

Modern liberalism: A tradition within liberalism that provides (in contrast to classical liberalism) a qualified endorsement for social and economic intervention as a means of promoting personal development.

State: A political association that establishes sovereign jurisdiction over a defined territory and typically possesses a monopoly of the means of armed conflict.

Individuality: Self-fulfilment achieved through the realisation of an individual's distinctive or unique identity qualities; what distinguishes one person from all others.

Rights: Entitlements to act or be treated in a particular way; rights may have a moral or legal character.

Justice: A moral standard of fairness and impartiality; social justice is the idea of a morally justifiable distribution of wealth and rewards in society.

Natural rights: God-given rights that are fundamental to human beings and are therefore inalienable (they cannot be taken away, as discussed later in the chapter).

Human rights: Rights to which people are entitled by virtue of being human; human rights are universal, fundamental and absolute.

Key concept ... INDIVIDUALISM

Individualism is the belief in the supreme importance of the individual over any social group or collective body. In the form of *methodological* individualism, this suggests that the individual is central to any political theory or social explanation – all statements about society should be made in terms of the individuals who compose them. *Ethical* individualism, on the other hand, implies that society should be constructed so as to benefit the individual, giving moral priority to individual rights, needs or interests. Classical liberals and the New Right subscribe to *egoistical* individualism, which places emphasis on self-interestedness and self-reliance. Modern liberals, in contrast, have advanced a *developmental* form of individualism that prioritises human flourishing over the quest for interest satisfaction.

moral worth, an idea sometimes referred to as 'foundational equality'. Such thinking not only provided inspiration for the writing of documents such as the US Declaration of Independence (1776), the French Declaration of the Rights of Man and the Citizen (1789) and, more recently, the UN's Universal Declaration of Human Rights, but it has also meant that liberalism has provided fertile ground for the growth of feminist thinking. Liberal feminism (discussed in greater detail in Chapter 7) has been articulated by thinkers ranging from Mary Wollstonecraft (see below) to Betty Friedan (see p. 14).

A further component of the liberal view of **human nature** is the belief that humans are reason-guided creatures, capable of personal self-development and of bringing about wider social and political development. In this sense, liberalism is, and remains, very much part of the **Enlightenment** project. The central theme of the Enlightenment was the desire to release humankind from its bondage to superstition and ignorance, and unleash an 'age of reason'. Enlightenment rationalism (see below) has influenced liberalism in a number of ways. For example, it strengthened its faith in both the individual and **freedom**. To the extent that human beings are rational, thinking creatures, they are capable of

Human nature: The essential and innate character of all human beings: what the individual owes to nature rather than to society.

Enlightenment: An intellectual movement that reached its height in the eighteenth century which challenged traditional beliefs in religion, politics and learning in general in the name of reason and progress.

Freedom (or liberty): The ability to think and act as one wishes, a capacity that can be associated with the individual, a social group or a nation.

KEY FIGURE

Mary Wollstonecraft (1759–97)

A British philosopher and novelist, Wollstonecraft developed the first systematic feminist critique some 50 years before the emergence of the female suffrage movement. Her *A Vindication of the Rights of Men* (1790) was a response to Burke's (see p. 40) views on the French Revolution. Wollstonecraft's most famous work, *A Vindication of the Rights of Women* (1792), advanced an agenda for women's emancipation based on the assertion that, as human beings, women are rational creatures. As such, they are entitled to the same rights of liberty and self-determination as male rational creatures claim for themselves. Wollstonecraft placed a particular emphasis on the capacity of education to develop women's talents and character. Wollstonecraft's writings are widely seen to have established the basis for the tradition of liberal feminism, characterised as it is by a commitment to formal equality; that is, an equal distribution of both legal and political rights, and civil liberties, including the right to a career. For more on Wollstonecraft, see pp. 138 and 147.

Key concept ... RATIONALISM

Rationalism is the belief that the world has a rational structure, and that this can be disclosed through the exercise of human reason and critical enquiry. As a philosophical theory, rationalism is the belief that knowledge flows from reason rather than experience, and thus contrasts with empiricism. As a general principle, however, rationalism places a heavy emphasis on the capacity of human beings to understand and explain their world, and to find solutions to problems. While rationalism does not dictate the ends of human conduct, it certainly suggests how these ends should be pursued. It is associated with an emphasis on principle and reason-governed behaviour, as opposed to a reliance on custom or tradition, or on non-rational drives and impulses.

defining and pursuing their own best interests. By no means do liberals believe that individuals are infallible in this respect, but the belief in reason builds into liberalism a strong bias against paternalism (see p. 47). A faith in reason, moreover, inclines liberals to believe that conflict can generally be resolved by debate, discussion and argument, greatly reducing the need for force and bloodshed.

SOCIETY

Liberals subscribe to an individualist conception of society. They assume that society is a human artefact, constructed by individuals to serve their interests for purposes. In its extreme form, such a view amounts to **atomism**; indeed, it can lead to the belief that 'society' itself does not exist, but is merely a collection of self-sufficient individuals. Such radical individualism is based on the assumption that the individual is egoistical, essentially self-seeking and largely self-reliant. C. B. Macpherson (1973) characterised early liberalism as 'possessive individualism', in that it regarded the individual as 'the proprietor of his own person capabilities, owing nothing to society for them'. In contrast, later liberals have held a more optimistic view of human nature, and have been prepared to believe that **egoism** is tempered by a sense of social responsibility, especially a responsibility for those who are unable to look after themselves. Whether egoism is unrestrained or is qualified by a sense of social responsibility, liberals are united in their desire to create a society in which each person is capable of developing and flourishing to the fullness of his or her potential.

A further aspect of the liberal conception of society is that society is seen to be firmly distinct from the state. In this sense, society can be understood as '**civil society**'. From the liberal perspective, society is a 'realm of freedom', by comparison with the state, which is a 'realm of coercion'. Freedom is therefore the supreme social value of liberalism. Liberals, nevertheless, do not claim that individuals have an absolute entitlement to freedom. If liberty is unlimited it can degenerate into the abuse of others. In *On Liberty* ([1859] 1972), John Stuart Mill (see p. 27) argued that 'the only purpose for which power can be

Atomism: A belief that society is made up of a collection of self-interested and largely self-sufficient individuals, or atoms, rather than social groups.

Egoism: A concern for one's own welfare or interests, or the theory that the pursuit of self-interest is an ethical priority.

Civil society: A sphere of autonomous groups and associations, such as businesses, pressure groups, clubs, families and so on.

KEY FIGURE

Betty Friedan (1921–2006)

A US feminist political activist and founder of the National Organization for Women (NOW), Friedan was a key exponent of the liberal approach to women's liberation. Her *The Feminine Mystique* (1963) is often credited with having stimulated the emergence of second-wave feminism. In it, she examined 'the problem with no name': the sense of frustration and despair afflicting suburban American women. Defining women's liberation largely in terms of the establishment of a formally equal status with men in society and the widening of opportunities for women in education and careers in particular, Friedan argued that the root cause of female subordination was the embedded image of women as essentially feminine, and not human, beings. Her chief object of attack was therefore the 'feminine mystique', an image that encourages women to define themselves in relation to their husbands, home and children, and so discourages them from competing with men in the public realm. For more on Friedan, see pp. 139 and 146–7.

PERSPECTIVES ON ...
FREEDOM

LIBERALS give priority to freedom as the supreme individualist value. While classical liberals support negative freedom, understood as the absence of constraints – or freedom of choice – modern liberals advocate positive freedom in the sense of personal development and human flourishing.

CONSERVATIVES have traditionally endorsed a weak view of freedom as the willing recognition of duties and responsibilities, negative freedom posing a threat to the fabric of society. The New Right, however, endorses negative freedom in the economic sphere, freedom of choice in the marketplace.

SOCIALISTS have generally understood freedom in positive terms to refer to self-fulfilment achieved through either free creative labour or cooperative social interaction. Social democrats have drawn close to modern liberalism in treating freedom as the realisation of individual potential.

ANARCHISTS regard freedom as an absolute value, believing it to be irreconcilable with any form of political authority. Freedom is understood to mean the achievement of personal autonomy, not merely being 'left alone' but being rationally self-willed and self-directed.

NATIONALISTS view freedom as national self-determination, the right of a nation to shape its own destiny by achieving independence from foreign control and establishing itself as a sovereign entity through constructing a nation-state.

FEMINISTS have understood freedom both in terms of women's emancipation, focusing on the acquisition of legal and political rights, and in terms of women's liberation, focusing on the overthrow of the patriarch, possibly also implying sexual fulfilment as subjects, not as objects.

ECOLOGISTS, particularly deep ecologists, treat freedom as the achievement of oneness, self-realisation through the absorption of the personal ego into the ecosphere or universe. In contrast with political freedom, this is sometimes seen as 'inner' freedom, freedom as self-actualisation.

rightfully exercised over any member of a civilised community, against his will, is to prevent harm to others'. Mill's position is libertarian in that it accepts only the most minimal restrictions on individual freedom, and then only in order to prevent 'harm to others'. This idea is sometimes described as the 'harm principle'. An alternative way in which liberals have highlighted legitimate constraints on freedom is through the notion of an equal right to liberty. This has been expressed by John Rawls (see p. 30) in the principle that everyone is entitled to the widest possible liberty consistent with a like liberty for all.

However, although liberals have agreed that individuals should enjoy the greatest possible freedom, they have not always agreed about what it means for an individual to be 'free'. In 'Two Concepts of Liberty' ([1958] 1969), Isaiah Berlin (see p. 196) distinguished between a 'negative' theory of liberty and a 'positive' one. Early or classical liberals have believed in **negative freedom**, in that freedom consists in each person being left alone, free from interference and able to act in whatever way he or she may choose. This conception of freedom is 'negative' in that it is based on the absence of external restrictions or

Negative freedom: The absence of external restrictions or constraints on the individual, allowing freedom of choice.

constraints on the individual. Modern liberals, on the other hand, have been attracted to a more 'positive' conception of liberty, **positive freedom**, defined by Berlin as the ability to be one's own master; to be autonomous. Self-mastery requires that the individual is able to develop skills and talents, broaden his or her understanding, and gain fulfilment. This led to an emphasis on the capacity of human beings to develop and ultimately achieve self-realisation. These rival conceptions of liberty have not merely stimulated academic debate within liberalism, but have also encouraged liberals to hold very different views about the desirable relationship between the individual and the state.

Finally, liberals have a distinctive view of the structure of society in terms of the distribution of wealth and other rewards. This is based on a commitment to **equality of opportunity**. For liberals, each and every individual should have the same chance to rise or fall in society. The game of life, in that sense, must be played on a 'level playing field'. This is not to say that there should be equality of outcome or reward, or that living conditions and social circumstances should be the same for all. Liberals believe social equality to be undesirable because people are not born the same. They possess different talents and skills, and some are prepared to work much harder than others. Liberals believe that it is right to reward merit (ability and the willingness to work); indeed, they think it is essential to do so if people are to have an incentive to realise their potential and develop the talents with which they were born. Equality, for a liberal, means that individuals should have an equal opportunity to develop their unequal skills and abilities. This leads to a belief in **meritocracy**. However, whereas classical liberals have endorsed strict meritocracy, on grounds of both fairness (some people *deserve* to be better off than others) and incentives, modern liberals are inclined to believe that equality of opportunity can only be ensured if material inequalities are relatively narrow.

THE STATE

Liberal thinking about politics focuses primarily on the nature and role of the state and the organisation of government power. Such thinking is underpinned by the core assumption that the liberty of one person is always in danger of becoming a licence to abuse another. Each person can be said to be both a threat to, and under threat from, every other member of society. Our liberty therefore requires that the other members of society are restrained from encroaching on our freedom and, in turn, their liberty requires that they are safeguarded from us. This protection is provided by a sovereign state, capable of restraining all individuals and groups within society. The classical form of this argument is found in the **social contract** theories that were developed in the seventeenth century by thinkers such as Thomas Hobbes (see p. 36) and John Locke (see p. 17). Hobbes and Locke constructed a picture of what life had been like before government was formed, in a stateless society or what they called a '**state of nature**'. As individuals are selfish, greedy and power-seeking, the state of nature would be characterised by an unending civil war of each against all, in which, in Hobbes' words, human life would be 'solitary, poor, nasty, brutish and short'. As a result, they argued, rational individuals would enter into an agreement, or

Positive freedom: Self-mastery or self-realisation; the achievement of autonomy or the development of human capacities.

Equality of opportunity: Equality defined in terms of life chances or opportunities, allowing people to rise or fall but only on the basis of personal differences.

Meritocracy: Literally, rule by those with merit, merit being intelligence plus effort; a society in which social position is determined exclusively by ability and hard work.

Social contract: A (hypothetical) agreement among individuals through which they form a state in order to escape from the disorder and chaos of the 'state of nature'.

State of nature: A pre-political society characterised by unrestrained freedom and the absence of established authority.

KEY FIGURE

John Locke (1632–1704)

Locke was an English philosopher and politician whose political views were developed against the backdrop of the English Revolution, and are often seen as providing justification for the 'Glorious Revolution' of 1688, which ended absolutist rule in Britain by establishing a constitutional monarchy. Locke was a key thinker of early liberalism, placing a particular emphasis on the idea of 'natural' or God-given rights, identified as the rights to life, liberty and property. On this basis, he argued that no one can become subject to the authority of anyone else, or, for that matter, any law, save by his consent, thereby embracing the principle of limited government. The foundation of such thinking was social contract theory, in which the state and government are seen to arise from a theoretical voluntary agreement made by all citizens. Locke's most important political work is *Two Treatises of Government* (1690). For more on Locke, see pp. 16, 18, 21–2, 97 and 106.

'social contract', to establish a sovereign government, without which orderly and stable life would be impossible.

The social contract argument embodies two important liberal attitudes towards the state in particular, and political authority in general. First, it emphasises that political authority comes, in a sense, 'from below'; it is fashioned by citizens themselves and exists to serve their needs and interests. This implies that citizens do not have an absolute obligation to obey all laws or accept any form of government. If government is based on a contract, made by the governed, government itself may break the terms of this contract. When the legitimacy of government evaporates, the people have the right of rebellion. Second, in social contract theory, the state is not created by a privileged elite, wishing to exploit the masses, but by an agreement among all the people. The state therefore embodies the interests of all its citizens and acts as a neutral referee when individuals or groups come into conflict with one another. The state is thus devoid of bias towards particular groups or interests

However, although liberals are convinced of the need for government, they are also acutely aware of the dangers that government embodies. In their view, all governments are potential tyrannies against the individual. This position reflects a distinctively liberal fear of power. As human beings are self-seeking creatures, if they have power – the ability to influence the behaviour of others – they will inevitably seek to use it for their own benefit and at the expense of others. Simply put, the liberal position is that egoism plus power equals corruption. This was expressed in Lord Acton's famous warning: 'Power tends to corrupt, and absolute power corrupts absolutely,' and in his conclusion: 'Great men are almost always bad men' (Acton, 1956). Liberals therefore support the principle of limited government, achieved through **constitutionalism** and **democracy**.

Constitutionalism can take two forms. In the first place, the powers of government bodies and politicians can be limited by the introduction of external and, usually, legal constraints. The most important of these is a so-called **written**

Constitutionalism: The theory or practice of limiting government power through the use of external (legal) and internal (institutional) constraints.

Democracy: Rule by the people; democracy implies both popular participation and government in the public interest, and can take a wide variety of forms (see p. 19).

Written constitution: A single authoritative document that defines the duties, powers and functions of government institutions and so constitutes 'higher' law.

constitution, which codifies the major powers and responsibilities of government institutions within a single document. Second, constitutionalism can be established by the introduction of internal constraints which disperse political power among a number of institutions and create a network of 'checks and balances'. As the French political philosopher Montesquieu (1689–1775) put it, 'power should be a check to power' (Montesquieu, [1748] 1969). All liberal political systems exhibit some measure of internal fragmentation, most particularly through the application of the doctrine of the **separation of powers**, proposed by Montesquieu himself.

The liberal approaches to democracy have been characterised by ambivalence. This has been evident in the type of democracy they endorse – liberal democracy (see below) – which qualifies a 'democratic' emphasis on free, fair and competitive elections, based on universal suffrage, through 'liberal' stress on the need to guarantee **civil liberty** and ensure a healthy **civil society**. The central liberal concern about democracy is that popular rule ultimately boils down to the rule of the 51 per cent, a prospect that the French politician and social commentator Alexis de Tocqueville (1805–59) famously described as 'the tyranny of the majority'. Individual liberty and minority rights can thus be crushed in the name of the people. By the twentieth century, however, most liberal thinkers had come to accept the broader benefits of democracy. The earliest liberal argument in favour of democracy was that voting rights protect citizens from the encroachment of government. John Locke thus developed a limited theory of democracy by arguing that the franchise should be extended to the propertied, who could then defend their natural rights against government. Such thinking was later revised to encompass all adult citizens, and not just the propertied few. Liberals have nevertheless also supported democracy on the more radical grounds that it promotes what J. S. Mill called the 'highest and most harmonious development of human capacities'. In this view, participation in political life enables citizens to enhance their understanding, strengthen their sensibilities and achieve a higher level of personal development. (For a fuller account to the nature and types of democracy, see Chapter 2 of *Essentials of UK Politics*.)

Separation of powers: The principle that legislative, executive and judicial power should be separated through the construction of three independent branches of government.

Civil liberty: The private sphere of existence, belonging to the citizen, not to the state; freedom from government.

Civil society: A realm of autonomous associations and groups, formed by private citizens and enjoying independence from the government; civil society includes businesses, clubs, families and so on.

Key concept ... LIBERAL DEMOCRACY

A liberal democracy is a political regime in which a 'liberal' commitment to limited government is blended with a 'democratic' belief in popular rule. Its key features are: (1) the right to rule being gained through success in regular and competitive elections based on universal adult suffrage; (2) constraints on government imposed by a constitution, institutional checks and balances, and protections for individual rights; and (3) a vigorous civil society including a private enterprise economy, independent trade unions and a free press. While liberals view liberal democracy as being universally applicable, on the grounds that it allows for the expression of the widest possible range of views and beliefs, critics regard it as the political expression of either western values or capitalist economic structures.

PERSPECTIVES ON ...
DEMOCRACY

LIBERALS understand democracy in individualist terms as consent expressed through the ballot box, democracy being equated with regular and competitive elections. While democracy constrains abuses of power, it must always be conducted within a constitutional framework to prevent majoritarian tyranny.

CONSERVATIVES endorse liberal-democratic rule but with qualifications about the need to protect property and traditional institutions from the untutored will of 'the many'. The New Right, however, has linked electoral democracy to the problems of over-government and economic stagnation.

SOCIALISTS traditionally endorsed a form of radical democracy based on popular participation and the desire to bring economic life under public control, dismissing liberal democracy as simply capitalist democracy. Nevertheless, modern social democrats are now firmly committed to liberal-democratic structures.

ANARCHISTS endorse direct democracy and call for continuous popular participation and radical decentralisation. Electoral or representative democracy is merely a façade that attempts to conceal elite domination and reconcile the masses to their oppression.

ECOLOGISTS have often supported radical or participatory democracy. 'Dark' greens have developed a particular critique of electoral democracy that portrays it as a means of imposing the interests of the present generation of humans on (unenfranchised) later generations, other species and nature as a whole.

MULTICULTURALISTS commonly argue that the majoritarian bias in conventional forms of democracy denies minority groups and minority cultures a political voice.

THE ECONOMY

Liberal thinking on the economy largely derives from the work of figures such as the Scottish economist and philosopher Adam Smith (1723–90), and David Ricardo (1770–1823), the British political economist and politician. Smith's *The Wealth of Nations* ([1776] 1976) was in many respects the first economics textbook. His ideas drew heavily on liberal and rationalist assumptions about human nature and made a powerful contribution to the debate about the desirable role of government within civil society. Smith wrote at a time of wide-ranging government restrictions on economic activity. **Mercantilism**, the dominant economic idea of the sixteenth and seventeenth centuries, had encouraged governments to intervene in economic life in an attempt to encourage the export of goods and restrict imports. Smith's economic writings were designed to attack mercantilism, arguing instead for the principle that the economy works best when it is left alone by government.

Smith thought of the economy as a **market**, indeed as a series of inter-related markets. He believed that the market operates according to the wishes and decisions of free individuals. Freedom within the market means freedom of choice: the ability of businesses to choose what goods to make, the ability of workers to choose an employer, and the ability of consumers to choose what goods or

Mercantilism: A school of economic thought that emphasises the state's role in managing international trade and delivering prosperity.

Market: A system of commercial exchange between buyers and sellers, controlled by impersonal economic forces: 'market forces'.

services to buy. Relationships within such a market – between employers and employees, and between buyers and sellers – are thus voluntary and contractual, made by self-interested individuals for whom pleasure is equated with the acquisition and consumption of wealth. Economic theory therefore drew on utilitarianism (see p. 23) in constructing the idea of 'economic man', the notion that human beings are essentially egoistical and bent on material acquisition.

However, liberalism encompasses two contrasting economic traditions. Classical liberals have viewed the market economy as a vast network of commercial relationships, in which both consumers and producers indicate their wishes through the price mechanism. The clear implication of this is that government is relieved of the need to regulate or plan economic activity; economic organisation can simply be left to the market itself. Indeed, if government interferes with economic life, it runs the risk of upsetting the delicate balance of the market. In this view, so long as the economy operates as a **free market**, efficiency and prosperity are guaranteed by the irresistible tendency of the market mechanism to draw resources to their most profitable use. Modern liberals, on the other hand, reject the idea of a self-regulating market economy, arguing instead that the economy should be regulated, or 'managed', by government. In this view, although it remains the ultimate source of economic dynamism, the market, if left to its own devices, is flawed, tending, as it does, towards short-termism, unemployment and inequality. This helps to explain the attraction of Keynesianism (see p. 31) to many modern liberals.

TYPES OF LIBERALISM

CLASSICAL LIBERALISM

Classical liberalism was the earliest liberal tradition. Classical liberal ideas developed during the transition from feudalism to capitalism, and reached their high point during the early industrialisation of the nineteenth century. As a result, classical liberalism has sometimes been called 'nineteenth-century liberalism'. The cradle of classical liberalism was the UK, where the capitalist and industrial revolutions were the most advanced. Its ideas have always been more deeply rooted in Anglo-Saxon countries, particularly the UK and the USA, than in other parts of the world. However, classical liberalism is not merely a nineteenth-century form of liberalism, whose ideas are now only of historical interest. Its principles and theories, in fact, have had growing appeal from the second half of the twentieth century onwards. Though what is called 'neoclassical liberalism', or 'neoliberalism' (see p. 51), initially had the greatest impact in the UK and the USA, its influence has spread much more broadly, in large part fuelled by the advance of globalisation.

Classical liberal ideas have taken a variety of forms, but they have a number of common characteristics. Classical liberals:

▶ subscribe to egoistical individualism. They view human beings as rationally self-interested creatures, with a pronounced capacity for self-reliance.

Free market: The principle or policy of unfettered market competition, free from government interference.

Society is therefore seen as atomistic, composed of a collection of largely self-sufficient individuals, meaning that the characteristics of society can be traced back to the more fundamental features of human nature.

▶ believe in negative freedom. The individual is free in so far as he or she is left alone, not interfered with or coerced by others. As stated earlier, freedom in this sense is the absence of external constraints on the individual.

▶ regard the state as, in Thomas Paine's words, a 'necessary evil'. It is necessary in that, at the very least, it lays down the conditions for orderly existence; and it is evil in that it imposes a collective will on society, thereby limiting the freedom and responsibilities of the individual. Classical liberals thus believe in a minimal state, which acts, using Locke's metaphor, as a 'night watchman'. In this view, the state's proper role is restricted to the maintenance of domestic order, the enforcement of contracts, and the protection of society against external attack.

▶ have an essentially positive view of civil society. Civil society is not only regarded as a realm of choice, personal freedom and individual responsibility, but it is also seen to reflect the principle of balance or equilibrium. This is expressed most clearly in the classical liberal belief in a self-regulating market economy.

Classical liberalism nevertheless draws on a variety of doctrines and theories. The most important of these are:

▶ natural rights

▶ utilitarianism

▶ economic liberalism

▶ social Darwinism.

Natural rights

The natural rights theorists of the seventeenth and eighteenth centuries, such as John Locke in England and Thomas Jefferson in America, had a considerable influence on the development of liberal ideology. Modern political debate is littered with references to 'rights' and claims to possess 'rights'. A right, most simply, is an entitlement to act or be treated in a particular way. Such entitlements may be either moral or legal in character. For Locke and Jefferson, rights are 'natural' in that they are invested in human beings by nature or God. Natural rights are now more commonly called 'human rights'. They are, in Jefferson's words, 'inalienable' because human beings are entitled to them by virtue of being human: they cannot, in that sense, be taken away. Natural rights are thus thought to establish the essential conditions for leading a truly human existence. For Locke, there were three such rights: 'life, liberty and property'. Jefferson did not accept that property was a natural or God-given right, but rather, claimed it was one that had developed for human convenience. In the US Declaration of Independence he therefore described inalienable rights as those of 'life, liberty and the pursuit of happiness'.

The idea of natural or human rights has affected liberal thought in a number of ways. For example, the weight given to such rights distinguishes authoritarian thinkers such as Thomas Hobbes from early liberals such as John Locke. As explained earlier, both Hobbes and Locke believed that government was formed through a 'social contract'. However, Hobbes ([1651] 1968) argued that only a strong government, preferably a monarchy, would be able to establish order and security in society. He was prepared to invest the king with sovereign or absolute power, rather than risk a descent into a 'state of nature'. The citizen should therefore accept *any* form of government because even repressive government is better than no government at all. Locke, on the other hand, argued against arbitrary or unlimited government. Government is established in order to protect natural rights. When these are protected by the state, citizens should respect the government and obey the law. However, if government violates the rights of its citizens, they in turn have the right of rebellion. Locke thus approved of the English Revolution of the seventeenth century, and applauded the establishment of a constitutional monarchy in 1688.

For Locke, moreover, the contract between state and citizen is a specific and limited one: its purpose is to protect a set of defined natural rights. As a result, Locke believed in limited government. The legitimate role of government is limited to the protection of 'life, liberty and property'. Therefore, the realm of government should not extend beyond its three 'minimal' functions:

▶ maintaining public order and protecting property

▶ providing defence against external attack

▶ ensuring that contracts are enforced.

Other issues and responsibilities are properly the concern of private individuals. Thomas Jefferson expressed a similar sentiment a century later when he declared: 'That government is best which governs least.'

Utilitarianism

Natural rights theories were not the only basis of early liberalism. An alternative and highly influential theory of human nature was put forward in the early nineteenth century by the utilitarian thinkers, notably Jeremy Bentham (1748–1832) and James Mill (1773–1836). Bentham regarded the idea of rights as 'nonsense' and called natural rights 'nonsense on stilts'. In their place, he proposed what he believed to be the more scientific and objective idea that individuals are motivated by self-interest, and that these interests can be defined as the desire for pleasure, or happiness, and the wish to avoid pain, both calculated in terms of **utility**. The principle of utility is, furthermore, a moral principle in that it suggests that the 'rightness' of an action, policy or institution can be established by its tendency to promote happiness. Just as each individual can calculate what is morally good by the quantity of pleasure an action will produce, so the principle of 'the greatest happiness for the greatest number' can be used to establish which policies or institutions will benefit society at large.

Utility: Use-value; in economics, 'utility' describes the satisfaction that is gained from the consumption of material goods and services.

Utilitarian ideas have had a considerable impact on classical liberalism. In particular, they have provided a moral philosophy that explains how and why individuals act as they do. The utilitarian conception of human beings as rationally self-interested creatures was adopted by later generations of liberal thinkers. Moreover, each individual is thought to be able to perceive his or her own best interests. This cannot be done on their behalf by some paternal authority, such as the state. Bentham argued that individuals act so as to gain pleasure or happiness in whatever way they choose. No one else can judge the quality or degree of their happiness. If each individual is the sole judge of what will give him or her pleasure, then the individual alone can determine what is morally right. On the other hand, utilitarian ideas can also have illiberal implications. Bentham held that the principle of utility could be applied to society at large and not merely to individual human behaviour. Institutions and legislation can be judged by the yardstick of 'the greatest happiness'. However, this formula has majoritarian implications, because it uses the happiness of 'the greatest number' as a standard of what is morally correct, and therefore allows that the interests of the majority outweigh those of the minority or the rights of the individual.

Economic liberalism

The development of classical political economy in the late eighteenth and early nineteenth centuries was powerfully shaped by liberal ideas and assumptions, so much so that it is often portrayed as economic liberalism. The attraction of classical economic thinking was that, while each individual is materially self-interested, the economy itself is thought to operate according to a set of impersonal pressures – market forces – that tend naturally to promote economic prosperity and well-being. For instance, no single producer can set the price of a commodity – prices are set by the market, by the number of goods offered for sale and the number of consumers who are willing to buy. These are the forces of supply and demand. The market is a self-regulating mechanism; it needs no guidance from outside. The market should be 'free' from government interference because it is managed by what Adam Smith referred to as an 'invisible hand'. This idea of a self-regulating market reflects the liberal belief

---

Key concept ... UTILITARIANISM

Utilitarianism is a moral philosophy that was developed by Jeremy Bentham and James Mill. It equates 'good' with pleasure or happiness, and 'evil' with pain or unhappiness. Individuals are therefore assumed to act so as to maximise pleasure and minimise pain, these being calculated in terms of utility or use-value, usually seen as satisfaction derived from material consumption. The 'greatest happiness' principle can be used to evaluate laws, institutions and even political systems. *Act* utilitarianism judges an act to be right if it produces at least as much pleasure-over-pain as any other act. *Rule* utilitarianism judges an act to be right if it conforms to a rule which, if generally followed, produces good consequences.

in a naturally existing harmony among the conflicting interests within society. Smith ([1776] 1976) expressed the economic version of this idea as follows:

> It is not from the benevolence of the butcher, the brewer or the baker that we expect our dinner, but from their regard to their own interests.

Free-market ideas became economic orthodoxy in the UK and the USA during the nineteenth century. The high point of free-market beliefs was reached with the doctrine of **laissez–faire**. This suggests that the state should have no economic role, but should simply leave the economy alone and allow businesspeople to act however they please. *Laissez-faire* ideas opposed all forms of factory legislation, including restrictions on the employment of children, limits to the number of hours worked, and any regulation of working conditions. Such economic individualism is usually based on a belief that the unrestrained pursuit of profit will ultimately lead to general benefit. *Laissez-faire* theories remained strong in the UK throughout much of the nineteenth century, and in the USA they were not seriously challenged until the 1930s.

However, since the late twentieth century, faith in the free market has been revived through the rise of neoliberalism. Neoliberalism was counter-revolutionary: it aimed to halt, and if possible reverse, the trend towards 'big' government that had dominated most western countries, especially since 1945. Although it had its greatest initial impact in the two countries in which free-market economic principles had been most firmly established in the nineteenth century, the USA and the UK, from the 1980s onwards neoliberalism exerted a wider influence. At the heart of neoliberalism's assault on the 'dead hand' of government lies a belief in **market fundamentalism**. In that light, neoliberalism can be seen to go beyond classical economic theory. For instance, while Adam Smith is rightfully viewed as the father of market economics, he also recognised the limitations of the market and certainly did not subscribe to a crude utility-maximising model of human nature. Thus, although some treat neoliberalism as a form of revived classical liberalism, others see it is a form of economic libertarianism (see p. 48), which perhaps has more in common with the anarchist tradition, and in particular anarcho-capitalism (discussed in Chapter 5), than it does with the liberal tradition. The matter is further complicated by the fact that in the case of both 'Reaganism' in the USA and 'Thatcherism' in the UK, neoliberalism formed part of a larger, New Right ideological project that sought to foster *laissez-faire* economics with an essentially conservative social philosophy. This project is examined in more detail in Chapter 3.

Social Darwinism

One of the distinctive features of classical liberalism is its attitude to poverty and social equality. An individualistic political creed will tend to explain social circumstances in terms of the talents and hard work of each individual human being. Individuals make what they want, and what they can, of their own lives. Those with ability and a willingness to work will prosper, while the incompetent or the lazy will not. This idea was memorably expressed in the title of Samuel Smiles' book *Self-Help* ([1859] 1986), which begins by reiterating

Laissez-faire: Literally, 'leave to do'; the doctrine that economic activity should be entirely free from government interference.

Market fundamentalism: An absolute faith in the market, reflecting the belief that the market mechanism offers solutions to all economic and social problems.

the well-tried maxim that 'Heaven helps those who help themselves'. Such ideas of individual responsibility were widely employed by supporters of *laissez-faire* in the nineteenth century. For instance, the UK economist and politician Richard Cobden (1804–65) advocated an improvement of the conditions of the working classes, but argued that it should come about through 'their own efforts and self-reliance, rather than from law'. He advised them to 'look not to Parliament, look only to yourselves'.

Ideas of individual self-reliance reached their boldest expression in Herbert Spencer's *The Man versus the State* ([1884] 1940). Spencer (1820–1904), a UK philosopher and social theorist, developed a vigorous defence of the doctrine of *laissez-faire*, drawing on ideas that the UK scientist Charles Darwin (1809–82) had developed in *On the Origin of Species* ([1859] 1972). Darwin developed a theory of evolution that set out to explain the diversity of species found on Earth. He proposed that each species undergoes a series of random physical and mental changes, or mutations. Some of these changes enable a species to survive and prosper: they are pro-survival. Other mutations are less favourable and make survival more difficult or even impossible. A process of 'natural selection' therefore decides which species are fitted by nature to survive, and which are not. By the end of the nineteenth century, these ideas had extended beyond biology and were increasingly affecting social and political theory.

Spencer, for example, used the theory of natural selection to develop the social principle of 'the survival of the fittest'. People who are best suited by nature to survive, rise to the top, while the less fit fall to the bottom. Inequalities of wealth, social position and political power are therefore natural and inevitable, and no attempt should be made by government to interfere with them. Spencer's US disciple William Sumner (1840–1910) stated this principle boldly in 1884, when he asserted that 'the drunkard in the gutter is just where he ought to be'.

MODERN LIBERALISM

Modern liberalism is sometimes described as 'twentieth-century liberalism'. Just as the development of classical liberalism was closely linked to the emergence of industrial capitalism in the nineteenth century, so modern liberal ideas were related to the further development of industrialisation. Industrialisation had brought about a massive expansion of wealth for some, but was also accompanied by the spread of slums, poverty, ignorance and disease. Moreover, social inequality became more difficult to ignore as a growing industrial working class was seen to be disadvantaged by low pay, unemployment and degrading living and working conditions. These developments had an impact on UK liberalism from the late nineteenth century onwards, but in other countries they did not take effect until much later; for example, US liberalism was not affected until the depression of the 1930s. In these changing historical circumstances, liberals found it progressively more difficult to maintain the belief that the arrival of industrial capitalism had brought with it general prosperity and liberty for all. Consequently, many came to revise the early liberal expectation that the unrestrained pursuit of self-interest produced a socially just society. As the idea of economic individualism came increasingly under attack, liberals rethought their attitude towards the state. The minimal state of classical theory was quite incapable of rectifying the injustices and inequalities of civil society. Modern liberals were therefore prepared to advocate the development of an interventionist or enabling state.

However, modern liberalism has been viewed in two, quite different, ways:

▶ Classical liberals have argued that modern liberalism effectively broke with the principles and doctrines that had previously defined liberalism, in particular that it had abandoned individualism and embraced collectivism (see p. 64).

▶ Modern liberals, however, have been at pains to point out that they built on, rather than betrayed, classical liberalism. In this view, whereas classical liberalism is characterised by clear theoretical consistency, modern liberalism represents a marriage between new and old liberalism, and thus embodies ideological and theoretical tensions, notably over the proper role of the state.

The distinctive ideas of modern liberalism include:

▶ individuality

▶ positive freedom

▶ social liberalism

▶ economic management.

Individuality

John Stuart Mill's ideas have been described as the 'heart of liberalism'. This is because he provided a 'bridge' between classical and modern liberalism: his ideas look both back to the early nineteenth century and forward to the twentieth century and beyond. Mill's interests ranged from political economy to the campaign for female suffrage, but it is the ideas developed in *On Liberty* ([1859] 1972) that show Mill most clearly as a contributor to modern liberal thought. This work contains some of the boldest liberal statements in favour of individual freedom. Mill suggested that, 'Over himself, over his own body and mind, the individual is sovereign', a conception of liberty that is essentially negative as it portrays freedom in terms of the absence of restrictions on an individual's 'self-regarding' actions. Mill believed this to be a necessary condition for liberty, but not in itself a sufficient one. He thought that liberty was a positive and constructive force. It gave individuals the ability to take control of their own lives, to gain autonomy or achieve self-realisation.

Mill was influenced strongly by European romanticism and found the notion of human beings as utility maximisers both shallow and unconvincing. He believed passionately in individuality. The value of liberty is that it enables indi-viduals to develop, to gain talents, skills and knowledge and to refine their sensibilities. Mill disagreed with Bentham's utilitarianism in so far as Bentham

KEY FIGURE

John Stuart Mill (1806–73)

A British philosopher, economist and politician, Mill was a key liberal thinker whose work straddles the divide between the classical and modern traditions. His distrust of state intervention was firmly rooted in nineteenth-century principles, but his emphasis on the quality of individual life (reflected in a commitment to individuality) looked forward to later developments. In *On Liberty* (1859), Mill argued that every society's code of justice should recognise a basic right to absolute liberty in purely self-regarding matters, restrictions on liberty being justified only in order to prevent harm to others. In moral philosophy, this is known as the 'harm principle'. Such thinking also encouraged him to defend toleration and raise concerns about democracy, especially as the latter implies that majority opinions are more worthwhile than minority ones. At the heart of Mill's case for toleration lies a belief in individuals as autonomous agents, free to exercise sovereign control over their own lives and circumstances. For more on J. S. Mill, see below, pp. 14–15, 18, 26, 125, 138, 146–7 and 172.

believed that actions could only be distinguished by the quantity of pleasure or pain they generated. For Mill, there were 'higher' and 'lower' pleasures. Mill was concerned to promote those pleasures that develop an individual's intellectual, moral or aesthetic sensibilities. He was clearly concerned not with simple pleasure-seeking, but with personal self-development, declaring that he would rather be 'Socrates dissatisfied than a fool satisfied'. As such, he laid the foundations for a developmental model of individualism that placed emphasis on human flourishing rather than the crude satisfaction of interests.

Positive freedom

The clearest break with early liberal thought came in the late nineteenth century with the work of the British philosopher and social theorist T. H. Green (1836–82), whose writing influenced a generation of so-called 'new liberals' such as L. T. Hobhouse (1864–1929) and J. A. Hobson (1854–1940). Green believed that the unrestrained pursuit of profit, as advocated by classical liberalism, had given rise to new forms of poverty and injustice. The economic liberty of the few had blighted the life chances of the many. Following J. S. Mill, he rejected the early liberal conception of human beings as essentially self-seeking utility maximisers, and suggested a more optimistic view of human nature. Individuals, according to Green, have sympathy for one another; their egoism is therefore constrained by some degree of **altruism**. The individual possesses social responsibilities and not merely individual responsibilities, and is therefore linked to other individuals by ties of caring and empathy. Such a conception of human nature was clearly influenced by socialist ideas that emphasised the sociable and cooperative nature of humankind. As a result, Green's ideas have been described as 'socialist liberalism'.

Green also challenged the classical liberal notion of freedom. Negative freedom merely removes external constraints on the individual, giving the individual freedom of choice. In the case of the businesses that wish to maximise profits, negative freedom justifies their ability to hire the cheapest labour possible; for

Altruism: Concern for the interests and welfare of others, based either on enlightened self-interest or on a belief in a common humanity.

example, to employ children rather than adults, or women rather than men. Economic freedom can therefore lead to exploitation, even becoming the 'freedom to starve'. Freedom of choice in the marketplace is therefore an inadequate conception of individual freedom.

In the place of a simple belief in negative freedom, Green proposed that freedom should also be understood in positive terms. In this light, freedom is the ability of the individual to develop and attain individuality; it involves people's ability to realise their individual potential, attain skills and knowledge, and achieve fulfilment. Thus, whereas negative freedom acknowledges only legal and physical constraints on liberty, positive freedom recognises that liberty may also be threatened by social disadvantage and inequality. This, in turn, implied a revised view of the state. By protecting individuals from the social evils that cripple their lives, the state can expand freedom, and not merely diminish it. In place of the minimal state of old, modern liberals therefore endorsed an enabling state, exercising an increasingly wide range of social and economic responsibilities.

While such ideas undoubtedly involved a revision of classical liberal theories, they did not amount to the abandonment of core liberal beliefs. Modern liberalism drew closer to socialism, but it did not place society before the individual. For Green, for example, freedom ultimately consisted in individuals acting morally. The state could not force people to be good; it could only provide the conditions in which they were able to make more responsible moral decisions. The balance between the state and the individual had altered, but the underlying commitment to the needs and interests of the individual remained. Modern liberals share the classical liberal preference for self-reliant individuals who take responsibility for their own lives; the essential difference is the recognition that this can only occur if social conditions allow it to happen. The central thrust of modern liberalism is therefore the desire to help individuals to help themselves.

Social liberalism

The twentieth century witnessed the growth of state intervention in most western states and in many developing ones. Much of this intervention took the form of social welfare: attempts by government to provide welfare support for its citizens by overcoming poverty, disease and ignorance. If the minimal state was typical of the nineteenth century, during the twentieth century modern states became **welfare states**. This occurred as a consequence of a variety of historical and ideological factors. Governments, for example, sought to achieve national efficiency, healthier work forces and stronger armies. They also came under electoral pressure for social reform from newly enfranchised industrial workers and, in some cases, the peasantry. However, the political argument for welfarism has never been the prerogative of any single ideology. It has been put, in different ways, by socialists, liberals, conservatives, feminists and even at times by fascists. Within liberalism, the case for social welfare has been made by modern liberals, in marked contrast to classical liberals, who extol the virtues of self-help and individual responsibility.

Welfare state: A state that takes primary responsibility for the social welfare of its citizens, discharged through a range of social-security, health, education and other services.

Modern liberals defend welfarism on the basis of equality of opportunity. If particular individuals or groups are disadvantaged by their social circumstances, then the state possesses a social responsibility to reduce or remove these disadvantages to create equal, or at least more equal, life chances. Citizens have thus acquired a range of welfare or social rights, such as the right to work, the right to education and the right to decent housing. Welfare rights are positive rights because they can only be satisfied by the positive actions of government, through the provision of state pensions, benefits and, perhaps, publicly funded health and education services. During the twentieth century, liberal parties and liberal governments were therefore converted to the cause of social welfare. For example, the expanded welfare state in the UK was based on the Beveridge Report (1942), which set out to attack the so-called 'five giants' – want, disease, ignorance, squalor and idleness. It memorably promised to protect citizens 'from the cradle to the grave'. In the USA, liberal welfarism developed in the 1930s during the administration of F. D. Roosevelt, but reached its height in the 1960s with the 'New Frontier' policies of John F. Kennedy, and Lyndon Johnson's 'Great Society' programme.

Social liberalism was further developed in the second half of the twentieth century with the emergence of so-called social-democratic liberalism, especially in the writings of John Rawls. Social-democratic liberalism is distinguished by its support for relative social equality, usually seen as the defining value of socialism. In *A Theory of Justice* (1970), Rawls developed a defence of redistribution and welfare based on the idea of 'equality as fairness'. He argued that if people were unaware of their social position and circumstances, they would view an egalitarian society as 'fairer' than an inegalitarian one, on the grounds that the desire to avoid poverty is greater than the attraction of riches. He therefore proposed the 'difference principle': that social and economic inequalities should be arranged so as to benefit the least well-off, recognising the need for some

Differences between ...
CLASSICAL AND MODERN LIBERALISM

CLASSICAL LIBERALISM	MODERN LIBERALISM
economic liberalism	social liberalism
egoistical individualism	developmental individualism
maximise utility	personal growth
negative freedom	positive freedom
minimal state	enabling state
free-market economy	managed economy
rights-based justice	justice as fairness
strict meritocracy	concern for the poor
individual responsibility	social responsibility
safety-net welfare	cradle-to-grave welfare

KEY FIGURE

John Rawls (1921–2002)

A US academic and philosopher, Rawls' major work, *A Theory of Justice* (1970), is regarded as the most important work of political philosophy written in English since World War II, influencing modern liberals and the social democrats, in particular. Rawls proposed a theory of 'justice as fairness', based on the belief that social inequality can be justified only if it is of benefit to the least advantaged. This presumption in favour of equality is rooted in the assumption that most people, deprived of knowledge about their talents and abilities, would choose to live in an egalitarian, rather than an inegalitarian, society. This use of the so-called 'veil of ignorance' supposedly ensures that views about justice do not just reflect narrow self-interest. Such ideas have been used to justify redistribution and social welfare, although Rawls also insisted that there is a continuing need for some level of material inequality to act as an incentive to enterprise and so to promote economic growth. For more on Rawls, see pp. 15, 29, 84, 190 and 194.

measure of inequality to provide an incentive to work. Nevertheless, such a theory of justice remains liberal rather than socialist, as it is rooted in assumptions about egoism and self-interest, rather than a belief in social solidarity.

Economic management

In addition to providing social welfare, twentieth-century western governments also sought to deliver prosperity by 'managing' their economies. This once again involved rejecting classical liberal thinking, in particular its belief in a self-regulating free market and the doctrine of *laissez-faire*. The abandonment of *laissez-faire* came about because of the increasing complexity of industrial capitalist economies and their apparent inability to guarantee general prosperity if left to their own devices. The Great Depression of the 1930s, sparked off by the Wall Street Crash of 1929, led to high levels of unemployment throughout the industrialised world and in much of the developing world. This was the most dramatic demonstration of the failure of the free market. After World War II, virtually all western states adopted policies of economic intervention in an attempt to prevent a return to the pre-war levels of unemployment. To a large extent these interventionist policies were guided by the work of the UK economist John Maynard Keynes (1883–1946).

In *The General Theory of Employment, Interest and Money* ([1936] 1963), Keynes challenged classical economic thinking and rejected its belief in a self-regulating market. Classical economists had argued that there was a 'market solution' to the problem of unemployment and, indeed, all other economic problems. Keynes argued, however, that the level of economic activity, and therefore of employment, is determined by the total amount of demand – aggregate demand – in the economy. He suggested that governments could 'manage' their economies by influencing the level of aggregate demand. Government spending is, in this sense, an 'injection' of demand into the economy. Taxation, on the other hand,

Key concept ... KEYNESIANISM

Keynesianism refers, narrowly, to the economic theories of J. M. Keynes (1883–1946) and, more broadly, to a range of economic policies that have been influenced by these theories. Keynesianism provides an alternative to neoclassical economics and, in particular, advances a critique of the 'economic anarchy' of *laissez-faire* capitalism. Keynes argued that growth and employment levels are largely determined by the level of 'aggregate demand' in the economy, and that government can regulate demand, primarily through adjustments to fiscal policy, so as to deliver full employment. Keynesianism came to be associated with a narrow obsession with 'tax and spend' policies, but this ignores the complexity and sophistication of Keynes' economic writings. Influenced by economic globalisation, a form of *neo-Keynesianism* has emerged that rejects 'top-down' economic management but still acknowledges that markets are hampered by uncertainty, inequality and differential levels of knowledge.

is a 'withdrawal' from the economy: it reduces aggregate demand and dampens down economic activity. At times of high unemployment, Keynes recommended that governments should 'reflate' their economies by either increasing public spending or cutting taxes. Unemployment could therefore be solved, not by the invisible hand of capitalism, but by government intervention, in this case by running a budget deficit, meaning that the government literally 'overspends'.

Keynesian demand management thus promised to give governments the ability to manipulate employment and growth levels, and hence to secure general prosperity. As with the provision of social welfare, modern liberals have seen economic management as being constructive in promoting prosperity and harmony in civil society. Keynes was not opposed to capitalism; indeed, in many ways, he was its saviour. He simply argued that unrestrained private enterprise is unworkable within complex industrial societies. The first, if limited, attempt to apply Keynes' ideas was undertaken in the USA during Roosevelt's 'New Deal'. By the end of World War II, Keynesianism was widely established as an economic orthodoxy in the West, displacing the older belief in *laissez-faire*. Keynesian policies were credited with being the key to the 'long boom', the historically unprecedented economic growth of the 1950s and 1960s, which witnessed the achievement of widespread affluence, at least in western countries. However, the re-emergence of economic difficulties in the 1970s generated renewed sympathy for the theories of classical political economy, and led to a shift away from Keynesian priorities. Nevertheless, the failure of the free-market revolution of the 1980s and 1990s to ensure sustained economic growth resulted in the emergence of the 'new' political economy, or neo-Keynesianism. Although this recognised the limitations of the 'crude' Keynesianism of the 1950s–1970s, it nevertheless marked a renewed awareness of the link between unregulated capitalism and low investment, short-termism and social fragmentation.

? QUESTIONS FOR DISCUSSION

- Does individualism necessarily imply egoism?
- In what sense is liberalism linked to the Enlightenment project?
- How, within liberalism, is freedom linked to rationalism?
- Why do liberals reject unlimited freedom?
- How convincing is the liberal notion that human beings are reason-guided creatures?
- What are the key implications of social contract theory?
- How do classical liberals defend unregulated capitalism?
- How far are modern liberals willing to go in endorsing social and economic intervention?
- Do modern liberals have a coherent view of the state?
- Is liberal democracy the final solution to the problem of political organisation?
- To what extent is cosmopolitanism based on liberal assumptions?
- Are liberal principles universally valid?

📖 FURTHER READING

Bellamy, R., *Liberalism and Modern Society: An Historical Argument* (1992). An analysis of the development of liberalism that focuses on the adaptations necessary to apply liberal values to new social realities.

Fawcett, E., *Liberalism: The Life of an Idea* (2015). A fluent and stimulating history of liberal thinking from the early nineteenth century to the present day.

Gray, J., *Liberalism*, 2nd edn (1995). A short and not uncritical introduction to liberalism as the political theory of modernity; contains a discussion of post-liberalism.

Kelly, P., *Liberalism* (2005). An engagingly written defence of liberalism as a normative political theory, which particularly examines its link to equality.

3 Conservatism

PREVIEW

In everyday language, the term 'conservative' has a variety of meanings. It can refer to moderate or cautious behaviour, a lifestyle that is conventional, even conformist, or a fear of or refusal to change, particularly denoted by the verb 'to conserve'. 'Conservatism' was first used in the early nineteenth century to describe a distinctive political position or ideology. In the USA, it implied a pessimistic view of public affairs. By the 1820s, the term was being used to denote opposition to the principles and spirit of the 1789 French Revolution. In the UK, 'Conservative' gradually replaced 'Tory' as a title of the principal opposition party to the Whigs, becoming the party's official name in 1835.

As a political ideology, conservatism is defined by the desire to conserve, reflected in a resistance to, or at least a suspicion of, change. However, while the desire to resist change may be the recurrent theme within conservatism, what distinguishes conservatism from rival political creeds is the distinctive way in which this position is upheld, in particular through support for tradition, a belief in human imperfection, and the attempt to uphold the organic structure of society. Conservatism nevertheless encompasses a range of tendencies and inclinations. The chief distinction within conservatism is between what is called 'traditional conservatism' and the New Right. Traditional conservatism defends established institutions and values on the ground that they safeguard the fragile 'fabric of society', giving security-seeking human beings a sense of stability and rootedness. The New Right is characterised by a belief in a strong but minimal state, combining economic libertarianism with social authoritarianism, as represented by neoliberalism and neoconservatism.

CONTENTS

HISTORICAL OVERVIEW

Conservative ideas arose in reaction to the growing pace of political, social and economic change, which, in many ways, was symbolised by the French Revolution. One of the earliest, and perhaps the classic, statement of conservative principles is contained in Edmund Burke's (see p. 40) *Reflections on the Revolution in France* ([1790] 1968), which deeply regretted the revolutionary challenge to the *ancien régime* that had occurred the previous year. During the nineteenth century, western states were transformed by the pressures unleashed by industrialisation and reflected in the growth of liberalism, socialism and nationalism. While these ideologies preached reform, and at times supported revolution, conservatism stood in defence of an increasingly embattled traditional social order.

Conservative thought varied considerably as it adapted itself to existing traditions and national cultures. UK conservatism, for instance, has drawn heavily on the ideas of Burke, who advocated not blind resistance to change, but rather a prudent willingness to 'change in order to conserve'. In the nineteenth century, UK conservatives defended a political and social order that had already undergone profound change, in particular the overthrow of the absolute monarchy, as a result of the English Revolution of the seventeenth century. Such pragmatic principles have also influenced the conservative parties established in other Commonwealth countries. Between 1942 and 2003, the Conservative Party of Canada adopted the title Progressive Conservative precisely to distance itself from reactionary ideas. In continental Europe, where some autocratic monarchies persisted throughout much of the nineteenth century, a very different and more authoritarian form of conservatism developed, which defended monarchy and rigid autocratic values against the rising tide of reform. Only with the formation of Christian Democratic parties after World War II did continental conservatives, notably in Germany and Italy, fully accept political democracy and social reform. The USA, on the other hand, has been influenced relatively little by conservative ideas. The US system of government and its political culture reflect deeply established liberal and progressive values, and politicians of both major parties – the Republicans and the Democrats – have traditionally resented being labelled 'conservative'. It is only since the 1960s that overtly conservative views have been expressed by elements within both parties, notably by southern Democrats and the wing of the Republican Party that was associated in the 1960s with Barry Goldwater, and which supported Ronald Reagan in the 1980s and later George W. Bush.

As conservative ideology arose in reaction to the French Revolution and the process of modernisation in the West, it is less easy to identify political conservatism outside Europe and North America. In Africa, Asia and Latin America, political movements have developed that sought to resist change and preserve traditional ways of life, but they have seldom employed specifically conservative arguments and values. An exception to this is perhaps the Japanese Liberal Democratic Party (LDP), which has dominated politics in Japan since 1955 (with just two brief periods in opposition). The LDP has close links with business interests and is committed to promoting a healthy private sector. At the same time, it has attempted to preserve traditional Japanese values and customs, and has therefore supported distinctively conservative principles such as loyalty, duty and **hierarchy**. In other countries, conservatism has exhibited a populist–authoritarian character. Juan Perón in Argentina and Ayatollah Khomeini in Iran, for instance, both established regimes based on strong central authority, but also mobilised mass popular support on issues such as nationalism, economic progress and the defence of traditional values.

While conservatism is the most intellectually modest of political ideologies, it has also been remarkably resilient, perhaps because of this fact. In many ways, conservatism has prospered because it has been unwilling to be tied down to a fixed system of ideas. Nevertheless, it has undergone major changes since the 1970s, shaped by growing concerns about the welfare state and economic management. Particularly prominent in this respect were the Thatcher governments in the UK, 1979–90, and the Reagan administration in the USA, 1981–9, both of which practised an unusually radical and ideological brand of conservatism, commonly termed the **New Right**. New Right ideas have drawn heavily on free-market economics and, in so doing, have exposed deep divisions within conservatism. Indeed, commentators argue that 'Thatcherism' and 'Reaganism', and the New Right project in general, do not properly belong within conservative ideology at all, so deeply are they influenced by classical liberal economics.

The New Right has challenged traditional conservative economic views, but it nevertheless remains part of conservative ideology. In the first place, it has not abandoned traditional conservative social principles such as a belief in order, authority and discipline, and in some respects it has strengthened them. Furthermore, the New Right's enthusiasm for the free market has exposed the extent to which conservatism had already been influenced by liberal ideas. From the late nineteenth century onwards, conservatism has been divided between paternalistic support for state intervention and a libertarian commitment to the free market. The significance of the New Right is that it sought to revive the electoral fortunes of conservatism by readjusting the balance between these traditions in favour of libertarianism (see p. 48).

CORE IDEAS AND PRINCIPLES

HUMAN NATURE

While liberals and socialists tend to assume that human beings are naturally 'good', or that they can be made 'good' if their social circumstances are improved, conservatives see human beings as both imperfect and unperfectible. Indeed, conservatism has been described as a 'philosophy of human imperfection' (O'Sullivan, 1976). This imperfection has taken three forms. In the first place, human beings have been thought of as *psychologically* limited and dependent creatures. In the view of conservatives, people fear isolation and instability. They are drawn psychologically to the safe and the familiar, and, above all, seek the security of knowing 'their place'. The belief that people desire security and belonging has led conservatives to emphasise the importance of social order, and to be suspicious of the attractions of liberty. Order ensures that human life is stable and predictable; it provides security in an uncertain world. Liberty,

Hierarchy: A pyramidically ranked system of command and obedience, in which social position is unconnected with individual ability.

New Right: An ideological trend within conservatism that embraces a blend of neoliberalism (see p. 51) and neoconservatism (see p. 55).

on the other hand, presents individuals with choices and can generate change and uncertainty. Conservatives have often echoed the views of Thomas Hobbes (see below) in being prepared to sacrifice liberty in the cause of social order.

Second, whereas other political philosophies trace the origins of immoral or criminal behaviour to society, conservatives believe it is rooted in the individual. Human beings are thought to be *morally* imperfect. Conservatives hold a pessimistic, even Hobbesian, view of human nature. Humankind is innately selfish and greedy, anything but perfectible; as Hobbes put it, the desire for 'power after power' is the primary human urge. Some conservatives explain this by reference to the Old Testament doctrine of 'original sin'. Crime is therefore not a product of inequality or social disadvantage, as socialists and modern liberals tend to believe; rather, it is a consequence of base human instincts and appetites. People can only be persuaded to behave in a civilised fashion if they are deterred from expressing their violent and anti-social impulses. And the only effective deterrent is law, backed up by the knowledge that it will be strictly enforced. This explains the conservative preference for strong government and for 'tough' criminal justice regimes, based, often, on long prison sentences and the use of corporal or even capital punishment. For conservatives, the role of law is not to uphold liberty, but to preserve order. The concepts of 'law' and 'order' are so closely related in the conservative mind that they have almost become a single, fused concept.

Third, humankind's *intellectual* powers are also thought to be limited. Conservatives have traditionally believed that the world is simply too complicated for human reason to grasp fully. The political world, as Michael Oakeshott (see p. 37) put it, is 'boundless and bottomless'. Conservatives are therefore suspicious of abstract ideas and systems of thought that claim to understand what is, they argue, simply incomprehensible. They prefer to ground their ideas in **tradition**, experience and history, adopting a cautious, moderate and above all pragmatic approach to the world, and avoiding, if at all possible, doctrinaire or dogmatic beliefs. High-sounding political principles such as the 'rights of man',

Tradition: Values, practices or institutions that have endured through time and, in particular, been passed down from one generation to the next.

KEY FIGURE

Thomas Hobbes (1588–1679)

An English political philosopher, Hobbes, in his masterwork *Leviathan* (1651), defended absolutist government as the only alternative to anarchy and disorder. He portrayed life in a stateless society, the state of nature, as a 'war of all against all', based on the belief that human beings are essentially power-seeking and self-interested creatures. In Hobbes' view, citizens have an unqualified obligation towards the state, on the grounds that to limit the power of government is to risk a descent into the state of nature. Any system of political rule, however tyrannical, is preferable to no rule at all. Hobbes' pessimistic view of human nature and his emphasis on the vital importance of authority have had a considerable impact on conservative thought. However, Hobbes' writings also resembled early liberalism in some respects. This can be seen most clearly in the fact that he reached his absolutist conclusions through the use of a rationalist device, social contract theory, rather than through a belief in the divine right of kings, For more on Hobbes, see above, pp. 16, 22, 97 and 106.

'equality' and 'social justice' are fraught with danger because they provide a blueprint for the reform or remodelling of the world. Conservatives have thus typically eschewed the 'politics of principle' and adopted instead a traditionalist political stance (see p. 5, for a discussion of the conservative view of ideology). Nevertheless, conservative support for both traditionalism and pragmatism (see below) has weakened as a result of the rise of the New Right. In the first place, the New Right is radical, in that it has sought to advance free-market reforms by dismantling inherited welfarist and interventionist structures. Second, the New Right's radicalism is based on rationalism (see p. 13) and a commitment to abstract theories and principles, notably those of economic liberalism.

SOCIETY

The conservative view of society is based on the belief, discussed earlier, that human beings are dependent and security-seeking creatures. This implies that they do not, and cannot, exist outside society, but desperately need to belong,

Key concept ... **PRAGMATISM**

Pragmatism, broadly defined, refers to behaviour that is shaped in accordance with practical considerations and goals, rather than principles or ideological objectives. As a philosophical tradition, associated with 'classical pragmatists' William James (1841–1910) and John Dewey (1859–1952), pragmatism is a method for settling metaphysical disputes that seeks to clarify the meaning of concepts and hypotheses by identifying their practical consequences. The benefits of pragmatism in politics are that it allows policies and political assertions to be judged 'on their merits' (on the basis of 'what works'), and that it prevents ideology from becoming divorced from reality and turning into mere wishful thinking. Critics, however, equate pragmatism with a lack of principle or a tendency to follow public opinion rather than leaders.

KEY FIGURE

Michael Oakeshott (1901–90)

A British political philosopher, Oakeshott's collection of essays, *Rationalism in Politics and Other Essays* (1962), and his more systematic work of political philosophy, *On Human Conduct* (1975), were key texts of conservative traditionalism, exploring both the nature and implications of human imperfection. By highlighting the importance of civil association and insisting on the limited province of politics, he developed themes closely associated with liberal thought. Oakeshott is nevertheless best known for his powerful defence of a pragmatic and non-ideological style of politics, upholding traditional values and established customs on the grounds that the conservative disposition is to prefer 'the familiar to the unknown'. Oakeshott's style of conservatism was also characterised by the belief that governing is a 'specific and limited activity', amounting only to a means of enabling individuals to pursue their chosen activities through the formation of civil associations. In this light, he influenced many of the thinkers of the New Right. For more on Oakeshott, see above, pp. 5 and 36.

PERSPECTIVES ON ...
HUMAN NATURE

LIBERALS view human nature as a set of innate qualities intrinsic to the individual, placing little or no emphasis on social or historical conditioning. Humans are self-seeking and largely self-reliant creatures; but they are also governed by reason and are capable of personal development, particularly through education.

CONSERVATIVES believe that human beings are essentially limited and security-seeking creatures, drawn to the known, the familiar, the tried and tested. Human rationality is unreliable, and moral corruption is implicit in each human individual. The New Right nevertheless embraces a form of self-seeking individualism (see p. 12).

SOCIALISTS regard humans as essentially social creatures, their capacities and behaviour being shaped more by nurture than by nature, and particularly by creative labour. Their propensity for cooperation, sociability and rationality means that the prospects for personal growth and social development are considerable.

ANARCHISTS advance a complex theory of human nature in which rival potentialities reside in the human soul. While the human 'core' may be morally and intellectually enlightened, a capacity for corruption lurks within each and every individual.

NATIONALISTS embrace a communitarian theory of human nature in which individual identity is shaped by the communities to which people belong, with a 'higher' loyalty and deeper political significance attaching to the nation than to any other social group. Humankind is therefore naturally divided into a collection of nations, each possessing a distinctive character and separate identity.

FEMINISTS usually hold that men and women share a common human nature, gender differences being culturally or socially imposed. Separatist feminists nevertheless argue that men are genetically disposed to domination and cruelty, while women are naturally sympathetic, creative and peaceful.

ECOLOGISTS, particularly deep ecologists, see human nature as part of the broader ecosystem, even as part of nature itself. Materialism, greed and egoism therefore reflect the extent to which humans have become alienated from the oneness of life and thus from their own true nature. Human fulfilment requires a return to nature.

Social conservatism: The belief that society is fashioned out of a fragile network of relationships which need to be upheld through duty, traditional values and established institutions.

Anomie: A weakening of values and normative rules, associated with feelings of isolation, loneliness and meaninglessness.

to have 'roots' in society. The individual cannot be separated from society, but is part of the social groups that nurture him or her: family, friends or peer group, workmates or colleagues, local community and even the nation. These groups provide individual life with security and meaning, a stance often called '**social conservatism**'. As a result, traditional conservatives are reluctant to understand freedom in 'negative' terms, in which the individual is 'left alone' and suffers, as the French sociologist Émile Durkheim (1856–1917) put it, from **anomie**. Freedom is, rather, a willing acceptance of social obligations and ties by individuals who recognise their value. Freedom involves 'doing one's duty'. When, for example, parents instruct children how to behave, they are not constraining their liberty, but providing guidance for their children's benefit. To act as a dutiful son or daughter and conform to parental wishes is to act freely, out of a recognition of one's obligations. Conservatives believe that a society in which individuals knew only their rights, and did not acknowledge their duties, would be rootless and atomistic. Indeed, it is the bonds of duty and obligation that hold society together.

Such ideas are based on a very particular view of society, sometimes called '**organicism**'. Conservatives have traditionally thought of society as a living thing, an organism, whose parts work together just as the brain, heart, lungs and liver do within a human organism. Organisms differ from artefacts or machines in two important respects. First, unlike machines, organisms are not simply a collection of individual parts that can be arranged or rearranged at will. Within an organism, the whole is more than a collection of its individual parts; the whole is sustained by a fragile set of relationships between and among its parts, which, once damaged, can result in the organism's death. Thus, a human body cannot be stripped down and reassembled in the same way as, say, a bicycle. Second, organisms are shaped by 'natural' factors rather than human ingenuity. An organic society is fashioned, ultimately, by natural necessity. For example, the family has not been 'invented' by any social thinker or political theorist, but is a product of natural social impulses such as love, caring and responsibility. In no sense do children in a family agree to a 'contract' on joining the family – they simply grow up within it and are nurtured and guided by it.

The tendency within conservatism to understand society on the basis of the 'organic metaphor' helps to explain the emphasis that conservative thinkers have placed on tradition and hierarchy. Conservatives venerate tradition on two grounds. First, they believe that it generates, for both society and the individual, a sense of identity. Established customs and practices are ones that individuals can recognise; they are familiar and reassuring. Tradition thus provides people with a feeling of 'rootedness' and belonging, which is all the stronger because it is historically based. It generates social cohesion by linking people to the past and providing them with a collective sense of who they are. Burke thus described society as a partnership between 'those who are living, those who are dead and those who are to be born'. Second, tradition is a vital guide to action. From the conservative perspective, tradition represents the accumulated wisdom of the past. The institutions and practices of the past have been 'tested by time', and should therefore be preserved for the benefit of the living and for generations to come. Such a notion of tradition reflects an almost Darwinian belief that those institutions and customs that have survived have only done so because they have worked and been found to be of value. They have been endorsed by a process of 'natural selection' and demonstrated their fitness to survive.

The final aspect of conservative thinking about society is a tendency to believe in hierarchy. This is also based on a belief in organic assumptions. Just as the brain, the heart and the liver all perform very different functions within the body, the various classes and groups that make up society also have their own specific roles. There must be leaders and there must be followers; there must be managers and there must be workers; for that matter, there must be those who go out to work and those who stay at home and bring up children. Genuine social equality is therefore a myth; in reality, there is a natural inequality

Organicism: A belief that society operates like an organism or living entity, the whole being more than a collection of its individual parts.

KEY FIGURE

Edmund Burke (1729–97)

A Dublin-born British statesman and political theorist, Burke's writings emphasise the need for political action to be rooted in tradition and experience. Deeply opposed to the attempt to recast French politics in accordance with the principles of liberty, equality and fraternity, he argued that wisdom resides largely in history and, in particular, in institutions and practices that have survived through time. Burke nevertheless held that the French monarchy had been partly responsible for its own fate, as it had refused to 'change in order to conserve'. Burke had a gloomy view of government, recognising that, although it may prevent evil, it rarely promotes good. His most important work is *Reflections on the Revolution in France* (1790). Burke also supported the classical economics of Adam Smith, regarding market forces as an example of 'natural law', and championed a theory of representation that stresses trusteeship and holds that representatives serve their constituents best when they think for themselves and use their own judgement. For more on Burke, see pp. 34, 39, 41, 43, 45 and 48–9.

PERSPECTIVES ON ...
SOCIETY

LIBERALS regard society not as an entity in its own right but as a collection of individuals. To the extent that society exists, it is fashioned out of voluntary and contractual agreements made by self-interested human beings. Nevertheless, there is a general balance of interests in society that tends to promote harmony and equilibrium.

CONSERVATIVES believe that society should be viewed as an organism, a living entity. Society thus has an existence outside the individual, and in a sense is prior to the individual; it is held together by the bonds of tradition, authority and a common morality. Neoliberals nevertheless subscribe to a form of liberal atomism.

SOCIALISTS have traditionally understood society in terms of unequal class power, economic and property divisions being deeper and more genuine than any broader social bonds. Marxists believe that society is characterised by class struggle, and argue that the only stable and cohesive society is a classless one.

ANARCHISTS believe that society is characterised by unregulated and natural harmony, based on the natural human disposition towards cooperation and sociability. Social conflict and disharmony are thus clearly unnatural, a product of political rule and economic inequality.

NATIONALISTS view society in terms of cultural or ethnic distinctiveness. Society is thus characterised by shared values and beliefs, ultimately rooted in a common national identity. This implies that multinational or multicultural societies are inherently unstable.

FEMINISTS have understood society in terms of patriarchy and an artificial division between the 'public' and 'private' spheres of life. Society may therefore be seen as an organised hypocrisy designed to routinise and uphold a system of male power.

MULTICULTURALISTS view society as a mosaic of cultural groups, defined by their distinctive ethnic, religious or historical identities. The basis for wider social bonds, cutting across cultural distinctiveness, is thus restricted, perhaps, to civic allegiance.

of wealth and social position, justified by a corresponding inequality of social responsibilities. The working class might not enjoy the same living standards and life chances as their employers, but, at the same time, they do not have the livelihoods and security of many other people resting on their shoulders. Hierarchy and organicism have thus invested in traditional conservatism a pronounced tendency towards paternalism (see p. 47).

However, the rise of the New Right has weakened support within conservatism for organic ideas and theories. In line with the robust individualism (see p. 12) of classical liberalism, libertarian conservatives, including neoliberals, have held that society is a product of the actions of self-seeking and largely self-reliant individuals. This position was memorably expressed in Margaret Thatcher's assertion, paraphrasing Jeremy Bentham (1748–1832), that 'There is no such thing as society; there are individual men and women and there are families.'

THE STATE

Traditional conservatives have a view of the state that is rooted in wider thinking about the nature and role of **authority**. Conservatives do not accept the liberal belief that authority (and therefore the state) arises out of contracts made by free individuals. In liberal theory, authority is thought to be established by individuals for their own benefit. In contrast, conservatives believe that authority, like society, develops naturally. For example, in the case of children, it arises from the need to ensure that they are cared for, kept away from danger, have a healthy diet, go to bed at sensible times and so on. Such authority can only be imposed 'from above', quite simply because children do not know what is good for them. It does not and cannot arise 'from below': in no sense can children be said to have agreed to be governed. Authority is therefore rooted in the nature of society and all social institutions. In schools, authority is exercised by the teacher; in the workplace, by the employer; and in society at large, by government and the institutions of the state.

In this light, conservatives have placed a special emphasis on the capacity of government and the state to provide society with leadership. Leadership is a vital ingredient in any society because it is the capacity to give direction and provide inspiration for others. Traditional conservatives have, moreover, often seen leadership in personal terms, seeing political judgement and the capacity to enthuse and inspire as either natural gifts or products of privileged family or educational circumstances. Such a view enabled thinkers such as Burke to embrace the idea of a '**natural aristocracy**'. This stress on leadership and privilege helps to explain why conservatives sometimes adjusted more slowly and with less enthusiasm than liberals or socialists to the advent of democracy.

Authority: The right to exert influence over others by virtue of an acknowledged obligation to obey.

Natural aristocracy: The idea that talent and leadership are innate or inbred qualities that cannot be acquired through effort or self-advancement.

The stress on the need for leadership created a pro-state tendency within conservative ideology. In the UK, this was evident in the impact of figures such as Joseph Chamberlain (1836–1914), the radical social reformer and advocate of municipal government who in the 1980s broke with the Liberals and effectively joined the Conservatives. In the USA, a tradition of strong-state conservatism can be traced back to the presidency of Theodore Roosevelt, 1901–9, which was reflected in an insistence that no private interest should be stronger than the US state. However, such tendencies have usually been countered by deeper fears within conservatism about the dangers of 'over-government'. These fears have nevertheless been substantially strengthened by the rise of the New Right. The New Right, or at least its neoliberal or libertarian wing, is distinguished by a strong antipathy towards government intervention, born out of the belief that the state is a parasitic growth which threatens both individual liberty and economic security. The state is no longer a neutral referee but has become a self-serving monster, a 'nanny' or 'leviathan' state, interfering in every aspect of life.

THE ECONOMY

There are two basic positions taken on the economy within conservative ideology. One of these is traditionalist and paternalist in character, and countenances at least qualified economic intervention, while the other is liberal or libertarian in character and is firmly opposed to intervention. Both positions, however, have been constructed on the basis of a defence of private **property**, albeit advanced through contrasting arguments. From the liberal perspective, property reflects merit: those who work hard and possess talent will, and should, acquire wealth. Property, therefore, is 'earned'. This doctrine has an attraction for those conservatives who regard the ability to accumulate wealth as an important economic incentive. Traditional conservatives nevertheless link property to a range of psychological and social advantages. For example, it provides security. In an uncertain and unpredictable world, property ownership gives people a sense of confidence and assurance, something to 'fall back on'. Property, whether the ownership of a house or savings in the bank, provides individuals with a source of protection. Another argument in favour of property associates it with the promotion of important social values. Those who possess and enjoy their own property are thus seen to be more likely to respect the property of others. Having a 'stake' in society, property owners therefore have an interest in maintaining law and order. In this sense, property ownership can promote what have been portrayed as the 'conservative' values of respect for law, authority and social order.

Traditional conservatives have used such ideas and arguments in support of a paternalist approach to economic matters. In particular, they have challenged the liberal view of property by insisting that all rights, including property rights, entail obligations. Property is not an issue for the individual alone, but is also of importance to society. This can be seen, for instance, in the social bonds that cut across generations. Property is not merely the creation of the present generation. Much of it – land, houses, works of art and so on – has been passed down from earlier generations. The present generation is, in that sense, the custodian of the wealth of the nation and has a duty to preserve and protect it for the benefit of future generations. Harold Macmillan, UK Conservative prime minister, 1957–63, expressed such a view during the 1980s when he objected to the Thatcher government's policy of **privatisation**, describing it as 'selling

Property: The ownership of physical goods or wealth, whether by private individuals, groups of people or the state.

Privatisation: The transfer of state assets from the public to the private sector, reflecting a contraction of the state's responsibilities.

off the family silver'. Social obligations do not just bind generations together but also suggest that the wealthy have a duty to attend to the interests of the less well-off, a stance that has been used to justify social welfare. Such thinking has been most clearly developed in the 'One Nation' conservative tradition, discussed later in this chapter.

Liberal or libertarian thinking about the economy within conservatism has been most clearly associated with the New Right. This differs from paternalist economic thinking in at least three respects. First, property rights are taken to be absolute, in the sense that they are unconstrained by obligations or wider social responsibilities. Having 'earned' their wealth (supposedly through talent and hard work), people have an unchecked right to use it however they wish. Such a stance is often seen to be incompatible with any system of welfare or redistribution. Second, while traditionalist or paternalist economic thinking is largely shaped by pragmatic considerations and a sense of 'what works', liberal or libertarian thinking is affirmatively rationalist, being grounded in the theories of market economics. Third, rather than accepting the notion of a balance between the economy and the state, liberals or libertarians insist that only an unregulated capitalist economy can deliver efficiency and generate prosperity. The thinking behind this view is examined later in the chapter in connection with neoliberalism (see p. 51).

TYPES OF CONSERVATISM

AUTHORITARIAN CONSERVATISM

Whereas all conservatives would claim to respect the concept of authority, few modern conservatives would accept that their views are authoritarian. Nevertheless, while contemporary conservatives are keen to demonstrate their commitment to democratic, particularly liberal-democratic, principles, there is a tradition within conservatism that has favoured authoritarian rule, especially in continental Europe. At the time of the French Revolution, the principal defender of autocratic rule was the French political thinker Joseph de Maistre (1753–1821). De Maistre was a fierce critic of the French Revolution, but, in contrast to Burke, he wished to restore absolute power to the hereditary monarchy. He was a reactionary and was quite unprepared to accept any reform of the *ancien régime*, which had been overthrown in 1789. His political philosophy was based on willing and complete subordination to 'the master'. In *Du Pape* (in Maistre, [1817] 1971) de Maistre went further and argued that above the earthly monarchies a supreme spiritual power should rule in the person of the pope. His central concern was the preservation of order, which alone, he believed, could provide people with safety and security. Revolution, and even reform, would weaken the chains that bind people together and lead to a descent into chaos and oppression.

Throughout the nineteenth century, conservatives in continental Europe remained faithful to the rigid and hierarchical values of autocratic rule, and stood unbending in the face of rising liberal, nationalist and socialist protest.

Nowhere was authoritarianism more entrenched than in Russia, where Tsar Nicholas I, 1825–55, proclaimed the principles of 'orthodoxy, autocracy and nationality', in contrast to the values that had inspired the French Revolution: 'liberty, equality and fraternity'. Nicholas's successors stubbornly refused to allow their power to be constrained by constitutions or the development of parliamentary institutions. In Germany, constitutional government did develop, but Otto von Bismarck, the imperial chancellor, 1871–90, ensured that it remained a sham. Elsewhere, authoritarianism remained particularly strong in Catholic countries. The papacy suffered not only the loss of its temporal authority with the achievement of Italian unification, which led Pope Pius IX to declare himself a 'prisoner of the Vatican', but also an assault on its doctrines with the rise of secular political ideologies. In 1864, Pius IX condemned all radical or progressive ideas, including those of nationalism, liberalism and socialism, as 'false doctrines of our most unhappy age', and when confronted with the loss of the Papal States and Rome, he proclaimed in 1870 the edict of papal infallibility. The unwillingness of continental conservatives to come to terms with reform and democratic government extended well into the twentieth century. For example, conservative elites in Italy and Germany helped to overthrow parliamentary democracy and bring Benito Mussolini and Adolf Hitler to power by providing support for, and giving respectability to, rising fascist movements.

In other cases, conservative–authoritarian regimes have looked to the newly enfranchised masses for political support. This happened in nineteenth-century France, where Louis Napoleon succeeded in being elected president, and later in establishing himself as Emperor Napoleon III, by appealing to the smallholding peasantry, the largest element of the French electorate. The Napoleonic regime fused authoritarianism with the promise of economic prosperity and social reform in the kind of plebiscitary dictatorship more commonly found in the twentieth century. Bonapartism has parallels with twentieth-century Peronism. Juan Perón was dictator of Argentina, 1946–55, and proclaimed the familiar authoritarian themes of obedience, order and national unity. However, he based his political support not on the interests of traditional elites, but on an appeal to

Key concept ... **AUTHORITARIANISM**

Authoritarianism is belief in or the practice of government 'from above', in which authority is exercised over a population with or without its consent. Authoritarianism thus differs from authority. The latter rests on legitimacy, and in that sense arises 'from below'. Authoritarian thinkers typically base their views on either a belief in the wisdom of established leaders or the idea that social order can only be maintained by unquestioning obedience. However, authoritarianism is usually distinguished from totalitarianism. The practice of government 'from above', which is associated with monarchical absolutism, traditional dictatorships and most forms of military rule, is concerned with the repression of opposition and political liberty, rather than the more radical goal of obliterating the distinction between the state and civil society.

the impoverished masses, the 'shirtless ones', as Perón called them. The Peronist regime was populist (see p. 57) in that it moulded its policies according to the instincts and wishes of the common people, in this case popular resentment against 'Yankee imperialism', and a widespread desire for economic and social progress. Similar regimes have developed in parts of Africa, Asia and the Middle East. However, although such regimes have tended to consolidate the position of conservative elites, and often embrace a distinctively conservative form of nationalism, authoritarian–populist regimes such as Perón's perhaps exhibit features that are associated more closely with fascism (see p. 130) than with conservatism.

PATERNALISTIC CONSERVATISM

While continental conservatives adopted an attitude of uncompromising resistance to change, a more flexible and ultimately more successful Anglo-American tradition can be traced back to Edmund Burke. The lesson that Burke drew from the French Revolution was that change can be natural or inevitable, in which case it should not be resisted. 'A state without the means of some change,' he suggested, 'is without the means of its conservation' (Burke, [1790] 1968). The characteristic style of Burkean conservatism is cautious, modest and pragmatic; it reflects a suspicion of fixed principles, whether revolutionary or reactionary. As Ian Gilmour (1978) put it, 'the wise Conservative travels light'. The values that conservatives hold most dear – tradition, order, authority, property and so on – will be safe only if policy is developed in the light of practical circumstances and experience. Such a position will rarely justify dramatic or radical change, but accepts a prudent willingness to 'change in order to conserve'. Pragmatic conservatives support neither the individual nor the state in principle, but are prepared to support either, or, more frequently, recommend a balance between the two, depending on 'what works'. In practice, the reforming impulse in conservatism has also been associated closely with the survival into the modern period of neo-feudal paternalistic values, as represented in particular by One Nation conservatism.

One Nation conservatism

Since 1945, in continental Europe in particular, conservative paternalism has been associated with Christian democracy (see p. 46). The Anglo-American paternalistic tradition is nevertheless much older. It can be traced back to Benjamin Disraeli (1804–81), UK prime minister in 1868 and again 1874–80. Disraeli developed his political philosophy in two novels, Sybil (1845) and Coningsby (1844), written before he assumed ministerial responsibilities. These novels emphasised the principle of social obligation, in stark contrast to the extreme individualism then dominant within the political establishment. Disraeli wrote against a background of growing industrialisation, economic inequality and, in continental Europe at least, revolutionary upheaval. He tried to draw attention to the danger of Britain being divided into 'two nations: the Rich and the Poor'. In the best conservative tradition, Disraeli's argument was based on a combination of prudence and principle.

Key concept ... **CHRISTIAN DEMOCRACY**

Christian democracy is a political and ideological movement that advances a moderate and welfarist brand of conservatism. The origins of Christian democracy lie in Catholic social theory, which, in contrast to Protestantism's stress on individualism, emphasises the importance of social groups, especially the family, and highlights a harmony of interests among these groups. While Christian democracy is ideologically vague and has adapted itself to different national cultures, its most influential idea, particularly associated with the German Christian Democratic Union (CDU), is the notion of the social market. A social market is an economy structured on market lines and largely free from government control, operating in the context of a society in which cohesion is maintained through a comprehensive welfare state and effective public services.

On the one hand, growing social inequality contains the seeds of revolution. A poor and oppressed working class, Disraeli feared, would not simply accept its misery. The revolutions that had broken out in Europe in 1830 and 1848 seemed to bear out this belief. Reform would therefore be sensible, because, in stemming the tide of revolution, it would ultimately be in the interests of the rich. On the other hand, Disraeli appealed to moral values. He suggested that wealth and privilege brought with them social obligations, in particular a responsibility for the poor or less well-off. In so doing, Disraeli drew on the organic conservative belief that society is held together by an acceptance of duty and obligations. He believed that society is naturally hierarchical, but also held that inequalities of wealth or social privilege give rise to an inequality of responsibilities. The wealthy and powerful must shoulder the burden of social responsibility, which, in effect, is the price of privilege. These ideas were based on the feudal principle of *noblesse oblige*, the obligation of the aristocracy to be honourable and generous. For example, the landed nobility claimed to exercise a paternal responsibility for their peasants, as the king did in relation to the nation. Disraeli recommended that these obligations should not be abandoned, but should be expressed, in an increasingly industrialised world, in social reform. Such ideas came to be represented by the slogan 'One Nation'. In office, Disraeli was responsible both for the Second Reform Act of 1867, which for the first time extended the right to vote to the working class, and for the social reforms that improved housing conditions and hygiene.

Disraeli's ideas had a considerable impact on conservatism and contributed to a radical and reforming tradition that appeals both to the pragmatic instincts of conservatives and to their sense of social duty. In the UK, these ideas provide the basis of so-called 'One Nation conservatism', whose supporters sometimes style themselves as 'Tories' to denote their commitment to pre-industrial, hierarchic and paternal values. Disraeli's ideas were subsequently taken up in the late nineteenth century by Randolph Churchill (1911–68) in the form of 'Tory democracy'. In an age of widening political democracy, Churchill stressed the need for traditional institutions – for example, the monarchy, the House of

Key concept ... PATERNALISM

'Paternalism' literally means to act in a fatherly fashion. As a political principle, it refers to power or authority being exercised over others with the intention of conferring benefit or preventing harm. Social welfare and laws such as the compulsory wearing of seat belts in cars are examples of paternalism. 'Soft' paternalism is characterised by broad consent on the part of those subject to paternalism. 'Hard' paternalism operates regardless of consent, and thus overlaps with authoritarianism. The basis for paternalism is that wisdom and experience are unequally distributed in society, and that those in authority 'know best'. Opponents argue that authority is not to be trusted and that paternalism restricts liberty and contributes to the 'infantilisation' of society.

Lords and the church – to enjoy a wider base of social support. This could be achieved by winning working-class votes for the Conservative Party by continuing Disraeli's policy of social reform. One Nation conservatism can thus be seen as a form of Tory welfarism.

The high point of the One Nation tradition was reached in the 1950s and 1960s, when conservative governments in the UK and elsewhere came to practise a version of Keynesian social democracy, managing the economy in line with the goal of full employment and supporting enlarged welfare provision. This stance was based on the need for a non-ideological, 'middle way' between the extremes of *laissez-faire* liberalism and socialist state planning. Conservatism was therefore the way of moderation, and sought to draw a balance between rampant individualism and overbearing collectivism (see p. 64). In the UK, this idea was most clearly expressed in Harold Macmillan's *The Middle Way* ([1938] 1966). Macmillan, who was to be prime minister from 1957 to 1963, advocated what he called 'planned capitalism', which he described as 'a mixed system which combines state ownership, regulation or control of certain aspects of

Key concept ... TORYISM

'Tory' was used in eighteenth-century Britain to refer to a parliamentary faction that (as opposed to the Whigs) supported monarchical power and the Church of England, and represented the landed gentry; in the USA, it implied loyalty to the British Crown. Although in the mid-nineteenth century the British Conservative Party emerged out of the Tories, and in the UK 'Tory' is still widely (but unhelpfully) used as a synonym for Conservative, Toryism is best understood as a distinctive ideological stance within broader conservatism. Its characteristic features are a belief in hierarchy, tradition, duty and organicism. While 'high' Toryism articulates a neo-feudal belief in a ruling class and a pre-democratic faith in established institutions, the Tory tradition is also hospitable to welfarist and reformist ideas, provided these serve the cause of social continuity.

economic activity with the drive and initiative of private enterprise'. Such ideas later resurfaced, in the USA and the UK, in the notions of 'compassionate conservatism'. However, paternalist conservatism only provides a qualified basis for social and economic intervention. The purpose of One Nationism, for instance, is to consolidate hierarchy rather than to remove it, and its wish to improve the conditions of the less well-off is limited to the desire to ensure that the poor no longer pose a threat to the established order.

LIBERTARIAN CONSERVATISM

Although conservatism draws heavily on pre-industrial ideas such as organicism, hierarchy and obligation, the ideology has also been much influenced by liberal ideas, especially classical liberal ideas. This is sometimes seen as a late twentieth-century development, neoliberals having in some way 'hijacked' conservatism in the interests of classical liberalism. Nevertheless, liberal doctrines, especially those concerning the free market, have been advanced by conservatives since the late eighteenth century, and can be said to constitute a rival tradition to conservative paternalism. These ideas are libertarian in that they advocate the greatest possible economic liberty and the least possible government regulation of social life. Libertarian conservatives have not simply converted to liberalism, but believe that liberal economics is compatible with a more traditional, conservative social philosophy, based on values such as authority and duty. This is evident in the work of Edmund Burke, in many ways the founder of traditional conservatism, but also a keen supporter of the **economic liberalism** of Adam Smith.

The libertarian tradition has been strongest in those countries where classical liberal ideas have had the greatest impact, once again the UK and the USA. As early as the late eighteenth century, Burke expressed a strong preference for free trade in commercial affairs and a competitive, self-regulating market economy in domestic affairs. The free market is efficient and fair, but it is also, Burke believed, natural and necessary. It is 'natural' in that it reflects a desire for wealth, a 'love of lucre', that is part of human nature. The laws of the market are therefore

Economic liberalism: A belief in the market as a self-regulating mechanism that tends naturally to deliver general prosperity and opportunities for all (see pp 23–4).

Key concept ... **LIBERTARIANISM**

Libertarianism refers to a range of theories that give strict priority to liberty (understood in negative terms) over other values, such as authority, tradition and equality. Libertarians thus seek to maximise the realm of individual freedom and minimise the scope of public authority, typically seeing the state as the principal threat to liberty. The two best-known libertarian traditions are rooted in the idea of individual rights (as with Robert Nozick, see p. 54) and in *laissez-faire* economic doctrines (as with Friedrich von Hayek, 1899–1992), although socialists have also embraced libertarianism. Libertarianism is sometimes distinguished from liberalism on the grounds that the latter, even in its classical form, refuses to give priority to liberty over order. However, it differs from anarchism in that libertarians generally recognise the need for a minimal state, sometimes styling themselves as 'minarchists'.

Differences between …

PATERNALISTIC AND LIBERTARIAN CONSERVATISM

PATERNALISTIC CONSERVATISM	**LIBERTARIAN CONSERVATISM**
• pragmatism	• principle
• traditionalism	• radicalism
• social duty	• egoism
• organic society	• atomistic individualism
• hierarchy	• meritocracy
• social responsibility	• individual responsibility
• natural order	• market order
• 'middle way' economics	• *laissez-faire* economics
• qualified welfarism	• anti-welfarism

'natural laws'. He accepted that working conditions dictated by the market are, for many, 'degrading, unseemly, unmanly and often most unwholesome', but insisted that they would suffer further if the 'natural course of things' were to be disturbed. The capitalist free market could thus be defended on the grounds of tradition, just like the monarchy and the church.

Libertarian conservatives are not, however, consistent liberals. They believe in economic individualism and 'getting government off the back of business', but are less prepared to extend this principle of individual liberty to other aspects of social life. Conservatives, even libertarian conservatives, have a more pessimistic view of human nature. A strong state is required to maintain public order and ensure that authority is respected. Indeed, in some respects libertarian conservatives are attracted to free-market theories precisely because they promise to secure social order. Whereas liberals have believed that the market economy preserves individual liberty and freedom of choice, conservatives have at times been attracted to the market as an instrument of social discipline. Market forces regulate and control economic and social activity. For example, they may deter workers from pushing for wage increases by threatening them with unemployment. As such, the market can be seen as an instrument that maintains social stability and works alongside the more evident forces of coercion: the police and the courts. While some conservatives have feared that market capitalism will lead to endless innovation and restless competition, upsetting social cohesion, others have been attracted to it in the belief that it can establish a 'market order', sustained by impersonal 'natural laws' rather than the guiding hand of political authority.

THE NEW RIGHT

During the early post-1945 period, pragmatic and paternalistic ideas dominated conservatism through much of the western world. The remnants of authoritarian conservatism collapsed with the overthrow of the Portuguese and Spanish dictatorships in the 1970s. Just as conservatives had come to accept political democracy during the nineteenth century, after 1945 they came to accept a qualified form of social democracy. This tendency was confirmed by the rapid and sustained economic growth of the post-war years, the 'long boom', which appeared to bear out the success of 'managed capitalism'. During the 1970s, however, a set of more radical ideas developed within conservatism, challenging directly the Keynesian–welfarist orthodoxy. These 'New Right' ideas had their greatest initial impact in the USA and the UK, but they also came to be influential in parts of continental Europe, Australia and New Zealand, and had some kind of effect on western states across the globe.

'The New Right' is a broad term and has been used to describe ideas that range from the demand for tax cuts to calls for greater censorship of television and films, and even campaigns against immigration or in favour of repatriation. In essence, the New Right is a marriage between two apparently contrasting ideological traditions:

▶ The first of these is classical liberal economics, particularly the free-market theories of Adam Smith, which were revived in the second half of the twentieth century as a critique of 'big' government and economic and social intervention. This is called the 'liberal New Right', or 'neoliberalism'.

▶ The second element in the New Right is traditional conservative – and notably pre-Disraelian – social theory, especially its defence of order, authority and discipline. This is called the 'conservative New Right', or 'neoconservatism' (see p. 55).

The New Right thus attempts to fuse economic libertarianism with state and social authoritarianism. As such, it is a blend of radical, reactionary and traditional features. Its radicalism is evident in its robust efforts to dismantle or 'roll back' interventionist government and liberal or permissive social values. This radicalism is clearest in relation to neoliberalism, which draws on rational theories and abstract principles, and so dismisses tradition. New Right radicalism is nevertheless reactionary, in that both neoliberalism and neoconservatism usually hark back to a nineteenth-century 'golden age' of supposed economic vigour and moral fortitude. However, the New Right also makes an appeal to tradition, particularly through the emphasis neoconservatives place on so-called 'traditional values'.

Neoliberalism

Neoliberalism was a product of the end of the 'long boom' of the post-1945 period, which shifted economic thinking away from Keynesianism (see p. 31) and re-awakened interest in earlier, free-market thinking. In this, it has operated at a national level but also at an international level, through what is called 'neoliberal globalisation'. Neoliberal thinking is most definitely drawn from classical rather than modern liberalism. It amounts to a restatement of the case for a minimal state. This has been summed up as 'private, good; public, bad'.

Key concept ... NEOLIBERALISM

Neoliberalism (sometimes called 'neoclassical liberalism') is widely seen as an updated version of classical liberalism, particularly classical political economy. Its central theme is that the economy works best when left alone by government, reflecting a belief in free-market economics and atomistic individualism. While unregulated market capitalism delivers efficiency, growth and widespread prosperity, the 'dead hand' of the state saps initiative and discourages enterprise. In short, the neoliberal philosophy is: 'market: good; state: bad'. Key neoliberal policies include privatisation, spending cuts (especially in social welfare), tax cuts (particularly corporate and direct taxes) and deregulation. Neoliberalism is often equated with a belief in market fundamentalism; that is, an absolute faith in the capacity of the market mechanism to solve all economic and social problems.

Neoliberalism is anti-statist. The state is regarded as a realm of coercion and unfreedom: collectivism restricts individual initiative and saps self-respect. Government, however benignly disposed, invariably has a damaging effect on human affairs. Instead, faith is placed in the individual and the market. Individuals should be encouraged to be self-reliant and to make rational choices in their own interests. The market is respected as a mechanism through which the sum of individual choices will lead to progress and general benefit. As such, neoliberalism has attempted to establish the dominance of libertarian ideas over paternalistic ones within conservative ideology.

The dominant themes within this libertarian doctrine are a sustained defence of capitalism, particularly free-market capitalism, and a robust critique of socialism. Key influences on emergent neoliberal thinking included Ayn Rand (see p. 52), Friedrich von Hayek (1899–1992) the Austrian economist and political philosopher, and the US economist Milton Friedman (1912–2006). In her essays and popular novels, Rand advanced a moral justification for private enterprise, proclaiming herself to be a 'radical for capitalism'. Influenced in particular by Friedrich Nietzsche's concept of the Übermensch, the 'over-man' or 'superman', and by social Darwinism, Rand was a vigorous defender of the virtue of selfishness, sometimes seen as 'ethical egoism', seeing the central purpose of life as a quest for excellence, achieved by the exercise of rational self-interest. While selfishness allows people to advance their life's project by striving to be outstanding (wealth being but a measure of success in this respect), selflessness represents failure, a squandering of one's chance of excellence. In her most famous work, The Fountainhead ([1943] 2007), feeling betrayed when government bureaucrats insist on adding a different façade to a public housing complex he has designed, the novel's 'hero', Howard Roark, destroys the buildings.

Although Rand became a cult figure among right-wing college students in the USA in the 1960s and, through her supporters, exerted an influence on the newly fledged Libertarian Party in the 1970s, neoliberal thinking gained its greatest impetus from the revival of interest in free-market economic theories.

KEY FIGURE

Ayn Rand (1905–82)

A Russian-born writer and philosopher who emigrated to the USA when she was 21, deeply alienated by the Bolshevik Revolution, Rand (Alice Rosenbaum) became a Hollywood screenwriter before developing a career as an essayist and novelist. Her philosophy of 'objectivism', which claimed to show people as they are (that is, as rationally self-interested creatures), rather than as we may like them to be, gave unabashed support to selfishness and condemned altruism. Rand defended pure *laissez-faire* capitalism on the grounds that it both guarantees freedom and, by establishing untrammelled competition, it provides for the emergence of the elites needed to govern society. Rand's most influential works were her best-selling novels, *The Fountainhead* ([1943] 2007) and *Atlas Shrugged* (1947). Strongly informed by her objectivist philosophy and Freidrich Nietzsche's 'superman' ideal, the former glorifies the struggles of the visionary architect, Howard Roark, to rise above the conformism and corruption of his peers. The latter develops a portrait of a dystopian USA, in which the the country has succumbed to over-government and rampant collectivism. For more on Rand, see p. 51.

Free-market ideas gained renewed credibility during the 1970s as governments experienced increasing difficulty in delivering economic stability and sustained growth. Doubts consequently developed about whether it was in the power of government at all to solve economic problems. Hayek and Friedman, for example, challenged the very idea of a 'managed' or 'planned' economy. They argued that the task of allocating resources in a complex, industrialised economy was simply too difficult for any set of state bureaucrats to achieve successfully. The virtue of the market, on the other hand, is that it acts as the central nervous system of the economy, reconciling the supply of goods and services with the demand for them. It allocates resources to their most profitable use and thereby ensures that consumer needs are satisfied. In the light of the re-emergence of unemployment and inflation in the 1970s, Hayek and Friedman argued that government was invariably the cause of economic problems, rather than the cure.

The ideas of Keynesianism were one of the chief targets of neoliberal criticism. Keynes had argued that capitalist economies were not self-regulating. He placed particular emphasis on the 'demand side' of the economy, believing that the levels of economic activity and employment were dictated by the level of 'aggregate demand' in the economy. Milton Friedman, on the other hand, argued that there is a 'natural rate of unemployment', which is beyond the ability of government to influence. He also argued that attempts to eradicate unemployment by applying Keynesian techniques merely cause other, more damaging, economic problems, notably **inflation**. Inflation, neoliberals believe, threatens the entire basis of a market economy because, in reducing faith in money, the means of exchange, it discourages people from undertaking commercial or economic activity. However, Keynesianism had, in effect, encouraged governments to 'print money', albeit in a well-meaning attempt to create jobs. The free-market solution to inflation is to control the supply of money by cutting public spending, a policy practised by both the Reagan and the Thatcher administrations during the 1980s. Both administrations also allowed unemployment to rise sharply, in the belief that only the market could solve the problem.

Inflation: A rise in the general price level, leading to a decline in the value of money.

Neoliberalism is also opposed to the mixed economy and public ownership, and practises so-called 'supply-side economics'. Starting under Thatcher in the UK in the 1980s but later extending to many other western states, and most aggressively pursued in postcommunist states in the 1990s, a policy of privatisation has effectively dismantled both mixed and collectivised economies by transferring industries from public to private ownership. Nationalised industries were criticised for being inherently inefficient, because, unlike private firms and industries, they are not disciplined by the profit motive. Neoliberalism's emphasis on the 'supply-side' of the economy was reflected in the belief that governments should foster growth by providing conditions that encourage producers to produce, rather than consumers to consume. The main block to the creation of an entrepreneurial, supply-side culture is high taxes. Taxes, in this view, discourage enterprise and infringe on property rights, a stance sometimes called **fiscal conservatism**.

Neoliberalism is not only anti-statist on the grounds of economic efficiency and responsiveness, but also because of its political principles, notably its commitment to individual liberty. Neoliberals claim to be defending freedom against 'creeping collectivism'. At the extreme, these ideas lead in the direction of anarcho-capitalism (discussed in Chapter 5) and the belief that all goods and services, including the courts and public order, should be delivered by the market. The freedom defended by neoliberals is negative freedom: the removal of external restrictions on the individual. As the collective power of government is seen as the principal threat to the individual, freedom can only be ensured by rolling back the state. This, in particular, means rolling back social welfare. In addition to economic arguments against welfare – for example, that increased social expenditure pushes up taxes, and that public services are inherently inefficient – neoliberals object to welfare on moral grounds. In the first place, the welfare state is criticised for having created a 'culture of dependency': it saps initiative and enterprise, and robs people of dignity and self-respect.

Welfare is thus the *cause* of disadvantage, not its cure. Such a theory resurrects the notion of the 'undeserving poor'. Charles Murray (1984) also argued that, as welfare relieves women of dependence on 'breadwinning' men, it is a major cause of family breakdown, creating an underclass largely composed of single mothers and fatherless children. A further neoliberal argument against welfare is based on a commitment to individual rights. Robert Nozick (1974) (see p. 54) advanced this most forcefully in condemning all policies of welfare and redistribution as a violation of property rights. In this view, so long as property has been acquired justly, to transfer it, without consent, from one person to another amounts to 'legalised theft'. Underpinning this view is egoistical individualism, the idea that people owe nothing to society and are, in turn, owed nothing by society, a stance that calls the very notion of society into question.

The fortunes of neoliberalism were substantially boosted by the global financial crisis which peaked in the autumn of 2008, with the world economy seemingly on the brink of systemic collapse. The financial crisis precipitated the steepest decline in global output since the 1930s, causing tax revenues to plummet

Fiscal conservatism: A political-economic stance that prioritises the lowering of taxes, cuts in public spending and reduced government debt.

KEY FIGURE

Robert Nozick (1938–2002)

A US political philosopher, Nozick developed a form of libertarianism that draws on the ideas of Immanuel Kant (1724–1804) and John Locke (see p. 17). At its core, is an entitlement theory of justice that takes certain rights to be inviolable, and rejects the notion that social justice requires that a society's income and wealth should be distributed according to a set pattern. In particular, Nozick argued that property rights should be strictly upheld, provided that wealth has been justly acquired in the first place or has been justly transferred from one person to another. On this basis, he rejected all forms of welfare and redistribution as theft. Nozick did not, nevertheless, embrace anarchism. Instead, he argued that the state of nature is unsustainable since competition between private protection agencies will inevitably result in the emergence of a single dominant agency, which, in effect, becomes a minimal state. Nozick's major work is *Anarchy, State and Utopia* (1974), although some of its conclusions were modified in *The Examined Life* (1989). For more on Nozick, see pp. 53 and 108.

and government debt to soar, and even bringing the creditworthiness of some countries into question. Although the initial response to the financial crisis was a return to Keynesianism, in the form of a US-led coordinated policy of '**fiscal stimulus**', the crisis also provided new opportunities stemming from neoliberalism. From a neoliberal perspective, soaring government debt is essentially a consequence of a failure to control state spending, implying that the solution to indebtedness is 'fiscal retrenchment' or '**austerity**'. For example, in the UK the election of a Conservative-led coalition government in 2010 led to a swift break with Keynesianism and the introduction of a programme of spending cuts more severe than those put in place under Thatcher in the 1980s. Whereas the adoption of austerity was essentially a political choice in the UK, in the case of Greece, Ireland, Spain, Portugal and Cyprus, a reordering of the economy along neoliberal lines was a condition of bailouts imposed during 2010–13 by the EU, the IMF and the European Central Bank.

Neoconservatism

Neoconservatism emerged in the USA in the 1970s as a backlash against the ideas and values of the 1960s. It was defined by a fear of social fragmentation or breakdown, which was seen as a product of liberal reform and the spread of '**permissiveness**'. In sharp contrast to neoliberalism, neoconservatives stress the primacy of politics and seek to strengthen leadership and authority in society. This emphasis on authority, allied to a heightened sensitivity to the fragility of society, demonstrates that neoconservatism has its roots in traditional or organic conservatism. However, it differs markedly from paternalistic conservatism, which also draws heavily on organic ideas. Whereas paternalistic conservatives believe, for instance, that community is best maintained by social reform and the reduction of poverty, neoconservatives look to strengthen community by restoring authority and imposing social discipline. Neoconservative authoritarianism is, to this extent, consistent with neoliberal libertarianism. Both of them accept the rolling back of the state's economic responsibilities.

Fiscal stimulus: An economic strategy designed to promote growth by either, lowering taxes or increasing government spending, or both.

Austerity: Sternness or severity; as an economic strategy, austerity refers to public spending cuts designed to eradicate a budget deficit, and underpinned by faith in market forces.

Permissiveness: The willingness to allow people to make their own moral choices; permissiveness suggests that there are no authoritative values.

Key concept ... NEOCONSERVATISM

'Neoconservatism' refers to developments within conservative ideology that relate to both domestic policy and foreign policy. In domestic policy, neoconservatism is defined by support for a minimal but strong state, fusing themes associated with traditional or organic conservatism with an acceptance of economic individualism and qualified support for the free market. Neoconservatives have typically sought to restore public order, strengthen 'family' or 'religious' values, and bolster national identity. In foreign policy, neoconservatism was closely associated with the Bush administration in the USA in the years following 9/11. Its central aim was to preserve and reinforce what was seen as the USA's 'benevolent global hegemony' by building up US military power and pursuing a policy of worldwide 'democracy promotion'.

Differences between ...
NEOLIBERALISM AND NEOCONSERVATISM

NEOLIBERALISM	NEOCONSERVATISM
• classical liberalism	• traditional conservatism
• atomism	• organicism
• radicalism	• traditionalism
• libertarianism	• authoritarianism
• economic dynamism	• social order
• self-interest/enterprise	• traditional values
• equality of opportunity	• natural hierarchy
• minimal state	• strong state
• internationalism	• insular nationalism
• pro-globalisation	• anti-globalisation

Neoconservatives have developed distinctive views about both domestic policy and foreign policy. The two principal domestic concerns of neoconservatism have been with social order and public morality. Neoconservatives believe that rising crime, delinquency and anti-social behaviour are generally a consequence of a larger decline of authority that has affected most western societies since the 1960s. They have therefore called for a strengthening of social disciplines and authority at every level. This can be seen in relation to the family. For neoconservatives, the family is an authority system: it is both naturally hierarchical – children should listen to, respect and obey their parents – and naturally patriarchal. The husband is the provider and the wife the home-maker. This social authoritarianism is matched by state authoritarianism, the desire for a strong state reflected in a 'tough' stance on law and order. This led, in the USA and the UK in particular, to a greater emphasis on custodial sentences and to longer prison sentences, reflecting the belief that 'prison works'.

Neoconservatism's concern about public morality is based on a desire to re-assert the moral foundations of politics. A particular target of neoconservative criticism has been the 'permissive 1960s' and the growing culture of 'doing your own thing'. In the face of this, Thatcher in the UK proclaimed her support for 'Victorian values', and in the USA organisations such as Moral Majority campaigned for a return to 'traditional' or 'family' values. Neoconservatives see two dangers in a permissive society. In the first place, the freedom to choose one's own morals or lifestyle could lead to the choice of immoral or 'evil' views. There is, for instance, a significant religious element in neoconservatism, especially in the USA. The second danger is not so much that people may adopt the *wrong* morals or lifestyles, but that they may simply choose *different* moral positions. In the neoconservative view, moral pluralism is threatening because it undermines the cohesion of society. A permissive society is a society that lacks ethical norms and unifying moral standards. It is a 'pathless desert', which provides neither guidance nor support for individuals and their families. If individuals merely do as they please, civilised standards of behaviour will be impossible to maintain.

The issue that links the domestic and foreign policy aspects of neoconservative thinking is a concern about the nation and the desire to strengthen national identity in the face of threats from within and without. The value of the nation, from the neoconservative perspective, is that it binds society together, giving it a common culture and civic identity, which is all the stronger for being rooted in history and tradition. National patriotism (see p. 112) thus strengthens people's political will. The most significant threat to the nation 'from within' is the growth of multiculturalism, which weakens the bonds of nationhood by threatening the political community and creating the spectre of ethnic and racial conflict. Neoconservatives have therefore often been in the forefront of campaigns for stronger controls on immigration and, sometimes, for a privileged status to be granted to the 'host' community's culture (as discussed in Chapter 9). Such concerns have widened and deepened as a result of the advance of globalisation, as discussed in the next section. The threats to the nation 'from without' are many and various. In the UK, the main perceived threat has come from the process of European integration; indeed, since the 1990s, UK conservatism has at times appeared to be defined by '**Euroscepticism**'.

However, the nationalist dimension of neoconservative thinking also gave rise to a distinctive stance on foreign policy, particularly in the USA. Neoconservatism, in this form, was an approach to foreign policy-making that sought to enable the USA to take advantage of its unprecedented position of power and influence in the post-Cold War era. It consisted of a fusion of neo-Reaganism and 'hard' Wilsonianism (after President Woodrow Wilson, 1913–21). Neo-Reaganism took the form of a Manichaean world-view, in which 'good' (represented by the USA) confronted 'evil' (represented by 'rogue' states and terrorist groups that possess, or seek to possess, weapons of mass destruction). This implied that the USA should deter rivals and extend its global reach by achieving a position of 'strength beyond challenge' in military terms. 'Hard' Wilsonianism was expressed through the desire to spread US-style

Euroscepticism: Hostility to European integration based on the belief that it is a threat to national sovereignty and/or national identity.

democracy throughout the world by a process of 'regime change', achieved by military means if necessary. Such 'neocon' thinking dominated US strategic thinking in the aftermath of the September 11 terrorist attacks on New York and Washington, particularly through the establishment of the 'war on terror' and the attacks on Afghanistan in 2001 and Iraq in 2003. Neoconservative foreign-policy thinking nevertheless declined in significance from about 2005 onwards, as the USA recognised the limitations of achieving strategic objectives through military means alone, as well as the drawbacks of adopting a unilateral foreign-policy stance.

NATIONAL CONSERVATISM

In recent decades, new fault lines have opened up within conservatism over its relationship to globalisation. While liberalism favours the construction of a market-based world economy in which there is the free movement of goods, services, capital and people, other tendencies within conservatism have served as a counter-globalisation force, a mechanism of resistance to a 'borderless world'. This trend has been increasingly apparent since the early 2000s, having been boosted by the 2007–10 global financial crisis, which led to the steepest decline in global output since the 1930s, and by the onset, in 2015, of the European migration crisis. Counter-globalisation conservatism has been most apparent in the rise of far-right and anti-immigration parties, which have drawn on **national conservatism** in adopting a 'backward-looking' and culturally, and perhaps ethnically, 'pure' model of national identity. In many ways, this development has been part of the wider revival of populism, which has seen growing disenchantment with conventional politics and the emergence of anti-establishment leaders and movements in many mature democracies, a phenomenon often called **anti-politics**. Right-wing, populist parties, articulating concerns about immigration and multiculturalism, have become a feature of politics in many European states, a trend sometimes entangled with growing disillusionment about EU integration, and especially monetary union.

Key concept ... POPULISM

'Populism' (from the Latin *populus*, meaning 'the people') has been used to describe both distinctive political movements and a particular tradition of political thought. Movements or parties described as populist have been characterised by their claim to support the common people in the face of 'corrupt' economic or political elites. As a political tradition, populism reflects the belief that the instincts and wishes of the people provide the principal legitimate guide to political action. Populist politicians therefore make a direct appeal to the people and claim to give expression to their deepest hopes and fears, all intermediary institutions being distrusted. Although populism may be linked to any cause or ideology, it is often seen as implicitly authoritarian, 'populist' democracy being the enemy of 'pluralist' democracy.

National conservatism: A form of conservatism that prioritises the defence of national, cultural and, sometimes, ethnic identity over other concerns, often based on parallels between the family and the nation.

Anti-politics: A rejection of, and/or alienation from, conventional politicians and mainstream political parties.

The *Front National* in France, led by Marine Le Pen, the daughter of the founder of the party, Jean-Marie Le Pen, has attracted growing electoral support since the 1980s for a platform largely based on resistance to immigration. In 2017, Le Pen gained 10.6 million votes (34 per cent) in the second round of the presidential election. Other anti-immigration and anti-multiculturalist parties include the Freedom Party in Austria, the UK Independence Party, the Northern League in Italy, the *Vlaams Blok* in Belgium, the two Progress Parties in Norway and Denmark, and the Danish People's Party, which broke away from the Progress Party in 1995. Such national conservative parties and movements tend to prosper in conditions of fear, insecurity and social dislocation, their strength being their capacity to represent unity and certainty, binding national identity to tradition and established values. In other cases, such tendencies have been evident within larger and more mainstream conservative parties. This was, for example, evident in the UK Conservative Party's swift conversion to the cause of leaving the EU (Brexit) following the 'Leave' victory in the 2016 EU referendum, and in the subsequent decision by Theresa May's government to prioritise, in negotiations with Brussels, the establishment of checks on immigration from the EU over the UK's continued membership of the European single market. The link between conservatism and nationalism is examined in greater depth in Chapter 6. (For a discussion of the ideas and policies of the modern UK Conservative Party, see Chapter 5 of *Essentials of UK Politics*.)

? QUESTIONS FOR DISCUSSION

- Why, and to what extent, have conservatives supported tradition?
- Is conservatism a 'disposition' rather than a political ideology?
- Why has conservatism been described as a philosophy of imperfection?
- What are the implications of the belief that society is an organic entity?
- How does the conservative view of property differ from the liberal view?
- How far do conservatives go in endorsing authority?
- Is conservatism merely a ruling class ideology?
- To what extent do conservatives favour pragmatism over principle?
- In what ways is One Nation conservatism rooted in the assumptions of traditional conservatism?
- How and why have neoliberals criticised welfare?
- To what extent are neoliberalism and neoconservatism compatible?
- Why and how have conservatives sought to resist globalisation?

📖 FURTHER READING

Aughey, A. et al., *The Conservative Political Tradition in Britain and the United States* (1992). A stimulating examination of similarities and difference between conservative thought in the USA and the UK.

Honderich, T., *Conservatism: Burke, Nozick, Bush, Blair?* (2005). A distinctive and rigorously unsympathetic account of conservative thought; closely argued and interesting.

O'Hara, K., *Conservatism* (2011). A defence of a small-c sceptical conservatism that draws heavily on the writings of Burke and Oakeshott.

Scruton, R., *The Meaning of Conservatism* (2001). A stylish and openly sympathetic study that develops a distinctive view of the conservative tradition.

4 Socialism

PREVIEW

The term 'socialist' derives from the Latin *sociare*, meaning to combine or to share. Its earliest known use was in 1827 in the UK, in an issue of the *Co-operative Magazine*. By the early 1830s, the followers of Robert Owen in the UK and Henri de Saint-Simon in France had started to refer to their beliefs as 'socialism' and, by the 1840s, the term was familiar in a range of industrialised countries, notably France, Belgium and the German states.

Socialism, as an ideology, has traditionally been defined by its opposition to capitalism and by the attempt to provide a more humane and socially worthwhile alternative. At the core of socialism is a vision of human beings as social creatures united by their common humanity. This highlights the degree to which individual identity is fashioned by social interaction and the membership of social groups and collective bodies. Socialists therefore prefer cooperation to competition. The central, and some would say defining, value of socialism is equality, especially social equality. Socialists believe that social equality is the essential guarantee of social stability and cohesion, and that it promotes freedom, in the sense that it satisfies material needs and provides the basis for personal development. Socialism, however, contains a bewildering variety of divisions and rival traditions. These divisions have been about both 'means' (how socialism should be achieved) and 'ends' (the nature of the future socialist society). For example, communists or Marxists have usually supported revolution and sought to abolish capitalism through the creation of a classless society based on the common ownership of wealth. In contrast, democratic socialists or social democrats have embraced gradualism and aimed to reform or 'humanise' the capitalist system through a narrowing of material inequalities and the abolition of poverty.

HISTORICAL OVERVIEW

Although socialists have sometimes claimed an intellectual heritage that goes back to Plato's *Republic* or Thomas More's *Utopia* ([1516] 1965), as with liberalism and conservatism, the origins of socialism lie in the nineteenth century. Socialism arose as a reaction against the social and economic conditions generated in Europe by the growth of industrial capitalism (see p. 62). Socialist ideas were quickly linked to the development of a new but growing class of industrial workers, who suffered the poverty and degradation that are so often features of early industrialisation. Although socialism and liberalism have common roots in the Enlightenment, and share a faith in principles such as reason and progress, socialism emerged as a critique of liberal market society and was defined by its attempt to offer an alternative to industrial capitalism.

The character of early socialism was influenced by the harsh and often inhuman conditions in which the industrial working class lived and worked. Wages were typically low, child and female labour were commonplace, the working day often lasted up to twelve hours and the threat of unemployment was ever-present. In addition, the new working class was disorientated, being largely composed of first-generation urban dwellers, unfamiliar with the conditions of industrial life and work, and possessing few of the social institutions that could give their lives stability or meaning. As a result, early socialists often sought a radical, even revolutionary alternative to industrial capitalism. For instance, Charles Fourier (1772–1837) in France and Robert Owen (1771–1858) in the UK subscribed to **utopianism** in founding experimental communities based on sharing and cooperation. The Germans Karl Marx (see p. 67) and Friedrich Engels (see p. 72) developed more complex and systematic theories, which claimed to uncover the 'laws of history' and proclaimed that the revolutionary overthrow of capitalism was inevitable.

In the late nineteenth century, the character of socialism was transformed by a gradual improvement in working-class living conditions and the advance of political democracy. The growth of trade unions, working-class political parties and sports and social clubs served to provide greater economic security and to integrate the working class into industrial society. In the advanced industrial societies of western Europe, it became increasingly difficult to continue to see the working class as a revolutionary force. Socialist political parties progressively adopted legal and constitutional tactics, encouraged by the gradual extension of the vote to working-class men. By World War I, the socialist world was clearly divided between those socialist parties that had sought power through the ballot box and preached reform, and those that proclaimed a continuing need for revolution. The Russian Revolution of 1917 entrenched this split: revolutionary socialists, following the example of V. I. Lenin (1870–1924) and the Bolsheviks, usually adopted the term '**communism**', while reformist socialists described their ideas as either 'socialism' or '**social democracy**'.

The twentieth century witnessed the spread of socialist ideas into African, Asian and Latin American countries with little or no experience of industrial

Utopianism: A belief in the unlimited possibilities of human development, typically embodied in the vision of a perfect or ideal society, a utopia (see p. 98).

Communism: The principle of the common ownership of wealth, or a system of comprehensive collectivisation; communism is often viewed as 'Marxism in practice' (see p. 71).

Social democracy: A moderate or reformist brand of socialism that favours a balance between the market and the state, rather than the abolition of capitalism.

Key concept ... CAPITALISM

Capitalism is an economic system as well as a form of property ownership. It has a number of key features. First, it is based on generalised commodity production, a 'commodity' being a good or service produced for exchange – it has market value rather than use-value. Second, productive wealth in a capitalist economy is predominantly held in private hands. Third, economic life is organised according to impersonal market forces, in particular the forces of demand (what consumers are willing and able to consume) and supply (what producers are willing and able to produce). Fourth, in a capitalist economy, material self-interest and maximisation provide the main motivations for enterprise and hard work. Some degree of state regulation is nevertheless found in all capitalist systems.

capitalism. Socialism in these countries often developed out of the anti-colonial struggle, rather than a class struggle. The idea of class exploitation was replaced by that of colonial oppression, creating a potent fusion of socialism and nationalism, which is examined more fully in Chapter 5. The Bolshevik model of communism was imposed on eastern Europe after 1945; it was adopted in China after the revolution of 1949 and subsequently spread to North Korea, Vietnam, Cambodia and elsewhere. More moderate forms of socialism were practised elsewhere in the developing world; for example, by the Congress Party in India. Distinctive forms of African and Arab socialism also developed, being influenced respectively by the communal values of traditional tribal life and the moral principles of Islam. In Latin America in the 1960s and 1970s, socialist revolutionaries waged war against military dictatorships, often seen to be operating in the interests of US imperialism. The Castro regime, which came to power after the Cuban revolution of 1959, developed close links with the Soviet Union, while the Sandinista guerrillas, who seized power in Nicaragua in 1979, remained non-aligned. In Chile in 1970, Salvador Allende became the world's first democratically elected Marxist head of state, but was overthrown and killed in a CIA-backed coup in 1973.

Since the late twentieth century, socialism has suffered a number of spectacular reverses, leading some to proclaim the 'death of socialism'. The most dramatic of these reverses was, of course, the collapse of communism in the eastern European revolutions of 1989–91. However, rather than socialists uniting around the principles of western social democracy, these principles were thrown into doubt as parliamentary socialist parties in many parts of the world embraced ideas and policies that are more commonly associated with liberalism or even conservatism.

CORE IDEAS AND PRINCIPLES

HUMAN NATURE

At its heart, socialism offers a unifying vision of human beings as social creatures, capable of overcoming social and economic problems by drawing on the power of the community rather than simply on individual effort. This is a collectivist vision because it stresses the capacity of human beings for collective action, their willingness and ability to pursue goals by working together, as opposed to striving for personal self-interest. Most socialists, for instance, would be prepared to echo the words of the English metaphysical poet John Donne (1571–1631):

> No man is an Island entire of itself;
> every man is a piece of the Continent, a part of the main …
> any man's death diminishes me, because I am involved in Mankind; and therefore never send to know for whom the bell tolls;
> it tolls for thee.

Human beings are therefore 'comrades', 'brothers' or 'sisters', tied to one another by the bonds of a common humanity. This is expressed in the principle of **fraternity**.

Socialists are far less willing than either liberals or conservatives to assume that human nature is unchanging and fixed at birth. Rather, they believe that human nature is malleable or 'plastic', shaped by the experiences and circumstances of social life. In the long-standing philosophical debate about whether 'nurture' or 'nature' determines human behaviour, socialists side resolutely with nurture. From birth – perhaps even while in the womb – each individual is subjected to experiences that mould and condition his or her personality. All human skills and attributes are learnt from society, from the fact that we stand upright, to the language we speak. Whereas liberals draw a clear distinction between the 'individual' and 'society', socialists believe that the individual is inseparable from society. Human beings are neither self-sufficient nor self-contained; to think of them as separate or atomised 'individuals' is absurd. Individuals can only be understood, and understand themselves, through the social groups to which they belong. The behaviour of human beings therefore tells us more about the society in which they live and have been brought up, than it does about any abiding or immutable human nature.

The radical edge of socialism derives not from its concern with what people are like, but with what they have the capacity to become. This has led socialists to develop utopian visions of a better society, in which human beings can achieve genuine emancipation and fulfilment as members of a community. African and Asian socialists have often stressed that their traditional, pre-industrial societies already emphasise the importance of social life and the value of community. In these circumstances, socialism has sought to preserve traditional social values in the face of the challenge from western individualism (see p. 12). As Julius Nyerere, president of Tanzania 1964–85, pointed out, 'We, in Africa, have no more real need to be "converted" to socialism, than we have of being "taught" democracy.' He therefore described his own views as 'tribal socialism'.

If human beings are social animals, socialists believe that the natural relationship among them is one of **cooperation** rather than competition. Socialists believe that competition pits one individual against another, encouraging each of them

Fraternity: Literally, brotherhood; bonds of sympathy and comradeship between and among human beings.

Cooperation: Working together; collective effort intended to achieve mutual benefit.

Key concept ... COLLECTIVISM

Collectivism is, broadly, the belief that collective human endeavour is of greater practical and moral value than individual self-striving. It thus reflects the idea that human nature has a social core, and implies that social groups, whether 'classes', 'nations', 'races' or whatever, are meaningful political entities. However, the term is used with little consistency. Mikhail Bakunin (see p. 97) and other anarchists used 'collectivism' to refer to self-governing associations of free individuals. Others have treated collectivism as strictly the opposite of individualism (see p. 12), holding that it implies that collective interests should prevail over individual ones. It is also sometimes linked to the state as the mechanism through which collective interests are upheld, suggesting that the growth of state responsibilities marks the advance of collectivism.

to deny or ignore their social nature rather than embrace it. As a result, competition fosters only a limited range of social attributes and, instead, promotes selfishness and aggression. Cooperation, on the other hand, makes moral and economic sense. Individuals who work together rather than against each other develop bonds of sympathy, caring and affection. Furthermore, the energies of the community rather than those of the single individual can be harnessed. The Russian anarchist Peter Kropotkin (see p. 104), for example, suggested that the principal reason why the human species had survived and prospered was because of its capacity for 'mutual aid'.

Socialists thus believe that human beings can be motivated by moral incentives, and not merely by material incentives. In theory, capitalism rewards individuals for the work they do: the harder they work, or the more abundant their skills, the greater their rewards will be. The moral incentive to work hard, however, is the desire to contribute to the common good, which develops out of a sympathy, or sense of responsibility, for fellow human beings, especially those in need. While few modern social democrats would contemplate the outright abolition of material incentives, they nevertheless insist on the need for a balance of some kind between material and moral incentives. For instance, socialists would argue that an important incentive for achieving economic growth is that it helps to finance the provision of welfare support for the poorest and most vulnerable elements in society.

The final aspect of the socialist approach to human nature is a stress on equality. This does not mean that socialists believe that all people are born identical, possessing precisely the same capabilities and skills. An egalitarian society would not, for instance, be one in which all students gained the same mark in their mathematics examinations. Rather, socialist **egalitarianism** is underpinned by the belief that the most significant forms of human inequality are a result of unequal treatment by society, instead of unequal endowment by nature. Justice, from a socialist perspective, therefore demands that people are

Egalitarianism: A theory or practice based on the desire to promote equality; egalitarianism is sometimes seen as the belief that equality is the primary political value.

treated equally (or at least more equally) by society in terms of their rewards and material circumstances. This implies a commitment to social equality, or equality of outcome, the liberal idea of equality of opportunity usually being dismissed by socialists on the grounds that it legitimises inequality by perpetuating the myth of innate inequality. Nevertheless, although socialists agree about the virtue of social equality, they disagree about the extent to which it can and should be brought about. Marxists and communists believe in *absolute* social equality, brought about by the abolition of private property and **collectivisation** of productive wealth. Perhaps the most famous experiment in such radical egalitarianism took place in China under the 'Cultural Revolution'. Social democrats, however, believe in *relative* social equality, achieved by the redistribution of wealth through the welfare state and a system of **progressive taxation**. The social-democratic desire to tame capitalism rather than abolish it, reflects an acceptance of a continuing role for material incentives, with egalitarianism being refocused on the task of eradicating poverty. This, in turn, has sometimes blurred the distinction between social equality and equality of opportunity.

Collectivisation: The abolition of private property and the establishment of a comprehensive system of common or public ownership, usually through the mechanisms of the state.

Progressive taxation: A system of taxation in which the rich pay a higher proportion of their income in tax than the poor.

PERSPECTIVES ON ...
EQUALITY

LIBERALS believe that people are 'born' equal in the sense that they are of equal moral worth. This implies formal equality, notably legal and political equality, as well as equality of opportunity; but social equality is likely to threaten freedom and penalise talent. Whereas classical liberals emphasise the need for strict meritocracy and economic incentives, modern liberals argue that genuine equal opportunities require relative social equality.

CONSERVATIVES have traditionally viewed society as naturally hierarchical and have thus dismissed equality as an abstract and unachievable goal. Nevertheless, the New Right evinces a strongly individualist belief in equality of opportunity while emphasising the economic benefits of material inequality.

SOCIALISTS regard equality as a fundamental value and, in particular, endorse social equality. Despite shifts within social democracy towards a liberal belief in equality of opportunity, social equality, whether in its relative (social democratic) or absolute (communist) sense, has been seen as essential to ensuring social cohesion and fraternity, establishing justice or equity, and enlarging freedom in a positive sense.

ANARCHISTS place a particular stress on political equality, understood as an equal and absolute right to personal autonomy, implying that all forms of political inequality amount to oppression. Anarcho-communists believe in absolute social equality achieved through the collective ownership of productive wealth.

FEMINISTS take equality to mean sexual equality, in the sense of equal rights and equal opportunities (liberal feminism) or equal social or economic power (socialist feminism) irrespective of gender. However, some radical feminists have argued that the demand for equality may simply lead to women being 'male identified'.

ECOLOGISTS advance the notion of biocentric equality, which emphasises that all life forms have an equal right to 'live and blossom'. Conventional notions of equality are therefore seen as anthropocentric, in that they exclude the interests of all organisms and entities other than humankind.

SOCIETY

By sharp contrast with the conservative belief that society is best understood as an 'organic whole', socialists typically embrace a conflict theory of society, in which **social class** has traditionally been viewed as the deepest and most politically significant of social divisions. Socialist class politics have been expressed in two ways, however. In the first, social class is an analytical tool. In pre-socialist societies at least, socialists have believed that human beings tend to think and act together with others with whom they share a common economic position or interest. In other words, social classes, rather than individuals, are the principal actors in history and therefore provide the key to understanding social and political change. This is demonstrated most clearly in the Marxist belief that historical change is the product of class conflict. The second form of socialist class politics focuses specifically on the working class, and is concerned with political struggle and emancipation. Socialism has often been viewed as an expression of the interests of the working class, and the working class has been seen as the vehicle through which socialism will be achieved. Nevertheless, social class has not been accepted as a necessary or permanent feature of society: socialist societies have been seen either as classless or as societies in which class inequalities have been substantially reduced. In emancipating itself from capitalist exploitation, the working class thus also emancipates itself from its own class identity, its members becoming, in the process, fully developed human beings.

Socialists have nevertheless been divided about the nature and importance of social class. In the Marxist tradition, class is linked to economic power, as defined by the individual's relationship to the means of production. From this perspective, class divisions are divisions between 'capital' and 'labour'; that is, between the owners of productive wealth (the **bourgeoisie**) and those who live off the sale of their labour power (the **proletariat**). This Marxist two-class model is characterised by irreconcilable conflict between the bourgeoisie and the proletariat, leading, inevitably, to the overthrow of capitalism through a proletarian revolution. Social democrats, on the other hand, have tended to define social class in terms of income and status differences between 'white collar' or non-manual workers (the middle class) and 'blue collar' or manual workers (the working class). From this perspective, the advance of socialism is associated with the *narrowing* of divisions between the middle class and the working class brought about through economic and social intervention. Social democrats have therefore believed in social amelioration and class harmony rather than social polarisation and class war.

However, the link between socialism and class politics has declined significantly since the mid-twentieth century. This has largely been a consequence of declining levels of class solidarity and, in particular, the shrinkage of the traditional working class or urban proletariat. The waning in class politics is a consequence of deindustrialisation, reflected in the decline of traditional labour-intensive industries such as coal, steel, shipbuilding and so on. Not only has this forced traditional socialist parties to revise their policies in order to appeal to

Social class: A social division based on economic or social factors; a social class is a group of people who share a similar socio-economic position.

Bourgeoisie: A Marxist term denoting the ruling class of a capitalist society, the owners of productive wealth.

Proletariat: A Marxist term denoting a class that subsists through the sale of its labour power; strictly speaking, the proletariat is not equivalent to the manual working class.

middle-class voters, but it has also encouraged them to define their radicalism less in terms of class emancipation and more in relation to issues such as gender equality, ecological sustainability, or peace and international development.

THE STATE

Socialism encompasses two quite different theories of the state, one Marxist and the other social democratic. Marxism offers an analysis of state power that fundamentally challenges the liberal image of the state as a neutral arbiter or umpire. Marxists argue that the state cannot be understood as separate from the economic structure of society: the state emerges out of the class system, its function being to maintain and defend the oppression and exploitation. The classic Marxist view is expressed in Marx and Engels' often-quoted dictum from *The Communist Manifesto* (1848; in Engels, [1848] 1976): 'the executive of the modern state is but a committee for managing the common affairs of the whole bourgeoisie'. This position was stated still more starkly by Lenin in *The State and Revolution* (1964), who referred to the state simply as 'an instrument for the oppression of the exploited class'. If the state is a '**bourgeois state**', inevitably biased in favour of capital over labour, political reform and gradual change are clearly pointless. Universal suffrage and regular and competitive elections are, at best, a façade, their purpose being to conceal the reality of an equal class power and to misdirect the political energies of the working class. A class-conscious proletariat thus has no alternative: in order to build socialism it has first to overthrow the bourgeois state through **revolution**.

The choice of revolutionary or insurrectionary political means had profound consequences for socialism. For instance, the use of revolution usually relates to the pursuit of fundamentalist ends. Revolution has the advantage that it allowed the remnants of the old order to be overthrown and an entirely new social system to be constructed. Capitalism could be abolished and a qualitatively different socialist society established in its place. Socialism, in this context, usually

Bourgeois state: A Marxist term denoting the state that is bound by the interests of the bourgeoisie and so perpetuates the system of unequal class power.

Revolution: A fundamental and irreversible change, often a brief but dramatic period of upheaval; systemic change.

KEY FIGURE

Karl Marx (1818–83)

A German philosopher, economist and political thinker, Marx developed a theory of history that highlighted the importance of economic life and the conditions under which people produce and reproduce their means of subsistence. This was reflected in the belief that the economic 'base', consisting essentially of the 'mode of production', or economic system, conditions or determines the ideological 'structure'. According to Marx, history is driven forward through a dialectical process in which contradictions within each mode of production give rise to class conflict. All class societies, including capitalism, are thus doomed to collapse, eventually leading to the establishment of a classless, communist society. Marx's classic work is the three-volume *Capital* (1867, 1885 and 1894), which painstakingly analyses the capitalist process of production and is based, some argue, on economic determinism. Marx's best-known and most accessible work is *The Communist Manifesto* (with Engels) ([1848] 1968). For more on Marx, see above, pp. 61, 70–84, 93, 101, 103, 106 and 134.

took the form of state collectivisation, modelled on the Soviet Union during the Stalinist period. The revolutionary 'road' was nevertheless also associated with a drift towards dictatorship and the use of political repression.

Social democrats, by contrast, came to believe that the spread of political democracy would fundamentally alter the nature of state power, allowing all social classes, and not merely the ruling bourgeoisie, to exercise influence through the state. They thus adopted an essentially liberal, or pluralist, theory of the state. Indeed, they came to the conclusion not only that socialism could be brought about through evolution, or **gradualism**, but that this process would be inevitable. Such a view was closely associated in the UK with the Fabian Society, formed in 1884. The Fabians, led by Beatrice Webb (see p. 68) and her husband Sidney Webb (1859–1947), and including noted intellectuals such as George Bernard Shaw (1856–1950) and H. G. Wells (1856–1946), took their name from the Roman general Fabius Maximus, who was noted for the patient and defensive tactics he employed in defeating Hannibal's invading armies. In their view, socialism would develop naturally and peacefully out of liberal capitalism through a combination of political action and education. Fabian confidence in what they called 'the inevitability of gradualism' was rooted in the belief that the progressive extension of the franchise would eventually place power in the hands of the numerically dominant class, the working class, and thereby ensure the electoral success of socialist parties. Once in power, these parties would be able to carry out a fundamental transformation of society through a process of social reform. In the Fabian view, the advance of socialism was linked to the progressive expansion of the state, allowing a class of experts and technocrats, who had been 'permeated' with socialist ideas, to manage society for the benefit of the working classes.

Such optimistic expectations have, however, not been borne out in reality. Some have even argued that evolutionary or democratic socialism is founded on a

Gradualism: Progress brought about by gradual, piecemeal improvements, rather than dramatic upheaval; change through legal and political reform.

KEY FIGURE

Beatrice Webb (1859–1947)

A British socialist, labour historian and social reformer, Webb was a leading member of the Fabian Society and a key exponent of the gradualist approach to political change. With her husband Sydney (1859–1947), she co-authored a number of books and pamphlets and championed a paternalistic form of socialism that relied on the 'permeation' of elite groups by 'rational' and 'humane' socialist ideas, supported, in the UK, by the advance of the Labour Party. In her 1909 minority report, the Royal Commission on the Poor Laws, Webb advocated bringing all kinds of social provision up to a national minimum, anticipating the post-1945 UK welfare state. In their later years, the Webbs fell under the spell of Stalinist-style Soviet communism. For Beatrice and Sydney Webb, socialism thus came to be associated with the expansion, rather than the contraction (and certainly not the overthrow) of the state. This was reflected in clause IV of the Labour Party's 1918 constitution (which they wrote) in a commitment to the 'common ownership of the means of production, consumption and exchange'. For more on Beatrice Webb, see above.

contradiction: in order to respond successfully to electoral pressures, socialists have been forced to revise or 'water down' their ideological beliefs. Democratic socialism has certainly encountered a number of problems not envisaged by its founding father. These include the fact that, as capitalism has developed, the electoral strength of the urban manual workforce has declined, forcing socialist parties to look for support to the growing ranks of the middle class; and that, in developed societies in particular, the socialist credentials of the working class have been brought into question by rising affluence.

THE ECONOMY

At the heart of the socialist approach to the economy is a preference for common or collective ownership over private ownership. Such a view sets socialism apart from liberalism and conservatism, which both regard private ownership as natural and proper. Socialists criticise private property for a number of reasons:

▶ Property is *unjust*: wealth is produced by the collective effort of human labour and should therefore be owned by the community, not by private individuals.

▶ It breeds acquisitiveness and so is *morally corrupting*. Private property encourages people to be materialistic, to believe that human happiness or

PERSPECTIVES ON ...
THE ECONOMY

LIBERALS see the economy as a vital part of civil society and have a strong preference for a market or capitalist economic order based on property, competition and material incentives. However, while classical liberals favour *laissez-faire* capitalism, modern liberals recognise the limitations of the market and accept limited economic management.

CONSERVATIVES show clear support for private enterprise but have traditionally favoured pragmatic, if limited, intervention, fearing the free-for-all of *laissez-faire* and the attendant risks of social instability. The New Right, however, endorses unregulated capitalism.

SOCIALISTS in the Marxist tradition have expressed a preference for common ownership and absolute social equality, which in orthodox communism was expressed in state collectivisation and central planning. Social democrats, though, support welfare or regulated capitalism, believing that the market is a good servant but a bad master.

ANARCHISTS reject any form of economic control or management. However, while anarcho-communists endorse common ownership and small-scale self-management, anarcho-capitalists advocate an entirely unregulated market economy.

ECOLOGISTS condemn both market capitalism and state collectivism for being growth-obsessed and environmentally unsustainable. Economics must therefore be subordinate to ecology, and the drive for profit at any cost must be replaced by a concern with long-term sustainability and harmony between humankind and nature.

fulfilment can be gained through the pursuit of wealth. Those who own property wish to accumulate more, while those who have little or no wealth long to acquire it.

▶ It is divisive. It fosters conflict in society; for example, between owners and workers, employers and employees, or simply the rich and the poor.

Socialists have therefore proposed that either the institution of private property be abolished and replaced by the common ownership of productive wealth, or, more modestly, that the right to property be balanced against the interests of the community. **Fundamentalist socialists**, such as Marx and Engels, envisaged the abolition of private property, and hence the creation of a classless, communist society in place of capitalism. Their clear preference was that property be owned collectively and used for the benefit of humanity. However, they said little about how this goal could be achieved in practice. When Lenin and the Bolsheviks seized power in Russia in 1917, they believed that socialism could be built through **nationalisation**. This process was not completed until the 1930s, when Stalin's 'second revolution' witnessed the construction of a centrally planned economy, a system of state collectivisation. 'Common ownership' came to mean 'state ownership', or what the Soviet constitution described as 'socialist state property'. The Soviet Union thus developed a form of **state socialism**.

Social democrats have also been attracted to the state as an instrument through which wealth can be collectively owned and the economy rationally planned. However, in the West, nationalisation has been applied more selectively, its objective being not full state collectivisation but the construction of a **mixed economy**. In the UK, for example, the Attlee Labour government, 1945–51, nationalised what it called the 'commanding heights' of the economy: major industries such as coal, steel, electricity and gas. Through these industries, the government hoped to regulate the entire economy without the need for comprehensive collectivisation. However, since the 1950s, parliamentary socialist parties have gradually distanced themselves from the 'politics of ownership', preferring to define socialism in terms of the pursuit of equality and social justice rather than the advance of public ownership.

TYPES OF SOCIALISM

COMMUNISM

The communist tradition within socialism has a variety of manifestations, even overlapping with anarchism, as in the case of anarcho-communism (discussed in Chapter 5). However, its historically most significant association has undoubtedly been with Marxism. Strictly speaking, 'Marxism' as a codified body of thought only came into existence after Marx's death in 1883. It was the product of the attempt, notably by Marx's life-long collaborator Freidrich Engels, the German SPD leader Karl Kautsky (1854–1938) and the Russian theoretician Georgi Plekhanov (1857–1918), to condense Marx's ideas and theories into a systematic and comprehensive world-view that suited the needs

Fundamentalist socialism: A form of socialism that seeks to abolish capitalism and replace it with a qualitatively different kind of society.

Nationalisation: The extension of state or public ownership over private assets or industries, either individual enterprises or the entire economy (often called 'collectivisation').

State socialism: A form of socialism in which the state controls and directs economic life, acting, in theory, in the interests of the people.

Mixed economy: An economy in which there is a mixture of publicly owned and privately owned industries.

Key concept ... COMMUNISM

Communism, in its simplest sense, refers to the communal organisation of social existence, especially through the collective ownership of property. For Marxists, communism is a theoretical ideal. In this sense, communism is characterised by classlessness (wealth is owned in common), rational economic organisation (production-for-use replaces production-for-exchange) and statelessness (in the absence of class conflict, the state 'withers away'). 'Orthodox' communism refers to the societies founded in the twentieth century supposedly on the basis of Marxist principles. In such societies: (1) Marxism–Leninism was used as an 'official' ideology; (2) the communist party had a monopoly of power, based on its 'leading and guiding' role in society; and (3) economic life was collectivised and organised through a system of central planning.

of the growing socialist movement. This 'orthodox' Marxism, which is often portrayed as '**dialectical materialism**' (a term coined by Plekhanov and not used by Marx), later formed the basis of Soviet communism. Some see Marx as an economic determinist, while others proclaim him to be a humanist socialist. Moreover, distinctions have also been drawn between his early and later writings, sometimes presented as the distinction between the 'young Marx' and the 'mature Marx'. It is nevertheless clear that Marx himself believed he had developed a new brand of socialism that was scientific, in the sense that it was primarily concerned with disclosing the nature of social and historical development, rather than with advancing an essentially ethical critique of capitalism.

At least three forms of Marxism can be identified. These are:

▶ classical Marxism

▶ orthodox communism

▶ neo-Marxism.

Classical Marxism
Philosophy

The core of classical Marxism – the Marxism of Marx – is a philosophy of history that outlines why capitalism is doomed and why socialism is destined to replace it, based on supposedly scientific analysis. But in what sense did Marx believe his work to be scientific? Marx criticised earlier socialist thinkers such as the French social reformer Saint-Simon (1760–1825), Fourier and Owen as 'utopians' on the basis that their socialism was grounded in a desire for total social transformation unconnected with the necessity of class struggle and revolution. Marx, in contrast, undertook a laborious empirical analysis of history and society, hoping thereby to gain insight into the nature of future developments. However, whether with Marx's help or not, Marxism as the attempt to gain historical understanding through the application of scientific methods, later developed

Dialectical materialism:
The crude and deterministic form of Marxism that dominated intellectual life in orthodox communist states.

KEY FIGURE

Friedrich Engels (1820–95)

A German industrialist and life-long friend and collaborator of Marx, Engels elaborated Marx's ideas and theories for the benefit of the growing socialist movement. By emphasising the role of the dialectic as a force operating in both social life and nature, he helped to establish dialectical materialism as a distinct brand of Marxism, portraying Marxism in terms of a specific set of historical laws. Engels' writings include *The Condition of the Working Class in England* (1845), a historical account of the industrial proletariat in Manchester, and *The Origins of the Family, Private Property and the State* (1884), which analysed the institution of monogamous marriage in terms of the workings of the capitalist class system. Engels' writings were highly influential in popularising the ideas of Marx, but they have also been criticised for advancing a mechanistic and determinist interpretation of Marxism that, some argue, is not faithful to Marx himself. For more on Engels, see below, pp. 4–5, 61, 67, 70, 73, 74, 75, 80, and 148.

into Marxism as a body of scientific truths, gaining a status more akin to that of a religion. Engels' declaration that Marx had uncovered the 'laws' of historical and social development was a clear indication of this transition.

What made Marx's approach different from that of other socialist thinkers was that he subscribed to what Engels called the 'materialist conception of history', or **historical materialism** (see Figure 4.1). Rejecting the idealism of the German philosopher G. W. F. Hegel (1770–1831), who believed that history amounted to the unfolding of the so-called 'world spirit', Marx held material circumstances to be fundamental to all forms of social and historical development. This reflected the belief that the production of the means of subsistence is the most crucial of all human activities. Since humans cannot survive without food, water, shelter and so on, the way in which these are produced conditions all other aspects of life; in short, 'social being determines consciousness'. In the preface to *A Contribution to the Critique of Political Economy* ([1859] 1968), Marx gave this theory its most succinct expression, by suggesting that social consciousness and the 'legal and political superstructure' arise from the 'economic base', the

Historical materialism: A Marxist theory that holds that material or economic conditions ultimately structure law, politics, culture and other aspects of social existence.

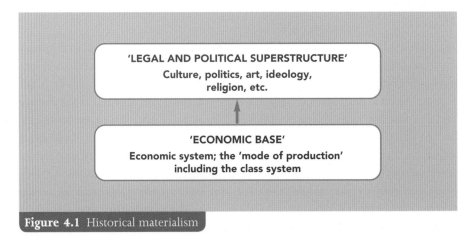

Figure 4.1 Historical materialism

real foundation of society. This 'base' consists essentially of the 'mode of production' or economic system – feudalism, capitalism, socialism and so on. This led Marx to conclude that political, legal, cultural, religious, artistic and other aspects of life could be explained primarily by reference to economic factors (see pp. 4–5 for an account of how this applies to Marx's theory of ideology).

While in other respects a critic of Hegel, Marx nevertheless embraced his belief that the driving force of historical change was the **dialectic**. In effect, progress is the consequence of internal conflict. For Hegel, this explained the movement of the 'world spirit' towards self-realisation through conflict between a thesis and its opposing force, an antithesis, producing a higher level, a synthesis, which in turn constitutes a new thesis. Marx, as Engels put it, 'turned Hegel on his head', by investing this Hegelian dialectic with a materialistic interpretation. Marx thus explained historical change by reference to internal contradictions within each mode of production, arising from the existence of private property. Capitalism is thus doomed because it embodies its own antithesis, the proletariat, seen by Marx as the 'grave digger of capitalism'. Conflict between capitalism and the proletariat will therefore lead to a higher stage of development in the establishment of a socialist, and eventually a communist, society.

Marx's theory of history is therefore teleological, in the sense that it invests history with meaning or a purpose, reflected in its goal: classless communism. This goal would nevertheless only be achieved once history had developed through a series of stages or epochs, each characterised by its own economic structure and class system. In *The German Ideology* ([1846] 1970) Marx identified four such stages:

- primitive communism or tribal society, in which material scarcity provided the principal source of conflict

- slavery, covering classical or ancient societies and characterised by conflict between masters and slaves

- feudalism, marked by antagonism between land owners and serfs

- capitalism, dominated by the struggle between the bourgeoisie and the proletariat.

Human history has therefore been a long struggle between the oppressed and the oppressor, the exploited and the exploiter. However, following Hegel, Marx envisaged an end of history, which would occur when a society was constructed that embodied no internal contradictions or antagonisms. This, for Marx, meant communism, a classless society based on the common ownership of productive wealth. With the establishment of communism, what Marx called 'the pre-history of mankind' would come to an end.

Economics

In Marx's early writings much of his critique of capitalism rests on the notion of **alienation**, which applies in four senses. Since capitalism is a system of production-for-exchange, it alienates humans from the *product* of their labour:

Dialectic: A process of development in which interaction between two opposing forces leads to a further or higher stage; historical change resulting from internal contradictions within a society.

Alienation: To be separated from one's genuine or essential nature; used by Marxists to describe the process whereby, under capitalism, labour is reduced to being a mere commodity.

they work to produce not what they need or what is useful, but 'commodities' to be sold for profit. They are also alienated from the *process* of labour, because most are forced to work under the supervision of foremen or managers. In addition, work is not social: individuals are encouraged to be self-interested and are therefore alienated from *fellow workers*. Finally, workers are alienated from *themselves*. Labour itself is reduced to a mere commodity and work becomes a depersonalised activity instead of a creative and fulfilling one.

However, in his later work, Marx analysed capitalism more in terms of class conflict and exploitation. Marx defined class in terms of economic power, specifically where people stand in relation to the ownership of the 'means of production', or productive wealth. He believed that capitalist society was being divided increasingly into 'two great classes facing one another: Bourgeoisie and Proletariat'. For Marx and later Marxists, the analysis of the class system provides the key to historical understanding and enables predictions to be made about the future development of capitalism: in the words of *The Communist Manifesto* (in Marx and Engels, 1968), 'The history of all hitherto existing societies is the history of class struggle.' Classes, rather than individuals, parties or other movements, are the chief agents of historical change.

Crucially, Marx believed that the relationship between classes is one of irreconcilable antagonism, the subordinate class being necessarily and systematically exploited by the '**ruling class**'. This he explained by reference to the idea of '**surplus value**'. Capitalism's quest for profit can only be satisfied through the extraction of surplus value from its workers, by paying them less than the value their labour generates. Economic exploitation is therefore an essential feature of the capitalist mode of production, and it operates regardless of the meanness or generosity of particular employers. Marx was concerned not only to highlight the inherent instability of capitalism, based on irreconcilable class conflict, but also to analyse the nature of capitalist development. In particular, he drew attention to its tendency to experience deepening economic crises. These stemmed, in the main, from cyclical crises of overproduction, plunging the economy into stagnation and bringing unemployment and immiseration to the working class. Each crisis would be more severe than the last, because, Marx calculated, in the long term the rate of profit would fall. This would eventually, and inevitably, produce conditions in which the proletariat, the vast majority of society, would rise up in revolution.

Politics

Marx's most important prediction was that capitalism was destined to be overthrown by a proletarian revolution. This would be not merely a political revolution that would remove the governing elite or overthrow the state machine, but a **social revolution** that would establish a new mode of production and culminate in the achievement of full communism. Such a revolution, he anticipated, would occur in the most mature capitalist countries – for example, Germany, Belgium, France or the UK – where the forces of production had expanded to their limit within the constraints of the capitalist system. Nevertheless, revolution would not simply be determined

Ruling class: A Marxist term denoting the class that owns the means of production, and so wields economic and political power.

Surplus value: A Marxist term denoting the value that is extracted from the labour of the proletariat by the mechanism of capitalist exploitation.

Social revolution: A qualitative change in the structure of society; for Marxists a social revolution involves a change in the mode of production and the system of ownership.

by objective conditions alone. The subjective element would be supplied by a 'class-conscious' proletariat, meaning that revolution would occur when both objective and subjective conditions were 'ripe'. As class antagonisms intensified, the proletariat would recognise the fact of its own exploitation and become a revolutionary force: a class for-itself and not merely a class in-itself. In this sense, revolution would be a spontaneous act, carried out by a proletarian class that would, in effect, lead or guide itself.

The initial target of this revolution was to be the bourgeois state. The state, in this view, is an instrument of oppression wielded by the economically dominant class. However, Marx recognised that there could be no immediate transition from capitalism to communism. A transitionary 'socialist' stage of development would last as long as class antagonisms persisted. This would be characterised by what Marx called the **dictatorship of the proletariat**. The purpose of this proletarian state was to safeguard the gains of the revolution by preventing counter-revolution carried out by the dispossessed bourgeoisie. However, as class antagonisms began to fade with the emergence of full communism, the state would 'wither away' once the class system had been abolished, the state would lose its reason for existence. The resulting communist society would therefore be stateless as well as classless, and would allow a system of commodity production to give way to one geared to the satisfaction of human needs.

Orthodox communism

The Russian Revolution and its consequences dominated the image of communism in the twentieth century. The Bolshevik Party, led by V. I. Lenin, seized power in a *coup d'état* in October 1917, and the following year adopted the name 'Communist Party'. As the first successful communist revolutionaries, the Bolshevik leaders enjoyed unquestionable authority within the communist world, at least until the 1950s. Communist parties set up elsewhere accepted the ideological leadership of Moscow and joined the Communist International, or 'Comintern', founded in 1919. The communist regimes established in eastern Europe after 1945, in China in 1949, in Cuba in 1959 and elsewhere, were consciously modelled on the structure of the Soviet Union. Thus, Soviet communism became the dominant model of communist rule, and the ideas of Marxism–Leninism became the ruling ideology of the communist world.

However, twentieth-century communism differed significantly from the ideas and expectations of Marx and Engels. In the first place, although the communist parties that developed in the twentieth century were founded on the theories of classical Marxism, they were forced to adapt these to the tasks of winning and retaining political power. Twentieth-century communist leaders had, in particular, to give greater attention to issues such as leadership, political organisation and economic management than Marx had done. Second, the communist regimes were shaped by the historical circumstances in which they developed. Communist parties did not achieve power, as Marx had anticipated, in the developed capitalist states of western Europe, but in backward, largely rural countries such as Russia and China. In consequence, the urban proletariat was invariably

Dictatorship of the proletariat: A Marxist term denoting the transitionary phase between the collapse of capitalism and the establishment of full communism, characterised by the establishment of a proletarian state.

small and unsophisticated, quite incapable of carrying out a genuine class revolution. Communist rule thus became the rule of a communist elite, and of communist leaders. Soviet communism, furthermore, was crucially shaped by the decisive personal contribution of the first two Bolshevik leaders, V. I. Lenin and Joseph Stalin (1879–1953).

Lenin was both a political leader and a major political thinker. His theories reflected his overriding concern with the problems of winning power and establishing communist rule. The central feature of **Leninism** was a belief in the need for a new kind of political party, a revolutionary party or vanguard party. Unlike Marx, Lenin did not believe that the proletariat would spontaneously develop revolutionary **class consciousness**, as the working class was deluded by **bourgeois ideology**. He suggested that only a 'revolutionary party' could lead the working class from 'trade union consciousness' to revolutionary class consciousness. Such a party should be composed of professional and dedicated revolutionaries. Its claim to leadership would lie in its ideological wisdom, specifically its understanding of Marxist theory. This party could therefore act as the 'vanguard of the proletariat' because, armed with Marxism, it would perceive the genuine interests of the proletariat and would act to awaken the proletarian class to its revolutionary potential. Lenin further proposed that the vanguard party should be organised according to the principles of **democratic centralism**. Lenin's theory of the party nevertheless attracted criticism from fellow Marxists. In particular, Rosa Luxemburg (see below) associated the notion of the vanguard party with the problem of 'substitutionism', in which a ruling party would substitute itself for the proletariat and, eventually, a supreme leader would substitute himself for the party.

When the Bolsheviks seized power in 1917 they did so as a vanguard party, and therefore in the name of the proletariat. If the Bolshevik Party was acting in the

Leninism: Lenin's theoretical contributions to Marxism, notably his belief in the need for a revolutionary or 'vanguard' party to raise the proletariat to class consciousness.

Class consciousness: A Marxist term denoting an accurate awareness of class interests and a willingness to pursue them; a class-conscious class is a class for-itself.

Bourgeois ideology: A Marxist term denoting ideas and theories that serve the interests of the bourgeoisie by concealing the contradictions of the capitalist class system.

Democratic centralism: The Leninist principle of party organisation, based on a supposed balance between freedom of discussion and strict unity of action.

KEY FIGURE

Rosa Luxemburg (1871–1919)

A Polish-born socialist and exponent of revolutionary Marxism, Luxemburg advanced the first Marxist critique of the Bolshevik tradition from the point of view of democracy. Emphasising the benefits of a broadly based democratic organisation, she condemned Lenin's conception of a tightly centralised vanguard party as an attempt to exert political control over the working class. By associating vanguardism with the rise of despotism, she predicted the subsequent course of Russian communism. In her most important theoretical work, *The Accumulation of Capital* (1913), Luxemburg examined the intrinsic connections between capitalism, nationalism, militarism and imperialism. In *Social Reform or Revolution* (1899), she condemned the revisionism of Bernstein and others for denying the objective foundations of the socialist project. Luxemburg therefore represented a form of Marxism that attempted to steer a course between Bolshevism and Marxist revisionism, and thus between the major two traditions of twentieth-century socialism: orthodox communism and social democracy. For more on Luxemburg, see above.

interests of the working class, it followed that opposition parties must represent the interests of classes hostile to the proletariat, in particular the bourgeoisie. The dictatorship of the proletariat required that the revolution be protected against its class enemies, which effectively meant the suppression of all parties other than the Communist Party. By 1920, Russia had become a one-party state. Leninist theory therefore implied the existence of a monopolistic party, which enjoys sole responsibility for articulating the interests of the proletariat and guiding the revolution towards its ultimate goal, that of 'building communism'.

Soviet communism was no less deeply influenced by the rule of Joseph Stalin, 1924–53, than by that of Lenin. Indeed more so, as the Soviet Union was affected more profoundly by Stalin's 'second revolution' in the 1930s than it had been by the October Revolution. Stalin's most important ideological shift was to embrace the doctrine of 'Socialism in One Country', initially developed by Nikolai Bukharin (1888–1938). Announced in 1924, this proclaimed that the Soviet Union could succeed in 'building socialism' without the need for international revolution. After consolidating himself in power, however, Stalin oversaw a dramatic economic and political upheaval, beginning with the announcement of the first Five Year Plan in 1928. Stalin's Five Year Plans brought about rapid industrialisation as well as the swift and total eradication of private enterprise. From 1929, agriculture was collectivised, and Soviet peasants were forced at the cost of literally millions of lives to give up their land and join state or collective farms. Economic **Stalinism** therefore took the form of state collectivisation or 'state socialism'. The capitalist market was entirely removed and replaced by a system of central planning, dominated by the State Planning Committee, 'Gosplan', and administered by a collection of powerful economic ministries based in Moscow.

Major political changes accompanied this 'second revolution'. During the 1930s, Stalin used his power to brutal effect, removing anyone suspected of disloyalty or criticism in an increasingly violent series of purges carried out by the secret police, the NKVD. The membership of the Communist Party was almost halved, over a million people lost their lives, including all the surviving members of Lenin's Politburo, and many millions were imprisoned in labour camps, or gulags. Political Stalinism was therefore a form of totalitarian dictatorship, operating through a monolithic ruling party, in which all forms of debate or criticism were eradicated by terror in what amounted to a civil war conducted against the party itself.

Neo-Marxism

While Marxism – or, more usually, Marxism–Leninism – was turned into a secular religion by the orthodox communist regimes of eastern Europe and elsewhere, a more subtle and complex form of Marxism developed in western Europe. Referred to as 'modern Marxism', 'western Marxism' or '**neo-Marxism**', this amounted to an attempt to revise or recast the classical ideas of Marx while remaining faithful to certain Marxist principles or aspects of Marxist methodology.

Stalinism: A centrally planned economy supported by systematic and brutal political oppression, based on the structures of Stalin's Russia.

Neo-Marxism: An updated and revised form of Marxism that rejects determinism, the primacy of economics and the privileged status of the proletariat.

Two principal factors shaped the character of neo-Marxism. First, when Marx's prediction about the imminent collapse of capitalism failed to materialise, neo-Marxists were forced to re-examine conventional class analysis. In particular, they took a greater interest in Hegelian ideas and in the stress on 'Man the creator' found in Marx's early writings. Neo-Marxists were thus able to break free from the rigid 'base/superstructure' straitjacket. In short, the class struggle was no longer treated as the beginning and end of social analysis. Second, neo-Marxists were usually at odds with, and sometimes profoundly repelled by, the Bolshevik model of orthodox communism. Not only were they critical of its authoritarian repressive character, but it also recoiled on its mechanistic and avowedly scientific pretensions.

The Hungarian Marxist Georg Lukacs (1885–1971) was one of the first to present Marxism as a humanistic philosophy, emphasising the process of 'reification', through which capitalism dehumanises workers by reducing them to passive objects or marketable commodities. The Italian Marxist revolutionary Antonio Gramsci (1891–1937) drew attention to the degree to which the class system is upheld not simply by unequal economic and political power, but also by bourgeois 'hegemony', the spiritual and cultural supremacy of the ruling class, brought about through the spread of bourgeois values and beliefs via civil society – the media, churches, youth movements, trade unions and so on. A more overtly Hegelian brand of Marxism was developed by the so-called Frankfurt School, whose leading early figures were Theodor Adorno (1903–69), Max Horkheimer (1895–1973) and Herbert Marcuse (1898–1979). Frankfurt theorists developed what was called 'critical theory', a blend of Marxist political economy, Hegelian philosophy and Freudian psychology, that came to have a considerable impact on the so-called 'New Left'. The leading exponent of the 'second generation' of the Frankfurt School is the German philosopher and social theorist Jürgen Habermas (born 1929). His wide-ranging work includes an analysis of 'crisis tendencies' in capitalist society that arise from tensions between capital accumulation and democracy.

Key concept ... NEW LEFT

The New Left comprises thinkers and intellectual movements that emerged in the 1960s and early 1970s, seeking to revitalise socialist thought by developing a radical critique of advanced industrial society. The New Left rejected both of the 'old' left alternatives: Soviet-style state socialism and de-radicalised western social democracy. Influenced by the humanist writings of the 'young' Marx, and by anarchism and radical forms of phenomenology and existentialism, New Left theories are often diffuse. Common themes nevertheless include a fundamental rejection of conventional society ('the system') as oppressive, a commitment to personal autonomy and self-fulfilment in the form of 'liberation', disillusionment with the role of the working class as the revolutionary agent, sympathy for identity politics (see p. 189), and a preference for decentralisation and participatory democracy.

The death of Marxism?

The year 1989 marked a dramatic watershed in the history of communism and in ideological history generally. Starting in April with student-led 'democracy movement' demonstrations in Tiananmen Square in Beijing and culminating in November in the fall of the Berlin Wall, the division of Europe into a capitalist West and a communist East was brought to an end. By 1991 the Soviet Union, the model of orthodox communism, had ceased to exist. Where communist regimes continue, as in China, Cuba, Vietnam, North Korea and elsewhere, they have either blended political Stalinism with market-orientated economic reform (most clearly in the case of China) or suffered increasing isolation (as in the case of North Korea). These developments were a result of a number of structural flaws from which orthodox communism suffered. Chief among these were that while central planning proved effective in bringing about early industrialisation, it could not cope with the complexities of modern industrial societies and, in particular, failed to deliver the levels of prosperity enjoyed in the capitalist West from the 1950s onwards.

There is, nevertheless, considerable debate about the implications of the collapse of communism for Marxism. On the one hand, there are those who, like the 'end of history' theorist Francis Fukuyama (1989, 1992), argue that the 'collapse of communism' is certain proof of the demise of Marxism as a world-historical force. On the other hand, there are those who argue that the Soviet-style communism that was rejected in the revolutions of 1989–91 differed markedly from the 'Marxism of Marx'. However, to point out that it was not Marxism but a Stalinist version of Marxism–Leninism that collapsed in 1989–91 is very far from demonstrating the continuing relevance of Marxism. A far more serious problem for Marxism is the failure of Marx's predictions (about the inevitable collapse of capitalism and its replacement by communism) to be realised. Quite simply, advanced industrial societies have not been haunted by the 'spectre of communism'. Even those who believe that Marx's views on matters such as alienation and exploitation continue to be relevant, have to accept that classical Marxism failed to recognise the remarkable resilience of capitalism and its capacity to recreate itself.

Some Marxists have responded to these problems by advancing 'post-Marxist' ideas and theories. Post-Marxism, nevertheless, has two implications. The first is that the Marxist project, and the historical materialism on which it is based, should be abandoned in favour of alternative ideas. This is evident in the writings of the one-time Marxist Jean-François Lyotard (1984), who suggested that Marxism as a totalising theory of history, and for that matter all other 'grand narratives', had been made redundant by the emergence of postmodernity. In its alternative version, post-Marxism consists of an attempt to salvage certain key Marxist insights by attempting to reconcile Marxism with aspects of postmodernism and poststructuralism. Ernesto Laclau and Chantal Mouffe (2014) accepted that the priority traditionally accorded to social class, and the central position of the working class in bringing about social change, were no longer sustainable. In so doing, they opened up space within Marxism for a wide range of other 'moments' of struggle, usually linked to so-called new social movements such as the women's movement, the ecological movement, the gay and lesbian movement, the peace movement, and so on.

SOCIAL DEMOCRACY

As an ideological stance, social democracy took shape around the mid-twentieth century, resulting from the tendency among western socialist parties not only to adopt parliamentary strategies, but also to revise their socialist goals. In particular, they abandoned the goal of abolishing capitalism and sought instead to reform or 'humanise' it. Social democracy therefore came to stand for a broad balance between the market economy, on the one hand, and state intervention, on the other.

Social democracy was most fully developed in the early post-1945 period, during which enthusiasm for social-democratic ideas and theories extended well beyond its socialist homeland, creating, in many western states, a social-democratic consensus. However, since the 1970s and 1980s, social democracy has struggled to retain its electoral and political relevance in the face of the advance of neoliberalism (see p. 51) and changed economic and social circumstances. The final decades of the twentieth century therefore witnessed a process of ideological retreat on the part of reformist socialist parties across the globe.

Ethical socialism

The theoretical basis for social democracy has been provided more by moral or religious beliefs than by scientific analysis. Social democrats have not accepted the materialist and highly systematic ideas of Marx and Engels, but rather advanced an essentially moral critique of capitalism. In short, socialism is portrayed as morally superior to capitalism because human beings are ethical creatures, bound to one another by the ties of love, sympathy and compassion. The moral vision that underlies ethical socialism has been based on both humanistic and religious principles. Socialism in France, the UK and other Commonwealth countries has been influenced more strongly by the **humanist** ideas of Fourier,

Humanism: A philosophy that gives moral priority to the satisfaction of human needs and aspirations.

Key concept ... SOCIAL DEMOCRACY

Social democracy is an ideological stance that supports a broad balance between market capitalism, on the one hand, and state intervention, on the other. Being based on a compromise between the market and the state, social democracy lacks a systematic underlying theory and is, arguably, inherently vague. It is nevertheless associated with the following views: (1) capitalism is the only reliable means of generating wealth, but it is a morally defective means of distributing wealth because of its tendency towards poverty and inequality; (2) the defects of the capitalist system can be rectified through economic and social intervention, the state being the custodian of the public interest; (3) social change can and should be brought about peacefully and constitutionally.

Owen and William Morris (1854–96) than by the 'scientific' creed of Karl Marx. However, ethical socialism has also drawn heavily on Christianity. For example, there is a long-established tradition of Christian socialism in the UK, reflected in the twentieth century in the works of the British socialist and historian R. H. Tawney (1880–1962). The Christian ethic that has inspired UK socialism is that of universal brotherhood, the respect that should be accorded to all individuals as creations of God, a principle embodied in the commandment 'Thou shalt love thy neighbour as thyself'. In *The Acquisitive Society* (1921), Tawney condemned unregulated capitalism because it is driven by the 'sin of avarice' rather than faith in a 'common humanity'.

Such religious inspiration has also been evident in the ideas of liberation theology, which has influenced many Catholic developing-world states, especially in Latin America. After years of providing support for repressive regimes in Latin America, Roman Catholic bishops meeting at Medellin, Colombia, in 1968 declared a 'preferential option for the poor'. The religious responsibilities of the clergy were seen to extend beyond the narrowly spiritual and to embrace the social and political struggles of ordinary people. Despite the condemnation of Pope John Paul II and the Vatican, radical priests in many parts of Latin America campaigned against poverty and political oppression and, at times, even backed socialist revolutionary movements. Similarly, socialist movements in the predominantly Muslim countries of North Africa, the Middle East and Asia have been inspired by religion. Islam is linked to socialism in that it exhorts the principles of social justice, charity and cooperation, and specifically prohibits usury or profiteering.

In abandoning scientific analysis in favour of moral or religious principles, however, social democracy weakened the theoretical basis of socialism. Social democracy has been concerned primarily with the notion of a just or fair distribution of wealth in society. This is embodied in the overriding principle of social democracy: **social justice**. Social democracy consequently came to stand for a broad range of views, extending from a left-wing commitment to extending equality and expanding the collective ownership of wealth, to a more right-wing acceptance of the need for market efficiency and individual self-reliance that may be difficult to distinguish from certain forms of liberalism or conservatism. Attempts have nevertheless been made to give social democracy a theoretical basis, usually involving re-examining capitalism itself and redefining the goal of socialism.

Revisionist socialism

The original, fundamentalist goal of socialism was that productive wealth should be owned in common by all, and therefore used for the common benefit. This required the abolition of private property and the transition from a capitalist mode of production to a socialist one, usually through a process of revolutionary change. Capitalism, in this view, is unredeemable: it is a system of class exploitation and oppression that deserves to be abolished altogether, not merely reformed. However, by the end of the nineteenth century, some socialists had come to believe that this analysis of capitalism was defective. The clearest

Social justice: A morally justifiable distribution of wealth, usually implying a commitment to greater equality.

theoretical expression of this belief was advanced by the German socialist politician and theorist Eduard Bernstein (1850–1932). In his *Evolutionary Socialism* ([1898] 1962), Bernstein undertook a comprehensive criticism of Marx and provided the foundation for **revisionist socialism**.

Bernstein's theoretical approach was largely empirical; he rejected Marx's method of analysis – historical materialism – because the predictions Marx had made had proved to be incorrect. Capitalism had shown itself to be both stable and flexible. Rather than class conflict intensifying, dividing capitalist society into 'two great classes' (the bourgeoisie and the proletariat), Bernstein suggested that capitalism was becoming increasingly complex and differentiated. In particular, the ownership of wealth had widened as a result of the introduction of joint stock companies, owned by a number of shareholders instead of a single powerful industrialist. The ranks of the middle classes had also been swollen by the growing number of salaried employees, technicians, government officials and professional workers, who were neither capitalists nor proletarians. In Bernstein's view, capitalism was no longer a system of naked class oppression. Capitalism could therefore be reformed by the nationalisation of major industries and the extension of legal protection and welfare benefits to the working class, a process which, Bernstein believed, could be achieved peacefully and democratically.

Western socialist parties have been revisionist in practice, if not always in theory, intent on 'taming' capitalism rather than abolishing it. In some cases they long retained a formal commitment to fundamentalist goals, as in the UK Labour Party's belief in 'the common ownership of the means of production, distribution and exchange', expressed in clause IV of its 1918 constitution. Nevertheless, as the twentieth century progressed, social democrats dropped their commitment to planning as they recognised the efficiency and vigour of the capitalist market. The Swedish Social Democratic Labour Party formally abandoned planning in the 1930s, as did the West German Social Democrats at the Bad Godesberg Congress of 1959, which accepted the principle of 'competition when possible; planning when necessary'. In the UK, a similar bid to embrace revisionism formally in the late 1950s ended in failure when the Labour Party conference rejected the then leader Hugh Gaitskell's attempt to abolish clause IV of the Labour constitution. Nevertheless, when in power, the Labour Party never revealed an appetite for wholesale nationalisation.

The abandonment of planning and comprehensive nationalisation left social democracy with three more modest objectives. Social democrats support:

Revisionist socialism: A form of socialism that has revised its critique of capitalism and seeks to reconcile greater social justice with surviving capitalist forms.

▶ The *mixed economy*, a blend of public and private ownership that stands between free-market capitalism and state collectivism. Nationalisation, when advocated by social democrats, is invariably selective and reserved for the 'commanding heights' of the economy, or industries that are thought to be 'natural monopolies'. The 1945–51 Attlee Labour government, for instance, nationalised the major utilities – electricity, gas, coal, steel, the railways and so on – but left most of UK industry in private hands.

Differences between ...

COMMUNISM AND SOCIAL DEMOCRACY

COMMUNISM	SOCIAL DEMOCRACY
• scientific socialism	• ethical socialism
• fundamentalism	• revisionism
• utopianism	• reformism
• revolution	• evolution/gradualism
• abolish capitalism	• 'humanise' capitalism
• common ownership	• redistribution
• classless society	• ameliorate class conflict
• absolute equality	• relative equality
• state collectivisation	• mixed economy
• central planning	• economic management
• vanguard party	• parliamentary party
• dictatorship of proletariat	• political pluralism
• proletarian/people's state	• liberal-democratic state

▶ *Economic management*, seeing the need for capitalism to be regulated in order to deliver sustainable growth. After 1945, most social democratic parties were converted to Keynesianism (see p. 31) as a device for controlling the economy and delivering full employment.

▶ The *welfare state*, viewing it as the principal means of reforming or humanising capitalism. Its attraction is that it acts as a redistributive mechanism that helps to promote social equality and eradicate poverty. Capitalism no longer needs to be abolished, only modified through the establishment of reformed or welfare capitalism.

An attempt to give theoretical substance to these developments, and in effect update Bernstein, was made by Anthony Crosland (see p. 84) in *The Future of Socialism* (1956). He subscribed to **managerialism**, in believing that modern capitalism bore little resemblance to the nineteenth-century model that Marx had had in mind. Crosland suggested that a new class of managers, experts and technocrats had supplanted the old capitalist class and come to dominate all advanced industrial societies, both capitalist and communist. The ownership of wealth had therefore become divorced from its control. Whereas shareholders, who own businesses, were principally concerned with profit, salaried managers, who make day-to-day business decisions, have a broader range of goals, including maintaining industrial harmony and upholding the public image of the company.

Such developments implied that Marxism had become irrelevant: if capitalism could no longer be viewed as a system of class exploitation, the fundamentalist goals of nationalisation and planning were simply outdated. Crosland thus

Managerialism: The theory that a governing class of managers, technocrats and state officials – those who possess technical and administrative skills – dominates both capitalist and communist societies.

KEY FIGURE

Anthony Crosland (1918–77)

A British Labour politician and social theorist, Crosland was a leading exponent of revisionist socialism. In *The Future of Socialism* (1956), he dismissed Marxism on the grounds that capitalism, in its classical sense, no longer existed, having been transformed by the spread of democracy, progressive taxation, the trade unions, welfare reforms and, above all, the divorce of ownership from effective control of industry. In this light, Crosland defined socialism in terms of ethical goals, notably equality and social justice, rather than class antagonism and common ownership. In *Socialism Now* (1974), he championed the idea of 'democratic equality', which, in recognising that some level of inequality is of benefit to all, prefigured the ideas of Rawls (see p. 30). Although Crosland revised the 'ends' of socialism in these ways, he supported a diverse and radical set of 'means' to advance them. These included a strengthened welfare state, Keynesian demand management, the wider use of progressive taxation and expanded social ownership (particularly through state investment in business). For more on Crosland, see pp. 83–5.

recast socialism in terms of the politics of social justice, rather than the politics of ownership. Wealth need not be owned in common, because it could be redistributed through a welfare state that is financed by progressive taxation. However, Crosland recognised that economic growth plays a crucial role in the achievement of socialism. A growing economy is essential to generate the tax revenues needed to finance more generous social expenditure, and the prosperous will only be prepared to finance the needy if their own living standards are underwritten by economic growth.

The crisis of social democracy

During the early post-1945 period, Keynesian social democracy – or traditional social democracy – appeared to have triumphed. Its strength was that it harnessed the dynamism of the market without succumbing to the levels of inequality and instability that Marx believed would doom capitalism. Nevertheless, Keynesian social democracy was based on an (arguably) inherently unstable compromise. On the one hand, there was a pragmatic acceptance of the market as the only reliable means of generating wealth. This reluctant conversion to the market meant that social democrats accepted that there was no viable socialist alternative to the market, meaning that the socialist project was reborn as an attempt to reform, not replace, capitalism. On the other hand, the socialist ethic survived in the form of a commitment to social justice. This, in turn, was linked to a weak notion of equality: distributive equality, the idea that poverty should be reduced and inequality narrowed through the redistribution of wealth from rich to poor.

At the heart of Keynesian social democracy there lay a conflict between its commitment to both economic efficiency and egalitarianism. During the 'long boom' of the post-1945 period, social democrats were not forced to confront this conflict because sustained growth, low unemployment and low inflation improved the living standards of all social groups and helped to finance more generous welfare provision. However, as Crosland had anticipated, recession in the 1970s and 1980s created strains within social democracy, polarising socialist thought into more clearly defined left-wing and right-wing positions. Recession precipitated a 'fiscal crisis of the welfare state', simultaneously increasing demand for welfare support as unemployment re-emerged, and squeezing the tax revenues that financed welfare spending (because fewer people were at work and businesses were less profitable). A difficult question had to be answered: should social democrats attempt to restore efficiency to the market economy, which might mean cutting inflation and possibly taxes, or should they defend the poor and the lower paid by maintaining or even expanding welfare provision?

This crisis of social democracy was intensified in the 1980s and 1990s by a combination of political, social and international factors. In the first place, the electoral viability of social democracy was undermined by deindustrialisation and the shrinkage of the traditional working class, the social base of Keynesian social democracy. Whereas in the early post-1945 period the tide of democracy had flowed with progressive politics, since the 1980s it has been orientated increasingly around the interests of what J. K. Galbraith (1992) called the 'contented majority'. Social democratic parties paid a high price for these social and electoral shifts. For instance, the UK Labour Party lost four successive general elections between 1979 and 1992; the SPD in Germany was out of power between 1982 and 1998; and the French Socialist Party suffered crushing defeats, notably in 1993 and 2002. Furthermore, the intellectual credibility of social democracy was badly damaged by the collapse of communism. Not only did this create a world without any significant non-capitalist economic forms, but it also undermined faith in the state as the principal agent of economic and social reform. In this light, Keynesian social democracy could be viewed as only a more modest version of the 'top-down' state socialism that had been discarded so abruptly in the revolutions of 1989–91.

Neo-revisionism and the 'third way'

Since the 1980s, reformist socialist parties across the globe, but particularly in countries such as the UK, the Netherlands, Germany, Italy, Australia and New Zealand, have undergone a further bout of revisionism, sometimes termed 'neo-revisionism'. In so doing, they have distanced themselves, to a greater or lesser extent, from the principles and commitments of traditional social democracy. The resulting ideological stance has been described in various ways, including 'new' social democracy, the '**third way**', the 'radical centre', the 'active centre' and the '*Neue Mitte*' (new middle). However, the ideological significance of neo-revisionism, and its relationship to traditional social democracy in particular and to socialism in general, have been shrouded in debate and confusion. This is partly because neo-revisionism has taken different forms in different countries. There have therefore been a number of contrasting neo-revisionist projects, including those associated with Tony Blair and New Labour in the UK and with Bill Clinton and the New Democrats in the USA, as well as those that have emerged in states such as Germany, the Netherlands, Italy, Australia and New Zealand. The central thrust

Third way: The notion of an alternative form of economics to both state socialism and free-market capitalism, sought at different times by conservatives, socialists and fascists.

Key concept ... COMMUNITARIANISM

Communitarianism is the belief that the self or person is constituted through the community, in the sense that individuals are shaped by the communities to which they belong and thus owe them a debt of respect and consideration – there are no 'unencumbered selves'. Though clearly at odds with liberal individualism, communitarianism nevertheless has a variety of political forms. *Left-wing* communitarianism holds that community demands unrestricted freedom and social equality (for example, anarchism). *Centrist* communitarianism holds that community is grounded in an acknowledgement of reciprocal rights and responsibilities (for example, social democracy/Tory paternalism). *Right-wing* communitarianism holds that a community requires respect for authority and established values (for example, neoconservatism, see p. 55).

of neo-revisionism is nevertheless encapsulated in the notion of the third way, highlighting the idea of an alternative to both capitalism and socialism. In its modern form, the third way represents, more specifically, an alternative to old-style social democracy and neoliberalism.

Although the third way is (perhaps inherently) imprecise and subject to competing interpretations, certain characteristic third-way themes can nevertheless be identified. The first of these is the belief that socialism, at least in the form of what Anthony Giddens (see p. 87) called the 'cybernetic model' of socialism (Giddens, 1994), in which the state, acting as the brain within society, is dead. This shift away from 'top-down' state intervention implied that there is no alternative to what the revised clause IV of the UK Labour Party's 1995 constitution refers to as 'a dynamic market economy'. With this goes a general acceptance of globalisation and the belief that capitalism has mutated into an 'information society' or '**knowledge economy**'. This general acceptance of the market over the state, and the adoption of a pro-business and pro-enterprise stance, means that the third way attempts to build on, rather than reverse, the neoliberal revolution of the 1980s and 1990s.

The second key third-way belief is its emphasis on community and moral responsibility. Community, of course, has a long socialist heritage, drawing as it does, like fraternity and cooperation, on the idea of a social essence. While the third way accepts many of the economic theories of neoliberalism, it firmly rejects its philosophical basis and its moral and social implications. The danger of market fundamentalism is that it generates a free-for-all that undermines the moral foundations of society. Some versions of the third way, notably the so-called 'Blair project' in the UK, nevertheless attempted to fuse communitarian ideas with liberal ones, creating a form of communitarian liberalism which, in many ways, resembled the 'new liberalism' of the late nineteenth century. The cornerstone belief of communitarian liberalism is that rights and responsibilities are intrinsically bound together: all rights must be balanced against responsibilities, and vice versa.

Knowledge economy: An economy in which knowledge is supposedly the key source of competitiveness and productivity, especially in the form of information and communication technology.

KEY FIGURE

Anthony Giddens (born 1938)

 A British academic and social theorist, Giddens had a strong impact on the development of a new social-democratic agenda in the UK and elsewhere, and was sometimes referred to as 'Tony Blair's guru'. In works such as *Beyond Left and Right* (1994) and *The Third Way* (1998), he explained the plight of the traditional forms of both socialism and conservatism in terms of sociological developments associated with the emergence of so-called 'high modernity'. Placing a particular emphasis on the impact of globalisation, Giddens argued that modern societies have become so complex and fluid that they have to be organised substantially through the market and networks, rather than by the state and social class. Giddens nevertheless insisted that such developments open up new opportunities for progressive politics. This occurs not least as the stretching of political horizons beyond the nation-state generates increased pressure for local autonomy and the building of regional cultural identities. For more on Giddens, see p. 86 and below.

Third, supporters of the third way tend to adopt a consensus view of society, in contrast to socialism's conflict view of society. This is evident, for example, in the tendency of community to highlight ties that bind all members of society, and thus to ignore, or conceal, class differences and economic inequalities. A faith in consensus and social harmony is also reflected in the value framework of the third way, which rejects the either/or approach of conventional moral and ideological thinking, and offers what almost amounts to a non-dualistic world-view. Third-way politicians thus typically endorse enterprise *and* fairness, opportunity *and* security, self-reliance *and* interdependence, and so on. While this may demonstrate that the third way goes 'beyond left and right', as Giddens (1994) argued, it also leaves it open to the criticism that it is at best ambiguous and at worst simply incoherent.

Differences between ...
SOCIAL DEMOCRACY AND THE THIRD WAY

SOCIAL DEMOCRACY	THIRD WAY
• ideological	• pragmatic
• nation-state	• globalisation
• industrial society	• information society
• class politics	• community
• mixed economy	• market economy
• full employment	• full employability
• concern for underdog	• meritocracy
• social justice	• opportunity for all
• eradicate poverty	• promote inclusion
• social rights	• rights and responsibilities
• cradle-to-grave welfare	• welfare-to-work
• social reformist state	• competition/market state

Fourth, the third way has substituted a concern with **social inclusion** for the traditional socialist commitment to equality. This is evident in the stress placed on liberal ideas such as opportunity, and even meritocracy. Egalitarianism is therefore scaled down to a belief in equality of opportunities or 'asset-based egalitarianism', the right of access to assets and opportunities that enable individuals to realise their potential. Third-way proposals for welfare reform therefore typically reject both the neoliberal emphasis on 'standing on your own two feet' and the social-democratic belief in 'cradle to grave' welfare. Instead, welfare should be targeted at the 'socially excluded' and should follow the modern liberal approach of 'helping people to help themselves', or as the former US President Bill Clinton put it, giving people 'a hand up, not a handout'. Welfare policies should, in particular, aim to widen access to work, in line with the US idea of 'workfare', the belief that welfare support should be conditional on an individual's willingness to seek work and become self-reliant.

Finally, the third way is characterised by new thinking about the proper role of the state. The third way embraces the idea of a **competition state** or market state. The state should concentrate on social investment, which means improving the infrastructure of the economy and, most important, strengthening the skills and knowledge of the country's workforce. Education rather than social security should therefore be the government's priority, with education being valued not in its own right, because it furthers personal development (the modern liberal view), but because it promotes employability and benefits the economy (the utilitarian or classical liberal view). From this perspective, the government is essentially a cultural actor, whose purpose is to shape or reshape the population's attitudes, values, skills, beliefs and knowledge, rather than to carry out a programme of economic and social engineering.

Revival of socialism?

Indications of a radical turn in socialist politics emerged in the 1990s through growth of the anti-globalisation, or 'anti-capitalist', movement. In this light, some proclaimed that socialism in the twenty-first century may be reborn as global anti-capitalism, a trend that has been particularly apparent since the global financial crisis of 2007–10. A resurgence of leftist radicalism was thus evident in the upsurge of the Occupy movement, which in 2011 organised demonstrations in some 82 countries protesting against the dominance of the '1 per cent'.

Evidence of a revival of socialism can nevertheless also be seen at the national level. In some cases, radical leftist parties have come from seemingly nowhere to challenge mainstream parties of both the centre-left and centre-right. For example, Syriza (the Coalition of the Radical Left), founded in 2004, became the largest party in the Greek parliament in elections in January and September 2015, its chairman, Alexis Tsipras, becoming prime minister. In Spain, the far-left party Podemos (We can), founded in 2014, gained the third largest number of votes and the second largest number of seats in the 2015 parliamentary elections. In other cases, upsurges of radicalism have occurred within established

Social inclusion: The acquisition of rights, skills and opportunities that enable citizens to participate fully in their society.

Competition state: A state whose principal role is to pursue strategies for national prosperity in conditions of intensifying global competition.

parties of the centre-left. In the UK, Jeremy Corbyn, a veteran of the Labour Party's hard left, emerged as the surprise victor in the party's 2015 leadership election, while in the USA Bernie Saunders, a self-declared socialist, was only narrowly defeated by Hillary Clinton in the contest to become the Democratic nominee in the 2016 presidential election. (For a discussion of the ideas and policies of the modern Labour Party, see Chapter 5 of *Essentials of UK Politics*.)

Despite national and regional differences, two wider explanations can be advanced for these developments. The first has been a backlash against the politics of austerity, a policy that was widely adopted as economies fell into recession and tax revenues plummeted in the aftermath of the global financial crisis. In countries such as Greece, Spain and Portugal, this was exacerbated by the terms of bailout arrangements that were negotiated with the EU, the IMF and the European Central Bank. The second factor is that far-left parties and movements have tapped into a growing mood of anti-establishment radicalism, sometimes called 'anti-politics', that stems, in part, from a narrowing of the ideological divide between left- and right-wing parties. This, in turn, has been one of the consequences of the advance of globalisation. In this light, resurgent socialism can be seen as part of the wider rise of populism (see p. 57) since the beginning of the twenty-first century.

? QUESTIONS FOR DISCUSSION

- What is distinctive about the socialist view of equality?
- Why do socialists favour collectivism, and how have they tried to promote it?
- Is class politics an essential feature of socialism?
- What are the implications of trying to achieve socialism through revolutionary means?
- How persuasive is the socialist critique of private property?
- What are the implications of trying to achieve socialism through democratic means?
- On what grounds have Marxists predicted the inevitable collapse of capitalism?
- How closely did orthodox communism reflect the classical ideas of Marx?
- To what extent is socialism defined by a rejection of capitalism?
- Is social democracy really a form of socialism?
- Is the social-democratic 'compromise' inherently unstable?
- Can there be a 'third way' between capitalism and socialism?

📖 FURTHER READING

McLellan, D., *Marxism after Marx* (2007). An authoritative and comprehensive account of twentieth-century Marxism and more recent developments that also contains useful biographical information.

Moschonas, G., *In the Name of Social Democracy – The Great Transformation: 1945 to the Present* (2002). An impressive and thorough account of the nature, history and impact of social democracy that focuses on the emergence of 'new' social democracy.

Sassoon, D., *One Hundred Years of Socialism* (2013). A very stylish and detailed account of the life and times of democratic socialist ideas and movements.

Wright, A., *Socialisms: Theories and Practices* (1996). A good, brief and accessible introduction to the basic themes of socialism, highlighting the causes of disagreement within the socialist family.

PART 2

OTHER POLITICAL IDEAS

These political ideas are associated with ideological traditions that either developed out of, or emerged to challenge, liberalism, conservatism or socialism. As their focus is generally narrower or more specific than that of the traditional ideologies, they do not always explicitly address the issues of human nature, society, the state and the economy.

5 | Anarchism

PREVIEW

The word 'anarchy' comes from the Greek *anarkhos* and literally means 'without rule'. The term 'anarchism' has been in use since the French Revolution, and was initially employed in a critical or negative sense to imply a breakdown of civilised or predictable order. In everyday language, anarchy implies chaos and disorder. Needless to say, anarchists themselves fiercely reject such associations. It was not until Pierre-Joseph Proudhon proudly declared in *What Is Property?* ([1840] 1970), 'I am an anarchist', that the word was clearly associated with a positive and systematic set of political ideas.

Anarchist ideology is defined by the central belief that political authority in all its forms, and especially in the form of the state, is both evil and unnecessary. Anarchists therefore look to the creation of a stateless society through the abolition of law and government. In their view, the state is evil because, as a repository of sovereign, compulsory and coercive authority, it is an offence against the principles of freedom and equality. Anarchism is thus characterised by principled opposition to certain forms of social hierarchy. Anarchists believe that the state is unnecessary because order and social harmony do not have to be imposed 'from above' through government. Central to anarchism is the belief that people can manage their affairs through voluntary agreement, without the need for top-down hierarchies or a system of rewards and punishments. However, anarchism draws from two quite different ideological traditions: liberalism and socialism. This has resulted in rival individualist and collectivist forms of anarchism. While both accept the goal of statelessness, they advance very different models of the future anarchist society.

CONTENTS

HISTORICAL OVERVIEW

Anarchist ideas have sometimes been traced back to Taoist or Buddhist ideas, to the Stoics and Cynics of Ancient Greece, or to the Diggers of the English Civil War. However, the first, and in a sense classic, statement of anarchist principles was produced by the British philosopher and novelist William Godwin (1756–1836) in his *Enquiry Concerning Political Justice* ([1793] 1971), although Godwin never described himself as an anarchist. During the nineteenth century, anarchism was a significant component of a broad but growing socialist movement. In 1864, Proudhon's (see p. 102) followers joined with Marx's (see p. 6) to set up the International Workingmen's Association, or First International. The International collapsed in 1871 because of growing antagonism between Marxists and anarchists, led by Mikhail Bakunin (see p. 97). In the late nineteenth century, anarchists sought mass support among the landless peasants of Russia and southern Europe and, more successfully, through anarcho-syndicalism, among the industrial working classes.

Syndicalism was popular in France, Italy and Spain, and helped to make anarchism a genuine mass movement in the early twentieth century. The powerful CGT union in France was dominated by anarchists before 1914, as was the CNT in Spain, which claimed a membership of over two million during the Civil War. Anarcho-syndicalist movements also emerged in Latin America in the early twentieth century, especially in Argentina and Uruguay, and syndicalist ideas influenced the Mexican Revolution, led by Emiliano Zapata. However, the spread of authoritarianism and political repression gradually undermined anarchism in both Europe and Latin America. The victory of General Franco in the Spanish Civil War (1936–9) brought an end to anarchism as a mass movement. The CNT was suppressed, and anarchists, along with left-wingers in general, were persecuted. The influence of anarchism was also undermined by the success of Lenin and the Bolsheviks in 1917, and thus by the growing prestige of communism (see p. 71) within the socialist and revolutionary movements.

Anarchism is unusual among political ideologies in that it has never succeeded in winning power, at least at the national level. Indeed, as anarchists seek to radically disperse and decentralise political power, this has never been their goal. No society or nation has therefore been remodelled according to anarchist principles. Hence, it is tempting to regard anarchism as an ideology of less significance than, say, liberalism, socialism, conservatism or fascism (see p. 130), each of which has proved itself capable of achieving power and reshaping societies. The nearest anarchists have come to winning power at a national level was during the Spanish Civil War. Consequently, anarchists have often looked back to historical societies that reflect their principles, such as the cities of Ancient Greece or medieval Europe, or to traditional peasant communes such as the Russian mir. Anarchists have also stressed the non-hierarchic and egalitarian nature of many traditional societies – for instance the Nuer in Africa – and supported experiments in small-scale, communal living within western society.

Syndicalism: A form of revolutionary trade unionism that focuses on labour syndicates as free associations of workers and emphasises the use of direct action and the general strike.

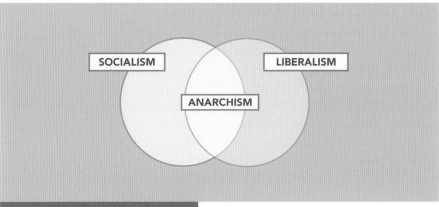

Figure 5.1 The nature of anarchism

Anarchism's appeal as a political movement has been restricted by both its ends and its means. The goal of anarchism – the overthrow of the state and dismantling of all forms of political authority – is widely considered to be unrealistic, if not impossible. Most, indeed, view the notion of a stateless society as, at best, a utopian dream. In terms of means, anarchists reject as corrupt, and corrupting, the conventional means of exercising political influence: forming political parties, standing for elections, seeking public office and so on. This does not, however, mean that they reject political organisation as such, but rather that they place their faith in non-hierarchical organisations, possibly supported by mass spontaneity and a popular thirst for freedom. Nevertheless, anarchism refuses to die. Precisely because of its uncompromising attitude to authority and political activism, it has an enduring, and often strong, moral appeal, particularly to the young. This can be seen, for example, in the prominence of anarchist ideas, slogans and groups within the emergent anti-capitalist or anti-globalisation movement.

CORE IDEAS AND PRINCIPLES

REJECTION OF THE STATE

The defining feature of anarchism is its opposition to hierarchy and domination, with the state often being seen as the paradigmatic form of hierarchy and domination. Anarchists have a preference for a stateless society in which free individuals manage their affairs by voluntary agreement, without compulsion or coercion. However, anarchism has been bedevilled by misleading stereotypes and distortions of various kinds. The most common of these is the idea that anarchism rests on little more than a faith in natural 'goodness', the belief that human beings are, at heart, moral creatures. Anarchists certainly believe that people are capable of leading productive and peaceful lives without the need for rulers or leaders, but this view is rarely sustained simply by optimistic assumptions about human nature (Marshall, 2007).

In the first place, anarchists do not share a common view of human nature. For example, despite sharing common individualist assumptions, Godwin stressed rational benevolence, while Max Stirner (see p. 107) emphasised conscious egoism. Second, rather than seeing human nature as fixed or determined, the majority of anarchists believe that human beings are products of their environment, even though they are also capable of changing it. Human beings can thus be either 'good' or 'evil' depending on the political and social circumstances in which they live. People who would otherwise be cooperative, sympathetic and sociable, become nothing less than impressive tyrants when raised up above others by power, privilege or wealth. Third, to the extent that anarchists have a theory of human nature, it can be said to be viewed as realistic, even pessimistic. In other words, anarchists replaced the liberal warning that 'power tends to corrupt and absolute power corrupts absolutely' (Acton, 1956) with the more radical and alarming warning that power in any shape or form will corrupt absolutely.

For anarchists, the state, as a repository of sovereign, compulsory and coercive authority, is a fundamental violation of the principles of liberty and equality. As such,

PERSPECTIVES ON …
THE STATE

LIBERALS see the state as a neutral arbiter among the competing interests and groups in society, a vital guarantee of social order. While classical liberals treat the state as a necessary evil and extol the virtues of a minimal or night watchman state, modern liberals recognise the state's positive role in widening freedom and promoting equal opportunities.

CONSERVATIVES link the state to the need to provide authority and discipline and to protect society from chaos and disorder, hence their traditional preference for a strong state. However, whereas traditional conservatives support a pragmatic balance between the state and civil society, neoliberals have called for the state to be 'rolled back', as it threatens economic prosperity and is driven, essentially, by bureaucratic self-interest.

SOCIALISTS have adopted contrasting views of the state. Marxists have stressed the link between the state and the class system, seeing it as either an instrument of class rule or as a means of ameliorating class tensions. Other socialists, however, regard the state as an embodiment of the common good, and thus approve of interventionism in either its social-democratic or state-collectivist form.

ANARCHISTS reject the state outright, believing it to be an unnecessary evil. The sovereign, compulsory and coercive authority of the state is seen as nothing less than legalised oppression operating in the interests of the powerful, propertied and privileged. As the state is inherently evil and oppressive, all states have the same essential character.

FEMINISTS have viewed the state as an instrument of male power, the patriarchal state serving to exclude women from, or subordinate them within, the public or 'political' sphere of life. Liberal feminists nevertheless regard the state as an instrument of reform that is susceptible to electoral and other pressures.

it is a concentrated form of evil. The flavour of the anarchist critique of the state is conveyed by one of Pierre-Joseph Proudhon's ([1851] 1923) famous diatribes:

> To be governed is to be watched over, inspected, spied on, directed, legislated, regimented, closed in, indoctrinated, preached at, controlled, assessed, evaluated, censored, commanded; all by creatures that have neither the right, nor the wisdom, nor the virtue.

The state is a *sovereign* body that exercises supreme authority over all individuals and associations living within a defined geographical area. Anarchists emphasise that the authority of the state is absolute and unlimited: law can restrict public behaviour, limit political activity, regulate economic life, interfere with private morality and thinking, and so on. The authority of the state is also *compulsory*. Anarchists reject the liberal notion that political authority arises from voluntary agreement, through some form of 'social contract', and argue instead that individuals become subject to state authority either by being born in a particular country or through conquest. Furthermore, the state is a *coercive* body, whose laws must be obeyed because they are backed up by the threat of punishment. For Emma Goldman (see below), government was symbolised by 'the club, the gun, the handcuff, or the prison' (Goldman, 1969, p. 58). The state can deprive individuals of their property, their liberty and ultimately, through capital punishment, their lives. The state is also *exploitative*, in that it robs individuals of their property through a system of taxation, once again backed up by the force of law and the possibility of punishment. Anarchists often argue that the state acts in alliance with the wealthy and privileged, and therefore serves to oppress the poor and weak. Finally, the state is *destructive*. 'War', as the US anarchist Randolph Bourne (1886–1918) suggested, 'is the health of the State' (1977). Individuals are required to fight, kill and die in wars that are invariably precipitated by a quest for territorial expansion, plunder or national glory by one state at the expense of others.

KEY FIGURE

Emma Goldman (1869–1940)

 A Russian-born propagandist, political agitator and revolutionary, Goldman was a prominent figure in US anarchist circles between 1890 and her deportation to the Soviet Union in 1919. She defined anarchism as 'the theory that all forms of government rest on violence, and are therefore wrong and harmful, as well as unnecessary'. Goldman developed an iconoclastic anarchist vision that drew from both the communist anarchism of Peter Kropotkin (see p. 104) and the individualism of Friedrich Nietzsche (1844–1900), Max Stirner (see p. 107) and others, being also one of the first to blend anarchism with feminism. Seeing political and economic freedom as incomplete without sexual and social freedom, she not only attacked the state as immoral and intrinsically corrupting, but also condemned the patriarchal family as the source of female dependence and inequality, denouncing, in the process, marriage, monogamy, homophobia and restrictions on birth control. Although Goldman continued to portray herself as a revolutionary, after WWI she became more sympathetic to gradualist politics. For more on Goldman, see above.

Although all anarchists reject the state in principle, they have disagreed about how the state can and should be challenged. For some anarchists, the violence that is implicit in the state system, as well as in the institutions of law and government, should be reflected back on itself in the form of 'revolutionary violence'. In the late nineteenth century, this sometimes led to a form of terrorist attacks and assassinations. One of the purposes of this was to rouse the 'oppressed masses' to insurrection and revolt, violence coming to be 'propaganda by the deed'. Short of a revolutionary assault on existing society, anarchists have also employed tactics of **direct action**. Anarcho-syndicalists, for example, refused to engage in conventional, representative politics, preferring instead to exert direct pressure on employers by boycotting their products, sabotaging machinery and organising strike action. The modern anti-capitalist movement, influenced by anarchism, also employed strategies of mass popular protest and direct political engagement. Other anarchists have, nevertheless, been attracted to the principles of **pacifism** and non-violence, although this has usually tended to apply to anarchists who have shied away from mass political activism.

ANARCHY IS ORDER

Anarchists regard the state not only as evil, but also as unnecessary. William Godwin sought to demonstrate this by, in effect, turning the most celebrated justification for the state – social contract theory – on its head. The social contract arguments of Hobbes (see p. 36) and Locke (see p. 17) suggest that a stateless society, the 'state of nature', amounts to a civil war of each against all, making orderly and stable life impossible. The source of such strife lies in human nature, which according to Hobbes and Locke is essentially selfish, greedy and potentially aggressive. Only a sovereign state can restrain such impulses and guarantee social order. In short, order is impossible without law. Godwin, in contrast, suggested that human beings are essentially rational creatures, inclined by education and enlightened judgement to live in accordance with truth and

Direct action: Physical action taken outside the constitutional and legal framework; direct action may range from passive resistance to terrorism.

Pacifism: A commitment to peace and a rejection of war and violence in any circumstances ('pacific' derives from the Latin, and means peace-making).

KEY FIGURE

Mikhail Bakunin (1814–76)

A Russian political agitator and revolutionary, Bakunin was one of the key proponents of collectivist anarchism and a leading figure within the nineteenth-century anarchist movement. Arguing that political power is intrinsically oppressive and placing his faith in human sociability, he proposed that freedom could only be achieved through collectivism, by which he meant self-governing communities based on voluntary cooperation, the absence of private property, and a system through which rewards would reflect contributions. An advocate of individual acts of terrorism, Bakunin extolled the 'sacred instinct of violence' as a necessary means of eliminating all political, social and religious institutions. Bakunin advanced an uncompromising critique of the statist implications of Marxist thinking. However, he was not a systematic thinker in terms of the consistency and coherence of the ideas he advanced, his writings exemplifying, not least, an uneasy balance between materialism and romanticism. For more on Bakunin, see pp. 93, 99, 100 and 101.

universal moral laws. He thus believed that people have a natural propensity to organise their own lives in a harmonious and peaceful fashion. Indeed, in his view it is the corrupting influence of government and unnatural laws, rather than any 'original sin' in human beings, that creates injustice, greed and aggression. Government, in other words, is not the solution to the problem of order, but its cause. Anarchists have often sympathised with the famous opening words of Jean-Jacques Rousseau's (see p. 119) *Social Contract* ([1762] 2012), 'Man was born free, yet everywhere he is in chains.'

At the heart of anarchism lies a distinctive tendency towards utopianism, at least in the sense that utopian thought has the imagination to visualise a society quite different from our own. As pointed out earlier, anarchists believe that human beings are capable of living together peacefully without the need for imposed order. Anarchist thought has thus sought to explain how social order can arise and be sustained in the absence of the machinery of 'law and order'. This has been done in two contrasting but usually interlocking ways. The first way in which anarchists have upheld the idea of natural, as opposed to political, order is through an analysis of human nature, or, more accurately, an analysis of the potentialities that reside in human nature. For example, collectivist anarchists have highlighted the human capacity for sociable and cooperative behaviour, while individualist anarchists have drawn attention to the importance of enlightened human reason.

For some anarchists, this potential for spontaneous harmony within human nature is linked to the belief that nature itself, and indeed the universe, is biased in favour of natural order. Anarchists have therefore sometimes been drawn to the ideas of non-western religions such as Buddhism and Daoism, which emphasise interdependence and oneness. An alternative basis for natural order can be found in the notion of ecology, particularly the 'social ecology' of thinkers such as Murray Bookchin (see p. 175). (Social ecology is discussed in Chapter 8, in relation to eco-anarchism.) However, anarchism does not merely stress positive human potentialities. As pointed out earlier, anarchist theories of human nature are often complex, and acknowledge that rival potentialities reside within the human soul.

Key concept ... **UTOPIANISM**

A utopia (from the Greek *outopia*, meaning 'nowhere', or *eutopia*, meaning 'good place') is usually taken to be a perfect, or at least a qualitatively better, society. Though utopias of various kinds can be envisaged, most are characterised by the abolition of want, the absence of conflict and the avoidance of oppression and violence. Utopianism is a style of political theorising that develops a critique of the existing order by constructing a model of an ideal or perfect alternative. Good examples are anarchism and Marxism. Utopian theories are usually based on assumptions about the unlimited possibilities of human self-development. However, utopianism is often used as a pejorative term to imply deluded or fanciful thinking, a belief in an unrealistic and unachievable goal.

The second way in which anarchists have supported the idea of natural order is through a stress on the social institutions that foster positive human potential. In this view, human nature is 'plastic', in the sense that it is shaped by the social, political and economic circumstances within which people live. Just as law, government and the state breed a domination/subordination complex, other social institutions nurture respect, cooperation and harmony. Collectivist anarchists thus endorse common ownership or mutualist institutions, while individualist anarchists have supported the market mechanism. Nevertheless, the belief in a stable and peaceful yet stateless society has often been viewed as the weakest and most contentious aspect of anarchist theory. Opponents of anarchism have argued that, however socially enlightened institutions may be, if selfish or negative impulses are basic to human nature and not merely evidence of corruption, the prospect of natural order is simply a delusion. This is why utopianism is most pronounced within the collectivist tradition of anarchism and least pronounced within the individualist tradition, with some anarcho-capitalists rejecting utopianism altogether (Friedman, 1973).

ANTI-CLERICALISM

Although the state has been the principal target of anarchist hostility, the same criticisms apply to any other form of compulsory authority. Indeed, anarchists have sometimes expressed as much bitterness towards the church as they have towards the state, particularly in the nineteenth century. This perhaps explains why anarchism has prospered in countries with strong religious traditions, such as Catholic Spain, France, Italy and the countries of Latin America, where it has helped to articulate anti-clerical sentiments.

Anarchist objections to organised religion serve to highlight broader criticisms of authority in general. Religion, for example, has often been seen as the source of authority itself. The idea of God represents the notion of a 'supreme being' who commands ultimate and unquestionable authority. For anarchists such as Proudhon and Bakunin, an anarchist political philosophy had to be based on the rejection of Christianity, because only then could human beings be regarded as free and independent. Moreover, anarchists have suspected that religious and political authority usually work hand in hand. Bakunin proclaimed that 'The abolition of the Church and the State must be the first and indispensable condition of the true liberation of society' (Bakunin, 1977). Anarchists view religion as one of the pillars of the state: it propagates an ideology of obedience and submission to both spiritual leaders and earthly rulers. As the Bible says, 'give unto Caesar that which is Caesar's'. Earthly rulers have often looked to religion to legitimise their power, most obviously in the doctrine of the divine right of kings.

Finally, religion seeks to impose a set of moral principles on the individual, and to establish a code of acceptable behaviour. Religious belief requires conformity to standards of 'good' and 'evil', which are defined and policed by figures of religious authority such as priests, imams or rabbis. The individual is thus robbed of moral autonomy and the capacity to make ethical judgements. Nevertheless, anarchists do not reject the religious impulse altogether. There is a clear mystical strain within anarchism. Anarchists can be said to hold an essentially spiritual conception of human nature, a utopian belief in the virtually unlimited possibilities of human self-development and in the bonds that unite humanity, and indeed all living things. Early anarchists were sometimes influenced by **millenarianism**; indeed, anarchism has often been portrayed as a form of political millenarianism. Modern anarchists have often been attracted to religions such as Daoism and Zen Buddhism, which offer the prospect of personal insight and preach the values of toleration, respect and natural harmony (Christoyannopoulos, 2011).

ECONOMIC FREEDOM

Anarchists have rarely seen the overthrow of the state as an end in itself, but have also been interested in challenging the structures of social and economic life. Bakunin (1973) argued that 'political power and wealth are inseparable'. In the nineteenth century, anarchists usually worked within the working-class movement and subscribed to a broadly socialist philosophy. Capitalism (see p. 62) was understood in class terms: a 'ruling class' exploits and oppresses 'the masses'. However, this 'ruling class' was not, in line with Marxism, interpreted in narrow economic terms, but was seen to encompass all those who command wealth, power or privilege in society. It therefore included kings and princes, politicians and state officials, judges and police officers, and bishops and priests, as well as industrialists and bankers. Bakunin thus argued that, in every developed society, three social groups can be identified: a vast majority who are exploited; a minority who are exploited but also exploit others in equal measure; and 'the supreme governing estate', a small minority of 'exploiters and oppressors pure and simple'. Hence, nineteenth-century anarchists identified themselves with the poor and oppressed and sought to carry out a social revolution in the name of the 'exploited masses', in which both capitalism and the state would be swept away.

However, it is the economic structure of life that most keenly exposes tensions within anarchism. While many anarchists acknowledge a kinship with socialism, based on a common distaste for property and inequality, others have defended property rights and even revered competitive capitalism. This highlights the distinction between the two major anarchist traditions, one of which is collectivist and the other individualist. Collectivist anarchists advocate an economy based on cooperation and collective ownership, while individualist anarchists support the market and private property.

Despite such fundamental differences, anarchists nevertheless agree about their distaste for the economic systems that dominated much of the twentieth century. All anarchists oppose the 'managed capitalism' that flourished in western countries after 1945. Collectivist anarchists argue that state intervention merely props up a system of class exploitation and gives capitalism a human face. Individualist anarchists suggest that intervention distorts the competitive market and creates economies dominated by both public and private monopolies. Anarchists have been even more united in their disapproval of Soviet-style 'state socialism'. Individualist anarchists object to the violation of property rights and

Millenarianism: A belief in a thousand-year period of divine rule; political millenarianism offers the prospect of a sudden and complete emancipation from misery and oppression.

Warren (1798–1874). In *What Is Property?* ([1840] 1970), Proudhon came up with the famous statement that 'Property is theft,' and condemned a system of economic exploitation based on the accumulation of capital. Nevertheless, unlike Marx, Proudhon was not opposed to all forms of private property, distinguishing between property and what he called 'possessions'. In particular, he admired the independence and initiative of small communities of peasants, craftsmen and artisans, especially the watchmakers of Switzerland, who had traditionally managed their affairs on the basis of mutual cooperation. Proudhon therefore sought, through mutualism, to establish a system of property ownership that would avoid exploitation and promote social harmony. Social interaction in such a system would be voluntary, mutually beneficial and harmonious, thus requiring no regulation or interference by government. Proudhon's followers tried to put these ideas into practice by setting up mutual credit banks in France and Switzerland, which provided cheap loans for investors and charged a rate of interest only high enough to cover the cost of running the bank, but not so high that it made a profit.

Anarcho-syndicalism

Although mutualism and anarcho-communism exerted significant influence within the broader socialist movement in the late nineteenth and early twentieth centuries, anarchism only developed into a mass movement in its own right in the form of anarcho-syndicalism. Syndicalism is a form of revolutionary trade unionism, drawing its name from the French word *syndicat*, meaning union or group. Syndicalism emerged first in France, and was embraced by the powerful CGT union in the period before 1914. Syndicalist ideas spread to Italy, Latin America, the USA and, most significantly, Spain, where the country's largest union, the CNT, supported them.

Syndicalism draws on socialist ideas and advances a theory of stark class war. Workers and peasants are seen to constitute an oppressed class, and industrialists, landlords, politicians, judges and the police are portrayed as exploiters. Workers defend themselves by organising syndicates or unions based on particular crafts, industries or professions. In the short term, these syndicates act as conventional trade unions, raising wages, shortening hours and improving working conditions. However, syndicalists are also revolutionaries, who look forward to the overthrow of capitalism and the seizure of power by the workers. In *Reflections on Violence* ([1908] 1950), Georges Sorel (1847–1922), an influential French syndicalist theorist, argued that such a revolution would come about through a general strike, a 'revolution of empty hands'. Sorel believed that the general strike was a '**political myth**', a symbol of working-class power, capable of inspiring popular revolt.

While syndicalist theory was at times unsystematic and confused, it nevertheless exerted a strong attraction for anarchists who wished to spread their ideas among the masses. As anarchists entered the syndicalist movement, they developed the distinctive ideas of anarcho-syndicalism. Two features of syndicalism inspired particular anarchist enthusiasm. First, syndicalists rejected conventional politics as corrupting and pointless. Working-class power, they believed, should be exerted through direct action, boycotts, sabotage and strikes, and ultimately a general strike. Second, anarchists saw the syndicate as a model

Political myth: A belief that has the capacity to provoke political action by virtue of its emotional power rather than through an appeal to reason.

103

for the decentralised, non-hierarchic society of the future. Syndicates typically exhibited a high degree of grassroots democracy and formed federations with other syndicates, either in the same area or in the same industry.

Although anarcho-syndicalism enjoyed genuine mass support, at least until the Spanish Civil War, it failed to achieve its revolutionary objectives. Beyond the rather vague idea of the general strike, anarcho-syndicalism did not develop a clear political strategy or a theory of revolution. Other anarchists have criticised syndicalism for concentrating too narrowly on short-term trade union goals, and therefore for leading anarchism away from revolution and towards reformism.

Anarcho-communism

In its most radical form, a belief in social solidarity leads in the direction of collectivism and full communism. Sociable and gregarious human beings should lead a shared and communal existence. For example, labour is a social experience, people work in common with fellow human beings and the wealth they produce should therefore be owned in common by the community, rather than by any single individual. In this sense, all forms of private property are theft: they represent the exploitation of workers, who alone create wealth, by employers who merely own it. Furthermore, private property encourages selfishness and, particularly offensive to the anarchist, promotes conflict and social disharmony. Inequality in the ownership of wealth fosters greed, envy and resentment, and therefore breeds crime and disorder.

Anarcho-communism stresses the human potential for cooperation, expressed most famously by Peter Kropotkin's theory of 'mutual aid'. Kropotkin attempted to provide a biological foundation for social solidarity via a re-examination of Darwin's theory of evolution. Whereas social thinkers such as Herbert Spencer (1820–1903) had used Darwinism to support the idea that humankind is naturally competitive and aggressive, Kropotkin argued that species are

KEY FIGURE

Peter Kropotkin (1842–1921)

A Russian aristocrat by birth, Kropotkin was an internationally respected physical geographer and one of the founding theorists of social or communist anarchism. In *Mutual Aid* (1902), Kropotkin sought to provide communist anarchism with a scientific basis. This involved taking issue with social Darwinism on the grounds that the quest for survival and human progress is more effectively served by mutual aid than it is by competition. His anarchism was focused on removing impediments to the development of mutual aid, notably the capitalist class system and government, and authoritarian relationships generally. For Kropotkin, the promotion of egalitarian relations through the creation of alternative institutions and modes of behaviour was the essence of revolution. His deep interest in geographical and biological ideas has lead to him being viewed as an early exponent of environmental anarchism. Kropotkin's other writings include *The Conquest of Bread* (1892) and *Fields, Factories and Workshops* (1897). For more on Kropotkin, see above, pp. 105, 159, 174 and 175.

successful precisely because they manage to harness collective energies through cooperation. The process of evolution thus strengthens sociability and favours cooperation over competition. Successful species, such as the human species, must, Kropotkin concluded, have a strong propensity for mutual aid. Kropotkin argued that while mutual aid had flourished in, for example, the city-states of Ancient Greece and medieval Europe, it had been subverted by competitive capitalism, threatening the further evolution of the human species.

Although Proudhon had warned that communism could only be brought about by an authoritarian state, anarcho-communists such as Kropotkin and Errico Malatesta (1853–1932) argued that true communism requires the abolition of the state. Anarcho-communists admire small, self-managing communities along the lines of the medieval city-state or the peasant commune. Kropotkin envisaged that an anarchic society would consist of a collection of largely self-sufficient communes, each owning its wealth in common. From the anarcho-communist perspective, the communal organisation of social and economic life has three key advantages. First, as communes are based on the principles of sharing and collective endeavour, they strengthen the bonds of compassion and solidarity, and help to keep greed and selfishness at bay. Second, within communes, decisions are made through a process of participatory or **direct democracy**, which guarantees a high level of popular participation and political equality. Popular self-government is the only form of government that would be acceptable to anarchists. Third, communes are small-scale or 'human-scale' communities, which allow people to manage their own affairs through face-to-face interaction. In the anarchist view, centralisation is always associated with depersonalised and bureaucratic social processes.

INDIVIDUALIST ANARCHISM

The philosophical basis of individualist anarchism (sometimes called 'anarcho-individualism') lies in the liberal idea of the sovereign individual. In many ways, anarchist conclusions are reached by pushing liberal individualism to its logical extreme. For example, William Godwin's anarchism amounts to a form of extreme classical liberalism. At the heart of liberalism is a belief in the primacy of the individual and the central importance of individual freedom. In the classical liberal view, freedom is negative: it consists in the absence of external constraints on the individual. When individualism is taken to its extreme, it therefore implies individual sovereignty: the idea that absolute and unlimited authority resides within each human being. From this perspective, any constraint on the individual is evil; but when this constraint is imposed by the state, by definition a sovereign, compulsory and coercive body, it amounts to an absolute evil. Quite simply, the individual cannot be sovereign in a society ruled by law and government. Individualism and the state are thus irreconcilable principles. As Wolff (1998) put it, 'The autonomous man, insofar as he is autonomous, is not subject to the will of another.'

Although these arguments are liberal in inspiration, significant differences exist between liberalism and individualist anarchism. First, while liberals accept the

Direct democracy: Popular self-government, characterised by the direct and continuous participation of citizens in the tasks of government.

importance of individual liberty, they do not believe this can be guaranteed in a stateless society. Classical liberals argue that a minimal or 'night watchman' state is necessary to prevent self-seeking individuals from abusing one another by theft, intimidation, violence or even murder. Law therefore exists to protect freedom, rather than constrain it. Modern liberals take this argument further, and defend state intervention on the grounds that it enlarges positive freedom. Anarchists, in contrast, believe that individuals can conduct themselves peacefully, harmoniously and prosperously without the need for government to 'police' society and protect them from their fellow human beings. Anarchists differ from liberals because they believe that free individuals can live and work together constructively because they are rational and moral creatures. Reason and morality dictate that where conflict exists it should be resolved by arbitration or debate, and not by violence.

Second, liberals believe that government power can be 'tamed' or controlled by the development of constitutional and representative institutions. Constitutions claim to protect the individual by limiting the power of government and creating checks and balances among its various institutions. Regular elections are designed to force government to be accountable to the general public, or at least a majority of the electorate. Anarchists dismiss the idea of limited, constitutional or representative government. All laws infringe on individual liberty, whether the government that enacts them is constitutional or arbitrary, democratic or dictatorial. In other words, all states are an offence against individual liberty. However, anarcho-individualism has taken a number of forms. The most important of these are:

▶ egoism

▶ libertarianism

▶ anarcho-capitalism.

Egoism

The boldest statement of anarchist convictions built on the idea of the sovereign individual is found in Max Stirner's *The Ego and His Own* ([1845] 1971). Like Marx, the German philosopher Stirner (see p. 107) was deeply influenced by ideas of Hegel (1770–1831), but the two arrived at fundamentally different conclusions. Stirner's theories represent an extreme form of individualism. The term 'egoism' can have two meanings. It can suggest that individuals are essentially concerned about their ego or 'self', that they are self-interested or self-seeking, an assumption that would be accepted by thinkers such as Hobbes or Locke. Self-interestedness, however, can generate conflict among individuals and justify the existence of a state, which would be needed to restrain each individual from harming or abusing others.

In Stirner's view, egoism is a philosophy that places the individual self at the centre of the moral universe. The individual, from this perspective, should simply act as he or she chooses, without any consideration for laws, social conventions, religious or moral principles. Such a position amounts to a form of

Nihilism: Literally a belief in nothing; the rejection of all moral and political principles.

KEY FIGURE

Max Stirner (1806–56)

 A German philosopher, Stirner (pseudonym of Johann Caspar Schmidt) developed an extreme form of individualism, based on egoism, which condemned all checks on personal autonomy. In contrast to other anarchists' stress on moral principles such as justice, reason and community, he emphasised solely the 'ownness' of the human individual, thereby placing the individual self at the centre of the moral universe. In proclaiming that no external authority has any objective force, Stirner held that the dictates of the amoral ego provide the basis for true emancipation. Such thinking influenced Nietzsche, especially through the idea that God is dead, and later provided a basis for existentialism. His most important political work is *The Ego and His Own* (1845). However, Stirner rejected the idea that egoism is necessarily anti-social, seeing in the future the possibility of a Union of Egoists, based on the mutual consent of all members, who, by an act of will, renew their membership on a constant basis and can withdraw from it at any time. For more on Stirner, see below, pp. 95 and 106.

nihilism. This is a position that clearly points in the direction of both atheism and an extreme form of individualist anarchism. However, as Stirner's anarchism also dramatically turned its back on the principles of the Enlightenment and contained few proposals about how order could be maintained in a stateless society, it had relatively little impact on the emerging anarchist movement. His ideas nevertheless influenced the German philosopher Friedrich Nietzsche and twentieth-century existentialism.

Libertarianism

The individualist argument was more fully developed in the USA by libertarian thinkers such as Henry David Thoreau (1817–62), Lysander Spooner (1808–87), Benjamin Tucker (1854–1939) and Josiah Warren. Thoreau's quest for spiritual truth and self-reliance led him to flee from civilised life and live for several years in virtual solitude, close to nature, an experience described in *Walden* ([1854] 1983). In his most political work, 'Civil Disobedience' ([1849] 1983), Thoreau approved of Jefferson's liberal motto 'That government is best which governs least,' but adapted it to conform with his own anarchist sentiment: 'That government is best which governs not at all.' For Thoreau, individualism leads in the direction of civil disobedience: the individual has to be faithful to his or her conscience and do only what each believes to be right, regardless of the demands of society or the laws made by government. Thoreau's anarchism places individual conscience above the demands of political obligation. In Thoreau's case, this led him to disobey a US government he thought was acting immorally, both in upholding slavery and in waging war against other countries.

Benjamin Tucker took **libertarianism** further by considering how autonomous individuals could live and work with one another without the danger of conflict or disorder. Two possible solutions to this problem are available to the individualist. The first emphasises human rationality, and suggests that when conflicts or disagreements develop they can be resolved by reasoned discussion. This, for

Libertarianism: A belief that the individual should enjoy the widest possible realm of freedom; libertarianism implies the removal of both external and internal constraints upon the individual (see p. 48).

example, was the position adopted by Godwin, who believed that truth will always tend to displace falsehood. The second solution is to find some sort of mechanism through which the independent actions of free individuals could be brought into harmony with one another. Extreme individualists such as Warren and Tucker believed that this could be achieved through a system of market exchange. Warren thought that individuals have a sovereign right to the property they themselves produce, but are also forced by economic logic to work with others in order to gain the advantages of the division of labour. He suggested that this could be achieved by a system of 'labour-for-labour' exchange, and set up 'time stores' through which one person's labour could be exchanged for a promise to return labour in kind. Tucker argued that 'Genuine anarchism is consistent Manchesterism,' referring to the nineteenth-century free-trade, free-market principles of Richard Cobden and John Bright (Nozick, 1974).

Anarcho-capitalism

The revival of interest in free-market economics in the late twentieth century led to increasingly radical political conclusions. New Right conservatives, attracted to classical economics, wished to 'get government off the back of business' and allow the economy to be disciplined by market forces, rather than managed by an interventionist state. Right-wing libertarians such as Robert Nozick (see p. 54) revived the idea of a minimal state, whose principal function is to protect individual rights. Other thinkers, for instance Ayn Rand (see p. 52), Murray Rothbard (1926–95) and David Friedman (1973), have pushed free-market ideas to their limit and developed a form of anarcho-capitalism. They have argued that government can be abolished and be replaced by unregulated market competition. Property should be owned by sovereign individuals, who may choose, if they wish, to enter into voluntary contracts with others in the pursuit of self-interest. The individual thus remains free and the market, beyond the control of any single individual or group, regulates all social interaction.

Differences between ...

INDIVIDUALIST AND COLLECTIVIST ANARCHISM

INDIVIDUALIST ANARCHISM	COLLECTIVIST ANARCHISM
• ultra-liberalism	• ultra-socialism
• extreme individualism	• extreme collectivism
• sovereign individual	• social solidarity
• civil disobedience	• social revolution
• atomism	• organicism
• egoism	• communalism
• market relations	• social obligations
• private property	• common ownership
• anarcho-capitalism	• anarcho-communism

Anarcho-capitalists go well beyond the ideas of free-market liberalism. Liberals believe that the market is an effective and efficient mechanism for delivering most goods, but argue that it also has its limits. Some services, such as the maintenance of domestic order, the enforcement of contracts and protection against external attack, are 'public goods', which must be provided by the state because they cannot be supplied through market competition. Anarcho-capitalists, however, believe that the market can satisfy all human wants. For example, Rothbard (1978) recognised that in an anarchist society individuals will seek protection from one another, but argued that such protection can be delivered competitively by privately owned 'protection associations' and 'private courts', without the need for a police force or a state court system.

Indeed, according to anarcho-capitalists, profit-making protection agencies would offer a better service than the present police force because competition would provide consumers with a choice, ensuring that agencies are cheap, efficient and responsive to consumer needs. Similarly, private courts would be forced to develop a reputation for fairness in order to attract custom from individuals wishing to resolve a conflict. Most important, unlike the authority of public bodies, the contracts thus made with private agencies would be entirely voluntary, regulated only by impersonal market forces. Radical though such proposals may sound, the policy of privatisation has already made substantial advances in many western countries. In the USA, several states already use private prisons, and experiments with private courts and arbitration services are well established. In the UK, private prisons and the use of private protection agencies have become commonplace, and schemes such as 'Neighbourhood Watch' have helped to transfer responsibility for public order from the police to the community.

? QUESTIONS FOR DISCUSSION

- Why do anarchists view the state as evil and oppressive?

- How and why is anarchism linked to utopianism?

- How, and how effectively, have anarchists sustained the idea of natural order?

- Is collectivist anarchism simply an extreme form of socialism?

- How do anarcho-communists and Marxists agree, and over what do they disagree?

- To what extent are anarchism and syndicalism compatible?

- How do individualist anarchists reconcile egoism with statelessness?

- Is anarcho-individualism merely free-market liberalism taken to its logical conclusion?

- To what extent do anarchists disagree about the nature of the future anarchist society?

- How can the political success of anarchism best be judged?

- Why have anarchist ideas been attractive to modern social movements?

- Do anarchists demand the impossible?

📖 FURTHER READING

Egoumenides, M., *Philosophical Anarchism and Political Obligation* (2014). An analysis of political obligation that challenges the notion of a special relationship between the government and the people from the perspective of philosophical anarchism.

Kinna, R., *Anarchism: A Beginner's Guide* (2009). A clear and insightful introduction to the nature, thinking, tactics and strategies, and various manifestations of anarchism.

Marshall, P., *Demanding the Impossible: A History of Anarchism* (2007). A very comprehensive, authoritative and engagingly enthusiastic account of the full range of anarchist theories and beliefs.

Purkis, J. and Bowen, J. (eds), *Changing Anarchism: Anarchist Theory and Practice in a Global Age* (2004). A wide-ranging collection that reflects on the nature and breadth of contemporary anarchist theory and practice in the light of the changes brought about by globalisation.

6 Nationalism

PREVIEW

The word 'nation' has been used since the thirteenth century and derives from the Latin *nasci*, meaning to be born. In the form of *natio*, it referred to a group of people united by birth or birthplace. In its original usage, 'nation' thus implied a breed of people or a racial group, but possessed no political significance. It was not until the late eighteenth century that the term acquired political overtones, as individuals and groups started to be classified as 'nationalists'. The term 'nationalism' was first used in print in 1789 by the anti-Jacobin French priest Augustin Barruel. By the mid-nineteenth century, nationalism was widely recognised as a political doctrine or movement; for example, as a major ingredient of the revolutions that swept across Europe in 1848.

Nationalism can be defined broadly as the belief that the nation is the central principle of political organisation. As such, it is based on two core assumptions. First, humankind is naturally divided into distinct nations, and second, the nation is the most appropriate, and perhaps only legitimate, unit of political rule. Classical political nationalism therefore set out to bring the borders of the state into line with the boundaries of the nation. Within so-called nation-states, nationality and citizenship would therefore coincide. However, nationalism is a complex and highly diverse ideological phenomenon. Not only are there distinctive political, cultural and ethnic forms of nationalism, but the political implications of nationalism have also been wide-ranging and sometimes contradictory. Although nationalism has been associated with a principled belief in national self-determination, based on the assumption that all nations are equal, it has also been used to defend traditional institutions and the established social order, as well as to fuel programmes of war, conquest and imperialism. Nationalism, moreover, has been linked to widely contrasting ideological traditions, ranging from liberalism to fascism.

CONTENTS

HISTORICAL OVERVIEW

The idea of nationalism was born during the French Revolution. Previously, countries had been thought of as 'realms', 'principalities' or 'kingdoms'. The inhabitants of a country were 'subjects', their political identity being formed by an allegiance to a ruler or ruling dynasty, rather than any sense of national identity or patriotism. However, the revolutionaries in France who rose up against Louis XVI in 1789 did so in the name of the people, and understood the people to be the 'French nation'. Their ideas were influenced by the writings of Jean-Jacques Rousseau (see p. 119) and the new doctrine of popular self-government. Nationalism was therefore a revolutionary and democratic creed, reflecting the idea that 'subjects of the crown' should become 'citizens of France'. The **nation** should be its own master. However, such ideas were not the exclusive property of the French. During the Revolutionary and Napoleonic Wars (1792–1815), much of continental Europe was invaded by France, giving rise to both resentment against France and a desire for **independence**. In Italy and Germany, long divided into a collection of states, the experience of conquest helped to forge, for the first time, a consciousness of national unity, expressed in a new language of nationalism, inherited from France. Nationalist ideas also spread to Latin America in the early nineteenth century, where Simon Bolivar (1783–1830), 'the Liberator', led revolutions against Spanish rule in what was then New Grenada, now the countries of Colombia, Venezuela and Ecuador, as well as in Peru and Bolivia.

In many respects, nationalism developed into the most successful and compelling of political creeds, helping to shape and reshape history in many parts of the world for over two hundred years. The rising tide of nationalism re-drew the map of Europe in the nineteenth century as the autocratic and multinational empires of Turkey, Austria and Russia started to crumble in the face of liberal and nationalist pressure. In 1848, nationalist uprisings broke out in the Italian states, among the Czechs and the Hungarians, and in Germany, where the desire for national unity was expressed in the creation of the short-lived Frankfurt parliament. The nineteenth century was a period of nation building.

Nation: A collection of people bound together by shared values and traditions, a common language, religion and history, and usually occupying the same geographical area (see p. 117).

Independence: The process through which a nation is liberated from foreign rule, usually involving the establishment of sovereign statehood.

Key concept ... PATRIOTISM

Patriotism (from the Latin *patria*, meaning 'fatherland') is a sentiment, a psychological attachment to one's nation, literally a 'love of one's country'. The terms 'nationalism' and 'patriotism' are often confused. Nationalism has a doctrinal character and embodies the belief that the nation is in some way the central principle of political organisation. Patriotism provides the affective basis for that belief, and thus underpins all forms of nationalism. It is difficult to conceive of a national group demanding, say, political independence without possessing at least a measure of patriotic loyalty or national consciousness. However, not all patriots are nationalists. Not all of those who identify with, or even love, their nation, see it as a means through which political demands can be articulated.

Italy, once dismissed by the Austrian Chancellor Metternich as a 'mere geographical expression', became a united state in 1861, the process of **unification** being completed with the acquisition of Rome in 1870. Germany, formerly a collection of 39 states, was unified in 1871, following the Franco-Prussian War.

Nevertheless, it would be a mistake to assume that nationalism was either an irresistible or a genuinely popular movement during this period. Enthusiasm for nationalism was largely restricted to the rising middle classes, who were attracted to the ideas of national unity and constitutional government. Although middle-class nationalist movements kept the dream of national unity or independence alive, they were nowhere strong enough to accomplish the process of nation building on their own. Where nationalist goals were realised, as in Italy and Germany, it was because nationalism coincided with the ambition of rising states such as Piedmont and Prussia. For example, German unification owed more to the Prussian army (which defeated Denmark in 1864, Austria in 1866 and France in 1870–1) than it did to the liberal nationalist movement.

However, by the end of the nineteenth century nationalism had become a truly popular movement, with the spread of flags, national anthems, patriotic poetry and literature, public ceremonies and national holidays. Nationalism became the language of mass politics, made possible by the growth of primary education, mass literacy and the spread of popular newspapers. The character of nationalism also changed. Nationalism had previously been associated with liberal and progressive movements, but was taken up increasingly by conservative and reactionary politicians. Nationalism came to stand for social cohesion, order and stability, particularly in the face of the growing challenge of socialism, which embodied the ideas of social revolution and international working-class solidarity. Nationalism sought to integrate the increasingly powerful working class into the nation, and so to preserve the established social structure. Patriotic fervour was no longer aroused by the prospect of political liberty or democracy, but by the commemoration of past national glories and military victories. Such nationalism became increasingly **chauvinistic** and **xenophobic**.

Key concept ... IMPERIALISM

Imperialism is, broadly, the policy of extending the power or rule of the state beyond its boundaries, typically through the establishment of an empire. In its earliest usage, imperialism was an ideology that supported military expansion and imperial acquisition, usually by drawing on nationalist and racialist doctrines. In its traditional form, imperialism involves the establishment of formal political domination or colonialism and reflects the expansion of state power through a process of conquest and (possibly) settlement. Neo-imperialism (sometimes called 'neocolonialism') is characterised less by political control and more by economic and ideological domination; it is often seen as a product of structural imbalances in the international economy and/or biases that operate within the institutions of global economic governance.

Unification: The process through which a collection of separate political entities, usually sharing cultural characteristics, are integrated into a single state.

Chauvinism: Uncritical and unreasoned dedication to a cause or group, typically based on a belief in its superiority, as in 'national chauvinism' or 'male chauvinism'.

Xenophobia: A fear or hatred of foreigners; pathological ethnocentrism.

Each nation claimed its own unique or superior qualities, while other nations were regarded as alien, untrustworthy, even menacing. This new climate of popular nationalism helped to fuel policies of imperialism (see p. 113) that intensified dramatically in the 1870s and 1880s and, by the end of the century, had brought most of the world's population under European control. It also contributed to a mood of international rivalry and suspicion, which led to world war in 1914.

The end of World War I saw the completion of the process of nation building in central and eastern Europe. At the Paris Peace Conference, US President Woodrow Wilson advocated the principle of national self-determination. The German, Austro-Hungarian and Russian empires were broken up and eight new states created, including Finland, Hungary, Czechoslovakia, Poland and Yugoslavia. These new countries were designed to be **nation–states** that conformed to the geography of existing national or ethnic groups. However, World War I failed to resolve the serious national tensions that had precipitated conflict in the first place. Indeed, the experience of defeat, and disappointment with the terms of the peace treaties, left an inheritance of frustrated ambition and bitterness. This was most evident in Germany, Italy and Japan, where fascist or authoritarian movements came to power in the inter-war period by promising to restore national pride through policies of expansion and **empire**. Nationalism was therefore a powerful factor leading to war in both 1914 and 1939.

During the twentieth century the doctrine of nationalism, which had been born in Europe, spread throughout the globe as the peoples of Asia and Africa rose in opposition to colonial rule. The process of colonialism had involved not only the establishment of political control and economic dominance, but also the importation of western ideas, including nationalism, which began to be used against the colonial masters themselves. Nationalist uprisings took place in Egypt in 1919 and quickly spread throughout the Middle East. The Anglo-Afghan war also broke out in 1919, and rebellions took place in India, the Dutch East Indies and Indochina. After 1945, the map of Africa and Asia was re-drawn as the British, French, Dutch and Portuguese empires each disintegrated in the face of nationalist movements that succeeded in either negotiating independence or winning wars of 'national liberation'.

Nation-state: A sovereign political association within which citizenship and nationality overlap; one nation within a single state.

Empire: A structure of domination in which diverse cultural, ethnic or nation groups are subjected to a single source of authority.

Anti-colonialism not only witnessed the spread of western-style nationalism to the developing world, but also generated new forms of nationalism. Nationalism in the developing world has embraced a wide range of movements. In China, Vietnam and parts of Africa, nationalism has been fused with Marxism, and national liberation has been regarded not simply as a political goal but as part of a social revolution. Elsewhere, developing-world nationalism has been anti-western, rejecting both liberal democratic and revolutionary socialist conceptions of nationhood. This has been particularly evident in the rise of forms of religious nationalism and especially in the emergence of religious fundamentalism (see p. 135). The relationship between nationalism and religious fundamentalism is examined later in the chapter, in association with postcolonial nationalism.

CORE IDEAS AND PRINCIPLES

THE NATION

The basic belief of nationalism is that the nation is, or should be, the central principle of political organisation. However, much confusion surrounds what nations are and how they can be defined. In everyday language, words such as 'nation', 'state', 'country' and even 'race' are often confused or used as if they are interchangeable. Many political disputes, moreover, are really disputes about whether a particular group of people should be regarded as a nation, and should therefore enjoy the rights and status associated with nationhood. This applies, for instance, to the Tibetans, the Kurds, the Palestinians, the Basques, the Tamils, and so on.

On the most basic level, nations are cultural entities, collections of people bound together by shared values and traditions, in particular a common language, religion and history, and usually occupying the same geographical area. From this point of view, the nation can be defined by 'objective' factors: people who satisfy a requisite set of cultural criteria can be said to belong to a nation; those who do not can be classified as non-nationals or members of foreign nations. However, to define a nation simply as a group of people bound together by a common culture and traditions raises some very difficult questions. Although particular cultural features are commonly associated with nationhood, notably language, religion, **ethnicity**, history and tradition, there is no blueprint nor any objective criteria that can establish where and when a nation exists.

Language is often taken to be the clearest symbol of nationhood. A language embodies distinctive attitudes, values and forms of expression that produce a sense of familiarity and belonging. German nationalism, for instance, has traditionally been founded on a sense of cultural unity, reflected in the purity and survival of the German language. Nevertheless, at the same time, there are peoples who share the same language without having any conception of a common national identity: Americans, Australians and New Zealanders may speak English as a first language, but certainly do not think of themselves as members of an 'English nation'. Other nations have enjoyed a substantial measure of national unity without possessing a national language, as is the case in Switzerland where, in the absence of a Swiss language, three major languages are spoken: French, German and Italian.

Religion is another major component of nationhood. Religion expresses common moral values and spiritual beliefs. In Northern Ireland, people who speak the same language have been divided along religious lines: most Protestants regard themselves as Unionists and wish to preserve their links with the UK, while many in the Catholic community favour a united Ireland. Islam has been a major factor in forming national consciousness in much of North Africa and the

Ethnicity: A sentiment of loyalty towards a particular population, cultural group or territorial area; bonds that are more often cultural rather than racial.

Middle East. On the other hand, religious beliefs do not always coincide with a sense of nationhood. Divisions between Catholics and Protestants in mainland UK do not inspire rival nationalisms, nor has the remarkable religious diversity found in the USA threatened to divide the country into a collection of distinct nations. At the same time, countries such as Poland, Italy, Brazil and the Philippines share a common Catholic faith but do not feel that they belong to a unified 'Catholic nation'.

Nations have also been based on a sense of *ethnic* or, in certain circumstances, *racial* unity. This was particularly evident in Germany during the Nazi period. However, nationalism usually has a cultural rather than a biological basis; it reflects an ethnic unity that may be based on race, but more usually draws on shared values and common cultural beliefs. The nationalism of US blacks, for example, is based less on colour than on their distinctive history and culture. Nations thus usually share a common *history and traditions*. Not uncommonly, national identity is preserved by recalling past glories, national independence, the birthdays of national leaders or important military victories. The USA celebrates Independence Day and Thanksgiving; Bastille Day is commemorated in France; in the UK, ceremonies continue to mark Armistice Day. However, nationalist feelings may be based more on future expectations than on shared memories or a common past. This applies in the case of immigrants who have been 'naturalised', and is most evident in the USA, a 'land of immigrants'. The journey of the *Mayflower* and the War of Independence have no direct relevance for most Americans, whose families arrived centuries after these events occurred.

The cultural unity that supposedly expresses itself in nationhood is therefore very difficult to pin down. It reflects a varying combination of cultural factors, rather than any precise formula. Ultimately, therefore, nations can only be defined 'subjectively', by their members, not by any set of external factors. In this sense, the nation is a psycho-political entity, a group of people who regard themselves as a natural political community and are distinguished by shared loyalty or affection in the form of patriotism. Objective difficulties such as the absence of land, a small population or lack of economic resources are of little significance if a group of people insists on demanding what it sees as 'national rights'. Latvia, for example, became an independent nation in 1991 despite having a population of only 2.6 million (barely half of whom are ethnic Lats), no source of fuel and very few natural resources. Likewise, the Kurdish peoples of the Middle East have nationalist aspirations, even though the Kurds have never enjoyed formal political unity and are at present spread over parts of Turkey, Iraq, Iran and Syria.

The fact that nations are formed through a combination of objective and subjective factors has given rise to rival concepts of the nation. While all nationalists agree that nations are a blend of cultural and psycho-political factors, they disagree strongly about where the balance between the two lies. On the one hand, 'exclusive' concepts of the nation stress the importance of ethnic unity and a shared history. By viewing national identity as 'given', unchanging

PERSPECTIVES ON ...
THE NATION

LIBERALS subscribe to a 'civic' view of the nation that places as much emphasis on political allegiance as on cultural unity. Nations are moral entities in the sense that they are endowed with rights, notably an equal right to self-determination.

CONSERVATIVES regard the nation as primarily an 'organic' entity, bound together by a common ethnic identity and a shared history. As the source of social cohesion and collective identity, the nation is perhaps the most politically significant of social groups.

SOCIALISTS tend to view the nation as an artificial division of humankind whose purpose is to disguise social injustice and prop up the established order. Political movements and allegiances should therefore have an international, not a national, character.

ANARCHISTS have generally held that the nation is tainted by its association with the state, and therefore with oppression. The nation is thus seen as a myth, designed to promote obedience and subjugation in the interests of the ruling elite.

MULTICULTURALISTS have rejected any form of nationalism that is based on the idea of cultural or ethnic unity, embracing instead a strictly civic model of national identity which blends cultural diversity with common political allegiances.

and indeed unchangeable, this implies that nations are characterised by common descent and so blurs the distinction between nations and races. Nations are thus held together by '**primordial** bonds', powerful and seemingly innate emotional attachments to a language, a religion, a traditional way of life and a homeland. To different degrees, conservatives and fascists adopt such a view of the nation. On the other hand, 'inclusive' concepts of the nation, as found in **civic nationalism**, highlight the importance of civic consciousness and patriotic loyalty. From this perspective, nations may be multi-racial, multi-ethnic, multi-religious and so forth. This, in turn, tends to blur the distinction between the nation and the state, and thus between nationality and citizenship. Liberals and socialists tend to adopt an inclusive view of the nation. These different approaches to the nation are illustrated in Figure 6.1.

Primordialism: The belief that nations are ancient and deep-rooted, fashioned variously out of psychology, culture and biology.

Civic nationalism: A form of nationalism that emphasises political allegiance based on a vision of a community of equal citizens, allowing for significant levels of ethnic and cultural diversity.

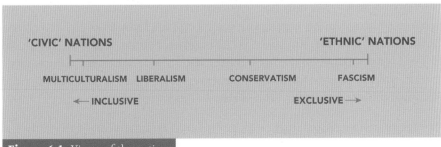

Figure 6.1 Views of the nation

ORGANIC COMMUNITY

Although nationalists may disagree about the defining features of the nation, they are unified by their belief that nations are organic communities. Humankind, in other words, is naturally divided into a collection of nations, each possessing a distinctive character and separate identity. This, nationalists argue, is why a 'higher' loyalty and deeper political significance attaches to the nation than to any other social group or collective body. Whereas, for instance, class, gender, religion and language may be important in particular societies, or may come to prominence in particular circumstances, the bonds of nationhood are more fundamental. National ties and loyalties are found in all societies, they endure over time, and they operate at an instinctual, even primordial, level. Nevertheless, different explanations have been provided for this, the most significant being based on the ideas of primordialism, modernism and constructivism.

Primordialist approaches to nationalism portray national identity as historically embedded: nations are rooted in a common cultural heritage and language that may long pre-date statehood or the quest for independence, and are character-ised by deep emotional attachments that resemble kinship ties. All nationalists, in that sense, are primordialists. Anthony Smith (1986) highlighted the impor-tance of primordialism by stressing the continuity between modern nations and pre-modern ethnic communities, which he called 'ethnies'. This implies that there is little difference between ethnicity and nationality, modern nations essentially being updated versions of long-established ethnic communities, although Smith rejected the idea that these proto-nations have existed from time immemorial.

In contrast, *modernist* approaches to nationalism suggest that national identity is forged in response to changing situations and historical challenges. Ernest Gellner (1983) thus emphasised the degree to which nationalism is linked to modernisation, and in particular to the process of industrialisation. He stressed that, while pre-modern or 'agro-literate' societies were structured by a network of feudal bonds and loyalties, emerging industrial societies promoted social mobility, self-striving and competition, and so required a new source of cul-tural cohesion. This was provided by nationalism. Although Gellner's theory suggests that nations coalesced in response to particular social conditions and circumstances, it also implies that the national community is deep-rooted and enduring, as a return to pre-modern loyalties and identities is unthinkable. Ben-edict Anderson (1983) also portrayed modern nations as a product of socio-economic change, in his case stressing the combined impact of the emergence of capitalism and the advent of modern mass communications, which he dubbed 'print-capitalism'. In his view, the nation is an 'imagined community', in that, within nations, individuals only ever meet a tiny proportion of those with whom they supposedly share a national identity.

The idea that nations are 'imagined', not organic, communities has nevertheless been seized on by critics of nationalism. *Constructivist* approaches to nationalism regard national identity as very largely an ideological construct, usually serving the interests of powerful groups. The Marxist historian Eric Hobsbawm (1983), for example, highlighted the extent to which nations are based on 'invented traditions'. Hobsbawm argued that a belief in historical continuity and cultural purity is invariably a myth, and, what is more, a myth created by nationalism itself. **Constructivism** suggests that nationalism creates nations, not the other way round. In the case of Marxism, nationalism has been viewed as a device through which the ruling class counters the threat of social revolution by ensuring that national loyalty is stronger than class solidarity, thereby binding the working class to the existing power structure.

SELF-DETERMINATION

Nationalism as a political ideology only emerged when the idea of national community encountered the doctrine of popular **sovereignty**. This occurred during the French Revolution and was influenced by the writings of Jean-Jacques Rousseau. Although Rousseau did not specifically address the question of the nation, or discuss the phenomenon of nationalism, his stress on popular sovereignty, expressed in the idea of the '**general will**', was the seed from which nationalist doctrines sprang. As a result of the Polish struggle for independence from Russia, he came to believe that this is vested in a culturally unified people. Rousseau argued that government should be based not on the absolute power of a monarch, but on the indivisible collective will of the entire community. During the French Revolution, these beliefs were reflected in the assertion that the French people were 'citizens' possessed of inalienable rights and duties, no longer merely 'subjects' of the crown. Sovereign power thus resided with the 'French nation'. The form of nationalism that emerged from the French Revolution was therefore based on the vision of a people or nation governing itself. In other words, the nation is not merely a natural community: it is a natural *political* community.

In this tradition of nationalism, nationhood and statehood are intrinsically linked. The litmus test of national identity is the desire to attain or maintain political independence, usually expressed in the principle of national self-determination.

Constructivism: The theory that meaning is imposed on the external world by the beliefs and assumptions we hold; reality is a social construct.

Sovereignty: The principle of absolute or unrestricted power expressed either as unchallengeable legal authority or unquestionable political power.

General will: The genuine interests of a collective body, equivalent to the common good; the will of all, provided each person acts selflessly.

KEY FIGURE

Jean-Jacques Rousseau (1712–78)

A Geneva-born French moral political philosopher, Rousseau was perhaps the principal intellectual influence on the French Revolution. His writing reflected a deep belief in the goodness of 'natural man' and the corruption of 'social man'. Rousseau's political teachings, developed in *The Social Contract* ([1762] 2012), advocate a radical form of democracy in which there is no distinction between free individuals and the process of government. His aim was to devise a form of authority to which people can be subject without losing their freedom. In this light, he proposed that government be based on the 'general will', as opposed to the 'particular', or selfish, will of each citizen. Rousseau is often seen as the 'father' of civic nationalism. This is because he took the general will to be the will of the nation, the people being bound together by patriotism or a sense of national *esprit de corps*. For Rousseau, nationalism was therefore inextricably linked to citizenship, democracy and the belief that the state's legitimacy derives from the active participation of its citizens. For more on Rousseau, see above, pp. 98, 112, 121 and 124.

The goal of nationalism is therefore the founding of a 'nation-state'. To date, this has been achieved in one of two ways. First, it may involve a process of unification. German history, for instance, has repeatedly witnessed unification. This occurred in medieval times under Charlemagne through the Holy Roman Empire; in the nineteenth century under Bismarck; and when the 'two Germanies' (East Germany and West Germany) were reunited in 1990. Second, nation-states can be created through the achievement of independence. For example, much of Polish history has witnessed successive attempts to achieve independence from the control of various foreign powers. Poland ceased to exist in 1793 when the Poles were partitioned by Austria, Russia and Prussia. Recognised by the Treaty of Versailles of 1919, Poland was proclaimed in 1918 and became an independent republic. However, in accordance with the Nazi–Soviet Pact of 1939, Poland was invaded by Germany and repartitioned, this time between Germany and the Soviet Union. Although Poland achieved formal independence in 1945, for much of the post-war period it remained firmly under Soviet control. The election of a non-communist government in 1989 therefore marked a further liberation of the country from foreign control.

For nationalists, the nation-state is the highest and most desirable form of political organisation. The great strength of the nation-state is that it offers the prospect of both cultural cohesion and political unity. When a people who share a common cultural or ethnic identity gain the right to self-government, nationality and citizenship coincide. Moreover, nationalism legitimises the authority of government. Political sovereignty in a nation-state resides with the people or the nation itself. Consequently, nationalism represents the notion of popular self-government, the idea that government is carried out either by the people or for the people, in accordance with their 'national interest'. This is why nationalists believe that the forces that have created a world of independent nation-states are natural and irresistible, and that no other social group could constitute a meaningful political community. The nation-state, in short, is the only viable political unit.

However, it would be misleading to suggest that nationalism is always associated with the nation-state or is necessarily linked to the idea of self-determination. Some nations, for instance, may be satisfied with a measure of political autonomy that stops short of statehood and full independence. This can be seen in the case of Welsh nationalism in the UK, and Breton and Basque nationalism in France. Nationalism is thus not always associated with **separatism**, but may instead be expressed through federalism or devolution. Nevertheless, it is unclear whether devolution, or even federalism, establishes a sufficient measure of self-government to satisfy nationalist demands. The granting of wide-ranging powers to the Basque region of Spain has failed to end ETA's separatist campaign, even though the organisation switched from military to democratic tactics in 2011 and completely disarmed in 2017. Similarly, the creation of a Scottish Parliament in the UK in 1999 has not ended the Scottish National Party's campaign to achieve an independent Scotland, which continues despite the failure of the 2015 independence referendum. In the case of the

Separatism: The quest to secede from a larger political formation with a view to establishing an independent state.

autonomous community of Catalonia in Spain, an independence referendum held in 2017, declared illegal by the Spanish government, resulted in a 91 per cent 'yes' vote and gave impetus to the long-standing struggle for secession.

CULTURALISM

Although 'classical' nationalism is associated with political goals – most commonly the pursuit, or defence, of independent statehood – other forms of nationalism are related more closely to ethnocultural aspirations and demands. This applies particularly in the case of **cultural nationalism** and **ethnic nationalism**. Cultural nationalism is a form of nationalism that emphasises the strengthening or defence of cultural identity over overt political demands. Its principal stress is on the regeneration of the nation as a distinctive civilisation, with the state being viewed as a peripheral, if not as an alien, entity. Whereas **political nationalism** is 'rational' and may be principled, cultural nationalism tends to be 'mystical', in that it is based on a romantic belief in the nation as a unique historical and organic whole. Typically, cultural nationalism is a 'bottom-up' form of nationalism that draws more on popular rituals, traditions and legends than on elite or 'higher' culture. Although it usually has an anti-modern character, cultural nationalism may also serve as an agent of modernisation, providing a people with a means of 'recreating' itself.

Whereas Rousseau is commonly seen as the 'father' of political civic national-ism, Johann Herder (see below) is usually viewed as the architect of cultural nationalism. Herder, together with writers such as Johann Fichte (1762–1814) and Friedrich Jahn (1778–1852), highlighted what they believed to be the uniqueness and superiority of German culture, in contrast to the ideas of the French Revolution. Herder believed that each nation possesses a **Volksgeist** which reveals itself in songs, myths and legends, and provides a nation with its source of creativity. Herder's nationalism therefore amounts to a form of **culturalism**. In this light, the role of nationalism is to develop an awareness and appreciation of national traditions and collective memories rather than to provide the basis for an overtly political quest for statehood. The tendency

---

Cultural nationalism: A form of nationalism that places primary emphasis on the regeneration of the nation as a distinctive civilisation, rather than on self-government.

Ethnic nationalism: A form of nationalism that is fuelled primarily by a keen sense of ethnic distinctiveness and the desire to preserve it.

Political nationalism: A form of nationalism that treats the nation as a natural political community, usually expressed with the idea of national self-determination.

Volksgeist: (German) Literally, the spirit of the people; the organic identity of a people reflected in their culture and particularly in their language.

Culturalism: The belief that human beings are culturally defined creatures, culture being the universal basis for personal and social identity.

KEY FIGURE

Johann Gottfried Herder (1744–1803)

A German poet, critic and philosopher, Herder was a powerful intellectual opponent of the Enlightenment and a crucial influence on the growth in Germany, and in central Europe generally, of the romantic movement. Herder placed an emphasis on the nation as an organic group characterised by a distinctive language, culture and 'spirit', which both helped to found cultural history and gave rise to a form of nationalism that stresses the intrinsic value of national culture. In this view, the *Volk* (the nation or 'the people') has a unique cultural identity, which is expressed through its distinctive national 'spirit', the *Volksgeist*. Herder placed a particular importance on the capacity of language to foster a people's historical identity and generate a sense of unity. Language is thus a repository of all that is precious to the group that speaks it. For more on Herder, see above and p. 187.

for nationalism to be expressed through cultural regeneration was particularly marked in nineteenth-century Germany, where it was reflected in the revival of folk traditions and the rediscovery of German myths and legends. The Brothers Grimm, for example, collected and published German folk tales, and the composer Richard Wagner (1813–83) based many of his operas on ancient myths.

Although cultural nationalism has often emerged within a European context, with early German nationalism sometimes being viewed as its archetypal form, cultural nationalism has been found in many parts of the world. It was, for instance, evident in black nationalism in the USA, as articulated by figures such as Marcus Garvey (see below) and by groups such as the Black Panthers and the Black Muslims (later the Nation of Islam). Similarly, it has been apparent in India, in forms of nationalism that have been based on the image of India as a distinctively Hindu civilisation. It is also evident in modern China in the increasing prominence given by party and state officials to the idea of 'Chinese-ness', expressed, among other things, in a revival of traditional cultural practices and an emphasis on 'Chinese' principles and moral values.

However, there has been disagreement about the implications of viewing nations primarily as cultural communities rather than political communities. On the one hand, cultural forms of nationalism have been viewed as being tolerant, and consistent with progressive political goals, in which case cultural nationalism clearly differs from ethnic nationalism, even though the terms 'culture' and 'ethnicity' overlap. 'Ethnicity' refers to loyalty towards a distinctive population, cultural group or territorial area. The term is complex because it has both racial and cultural overtones. Members of ethnic groups are often seen, correctly or incorrectly, to have descended from common ancestors, suggesting that ethnic groups are extended kinship groups, united by blood. A further indication of ethnic belonging is a link with an ancient or historic territory, a 'homeland', as in the case of Zionism (see p. 124).

KEY FIGURE

Marcus Garvey (1887–1940)

A Jamaican political thinker and activist, and an early advocate of black nationalism, Garvey was the founder in 1914 of the Universal Negro Improvement Association (UNIP). He left Jamaica for New York in 1916, where his message of black pride and economic self-sufficiency gained him a growing following, particularly in ghettos such as Harlem. Although his black business enterprises failed, and his call for a return to Africa was largely ignored, Garvey's emphasis on establishing black pride and his vision of Africa as a 'homeland' provided the basis for the later Black Power movement. Rastafarianism is also based largely on his ideas. Garvey's idea of Africa for the Africans was associated with a call to unite the continent from Cairo to the Cape, which had a profound impact on emerging pan-Africanism and inspired figures such as Kwame Nkrumah, the first prime minister and president of Ghana. Garvey was imprisoned for mail fraud in 1923, and was later deported, eventually dying in obscurity in London. For more on Garvey, see above and p. 183.

Key concept ... RACISM

Racism ('racism' and 'racialism' are now generally treated as synonymous) is, broadly, the belief that political or social conclusions can be drawn from the idea that humankind is divided into biologically distinct races. Racist theories are thus based on two assumptions. The first is that there are fundamental genetic, or species-type, differences among the peoples of the world – racial differences matter. The second is that these genetic divisions are reflected in cultural, intellectual and/or moral differences, making them politically or socially significant. Political racism is manifest in calls for racial segregation (for example, apartheid) and in doctrines of 'blood' superiority or inferiority (for example, Aryanism or anti-Semitism). 'Institutionalised' racism operates through the norms and values of an institution.

As it is not possible to 'join' an ethnic group (except perhaps through intermarriage), ethnic nationalism has a clearly exclusive character and tends to overlap with racism (see above). On the other hand, cultural and ethnic forms of nationalism have been viewed as closely related, even as part of the same phenomenon, commonly termed 'ethnocultural nationalism'. In this view, a distinction is drawn between inclusive or 'open' political nationalism and exclusive or 'closed' cultural nationalism. Cultural nationalism, from this perspective, is often taken to be, either implicitly or explicitly, chauvinistic or hostile towards other nations or minority groups, being fuelled by a mixture of pride and fear. To the extent that cultural nationalism is associated with demands for assimilation and cultural 'purity', it becomes incompatible with multiculturalism (the relationship between multiculturalism and nationalism is examined in greater depth in Chapter 9).

Differences between ...
CIVIC AND ETHNOCULTURAL NATIONALISM

CIVIC NATIONALISM	ETHNOCULTURAL NATIONALISM
• political nation	• cultural/historical nation
• inclusive	• exclusive
• universalism	• particularism
• equal nations	• unique nations
• rational/principled	• mystical/emotional
• national sovereignty	• national 'spirit'
• voluntaristic	• organic
• based on citizenship	• based on descent
• civic loyalty	• ethnic allegiance
• cultural diversity	• cultural unity

TYPES OF NATIONALISM

LIBERAL NATIONALISM

Political nationalism is a highly complex phenomenon, being characterised more by ambiguity and contradictions than by a single set of values and goals. For example, nationalism has been both liberating and oppressive: it has brought about self-government and freedom, and it has led to conquest and subjugation. Nationalism has been both progressive and regressive: it has looked to a future of national independence or national greatness, and it has celebrated past national glories and entrenched established identities. Nationalism has also been both rational and irrational: it has appealed to principled beliefs, such as national self-determination, and it has bred from non-rational drives and emotions, including ancient fears and hatreds. This reflects the capacity of nationalism to fuse with and absorb other political doctrines and ideas, thereby creating a series of rival nationalist traditions. The oldest and, some argue, 'classical' nationalist tradition is liberal nationalism.

Liberal nationalism dates back to the French Revolution and embodies many of its values. Its ideas spread quickly through much of Europe and were expressed most clearly by Giuseppe Mazzini (see p. 125). They also influenced the remarkable exploits of Simon Bolivar, who led the Latin American independence movement in the early nineteenth century and expelled the Spanish from much of Hispanic America. US President Woodrow Wilson's 'Fourteen Points', proposed as the basis for the reconstruction of Europe after World War I, were also based on liberal nationalist principles. Moreover, many twentieth-century anti-colonial leaders were inspired by liberal ideas, as in the case of Sun Yat-Sen (1866–1925), one of the leaders of China's 1911 Revolution, and Jawaharlal Nehru (1889–1964), the first prime minister of India.

The ideas of liberal nationalism were clearly shaped by Rousseau's defence of popular sovereignty, expressed in particular in the notion of the 'general will'. As the nineteenth century progressed, the aspiration for popular self-government

Key concept ... ZIONISM

Zionism (*Zion* is Hebrew for the Kingdom of Heaven) is the movement for the establishment of a Jewish homeland, usually seen as being located in Palestine. The idea was first advanced in 1897 by Theodore Herzl (1860–1904) at the World Zionist Congress in Basle, as the only means of protecting the Jewish people from persecution. Early Zionists had secularist and nationalistic aspirations, often associated with socialist sympathies. Since the foundation of the state of Israel in 1948, however, Zionism has come to be associated both with the continuing promise of Israel to provide a home for all Jews, and with attempts to promote sympathy for Israel and defend it against its enemies. In the latter sense, it has been recruited to the cause of fundamentalism, and, according to Palestinians, it has acquired an expansionist, anti-Arab character.

was fused progressively with liberal principles. This fusion was brought about by the fact that the multinational empires against which nationalists fought were also autocratic and oppressive. Mazzini, for example, wished the Italian states to unite, but this also entailed throwing off the influence of autocratic Austria. For many European revolutionaries in the mid-nineteenth century, liberalism and nationalism were virtually indistinguishable. Indeed, their nationalist creed was largely forged by applying liberal ideas, initially developed in relation to the individual, to the nation and to international politics.

Liberalism was founded on a defence of individual freedom, traditionally expressed in the language of rights. Nationalists believed nations to be sovereign entities, entitled to liberty, and also possessing rights, the most important being the right of self-determination. Liberal nationalism is therefore a liberating force in two senses. First, it opposes all forms of foreign domination and oppression, whether by multinational empires or colonial powers. Second, it stands for the ideal of self-government, reflected in practice in a belief in constitutionalism and representation. Woodrow Wilson, for example, argued in favour not only of a Europe composed of nation-states, but also one in which political democracy rather than autocracy ruled. For him, only a democratic republic, on the US model, could be a genuine nation-state.

Furthermore, liberal nationalists believe that nations, like individuals, are equal, at least in the sense that they are equally entitled to the right of self-determination. The ultimate goal of liberal nationalism is, therefore, the construction of a world of independent nation-states, not merely the unification or independence of a particular nation. In *Considerations on Representative Government* ([1861] 1972), John Stuart Mill (see p. 27) expressed this as the principle that 'the boundaries of government should coincide in the main with those of nationality'. Mazzini formed the clandestine organisation 'Young Italy' to promote the idea of a united Italy, but he also founded 'Young Europe' in the hope of spreading nationalist ideas throughout the continent. At the Paris Peace Conference, Woodrow Wilson advanced the principle of self-determination not

KEY FIGURE

Giuseppe Mazzini (1805–72)

An Italian nationalist and apostle of liberal republicanism, Mazzini is often portrayed as the 'prophet' of Italian unification. He came into contact with revolutionary politics as a member of a patriotic secret society, the Carbonari. After spells in France and Britain, Mazzini returned to Italy during the 1848 Revolutions, helping to liberate Milan and becoming head of the short-lived Roman Republic. Inspired by a distinctively liberal form of nationalism, Mazzini championed two principles, which he believed to be universally applicable: 'every nation a state' and 'only one state for the entire nation'. Although his influence on Italian unification faded once Piedmont assumed leadership of the movement, Mazzini's nationalism had a profound influence across Europe in strengthening the idea that freedom entails the creation of one's own nation-state. He nevertheless distrusted intellectualism and abstract thinking generally, arguing that thought must always be harnessed to action and vice versa, an idea he expressed through the concept of 'thought and action'. For more on Mazzini, see above, pp. 124 and 133.

Key concept ... INTERNATIONALISM

Internationalism is the theory or practice of politics based on transnational or global cooperation. It is rooted in universalist assumptions about human nature that put it at odds with political nationalism, the latter emphasising the degree to which political identity is shaped by nationality. However, internationalism is compatible with nationalism in the sense that it calls for cooperation or solidarity between or among pre-existing nations, rather than for the removal or abandonment of national identities altogether. Internationalism thus differs from cosmopolitanism (see p. 198), the latter implying the displacement of national allegiances by global allegiances. 'Weak' forms of internationalism can be seen in doctrines such as feminism, racism and religious fundamentalism, which hold that national ties are secondary to other political bonds. 'Strong' forms of internationalism have usually drawn on the universalist ideas of either liberalism or socialism.

simply because the break-up of the European empire served US national interests, but because he believed that the Poles, Czechs, Hungarians and so on all had the same right to political independence that Americans already enjoyed.

Liberals also believe that the principle of balance or natural harmony applies to the nations of the world, not just to individuals within society. The achievement of national self-determination is a means of establishing a peaceful and stable international order. Wilson believed that World War I had been caused by an 'old order', dominated by autocratic and militaristic empires. Democratic nation-states, on the other hand, would respect the national sovereignty of their neighbours and have no incentive to wage war or subjugate others. For a liberal, nationalism does not divide nations from one another, promoting distrust, rivalry and possibly war. Rather, it is a force that is capable of promoting both unity within each nation and brotherhood among all nations on the basis of mutual respect for national rights and characteristics. At heart, liberalism looks beyond the nation to the ideas of cosmopolitanism (see p. 198) and internationalism (see above).

Liberal internationalism is grounded in a fear of an international 'state of nature'. Liberals have long accepted that national self-determination is a mixed blessing. While it preserves self-government and forbids foreign control, it also creates a world of sovereign nation-states in which each nation has the freedom to pursue its own interests, possibly at the expense of other nations. Liberal nationalists have certainly accepted that constitutionalism and democracy reduce the tendency towards militarism and war, but when sovereign nations operate within conditions of 'international anarchy', self-restraint alone may not be sufficient to ensure what the German philosopher Immanuel Kant (1724–1804) called 'perpetual peace'. Liberals have generally proposed two means of preventing a recourse to conquest and plunder. The first is national interdependence, aimed at promoting mutual understanding and cooperation. This is why liberals have traditionally supported the policy of **free trade**: economic interdependence means that the material costs of international conflict are so great that warfare

Free trade: A system of trading between states that is unrestricted by tariffs or other forms of protectionism.

Differences between ...
LIBERAL AND EXPANSIONIST NATIONALISM

LIBERAL NATIONALISM	EXPANSIONIST NATIONALISM
• national self-determination	• national chauvinism
• inclusive	• exclusive
• voluntaristic	• organic
• progressive	• reactionary
• rational/principled	• emotional/instinctive
• human rights	• national interest
• equal nations	• hierarchy of nations
• constitutionalism	• authoritarianism
• ethnic/cultural pluralism	• ethnic/cultural purity
• cosmopolitanism	• imperialism/militarism
• collective security	• power politics
• supranationalism	• international anarchy

becomes virtually unthinkable. Second, Liberals have proposed that national ambition should be checked by the construction of international organisations capable of bringing order to an otherwise lawless international scene. This explains Woodrow Wilson's support for the first, if flawed, experiment in world government, the League of Nations, set up in 1919, and the far wider support for its successor, the United Nations, founded by the San Francisco Conference of 1945. Liberals have looked to these bodies to establish a law-governed state system to make possible the peaceful resolution of international conflicts.

However, critics of liberal nationalism have sometimes suggested that its ideas are naïve and romantic. Liberal nationalists see the progressive and liberating face of nationalism; their nationalism is rational and tolerant. However, they perhaps ignore the darker face of nationalism, the irrational bonds or **tribalism** that distinguish 'us' from a foreign and threatening 'them'. Liberals see nationalism as a universal principle, but have less understanding of the emotional power of nationalism, which has, in times of war, persuaded individuals to kill or die for their country, regardless of the justice of their nation's cause. Liberal nationalism is also misguided in its belief that the nation-state is the key to political and international harmony. The mistake of Wilsonian nationalism was the belief that nations live in convenient and discrete geographical areas, and that states can be constructed that coincide with these areas. In practice, all so-called 'nation-states' comprise a range of linguistic, religious, ethnic or regional groups, some of which may also consider themselves to be 'nations'. For example, in 1918 the newly created nation-states of Czechoslovakia and Poland contained a significant number of German speakers, and Czechoslovakia itself was a fusion of two major ethnic groups: the Czechs and the Slovaks. The former Yugoslavia, also created by the Treaty of Versailles, contained a bewildering

Tribalism: Group behaviour characterised by insularity and exclusivity, typically fuelled by hostility towards rival groups.

variety of ethnic groups – Serbs, Croats, Slovenes, Bosnians, Albanians and so on – which have subsequently realised their aspiration for nationhood. In fact, the ideal of a politically unified and culturally homogeneous nation-state can only be achieved by forcibly deporting minority groups and imposing an outright ban on immigration.

CONSERVATIVE NATIONALISM

In the early nineteenth century, conservatives regarded nationalism as a radical and dangerous force, a threat to order and political stability. However, as the century progressed, conservative statesmen such as Disraeli, Bismarck and even Tsar Alexander III became increasingly sympathetic towards nationalism, seeing it as a natural ally in maintaining social order and defending traditional institutions. In the modern period, nationalism has become an article of faith for most conservatives in most parts of the world.

Conservative nationalism tends to develop in established nation-states, rather than in those that are in the process of nation building. Conservatives care less for the principled nationalism of universal self-determination and more about the promise of social cohesion and public order embodied in the sentiment of national patriotism. For conservatives, society is organic: they believe that nations emerge naturally from the desire of human beings to live with others who possess the same views, habits and appearance as themselves. Human beings are thought to be limited and imperfect creatures, who seek meaning and security within the national community. Therefore, the principal goal of conservative nationalism is to maintain national unity by fostering patriotic loyalty and 'pride in one's country', especially in the face of the divisive idea of class solidarity preached by socialists. Indeed, by incorporating the working class into the nation, conservatives have often seen nationalism as the antidote to social revolution. Charles de Gaulle, French president 1959–69, harnessed nationalism to the conservative cause in France with particular skill. De Gaulle appealed to national pride by pursuing an independent, even anti-American, defence and foreign policy, and by attempting to restore order and authority to social life and build up a powerful state. In some respects, **Thatcherism** in the UK amounted to a British form of Gaullism, in that it fused an appeal based on nationalism, or at least national independence within Europe, with the promise of strong government and firm leadership.

The conservative character of nationalism is maintained by an appeal to tradition and history; nationalism thereby becomes a defence for traditional institutions and a traditional way of life. Conservative nationalism is essentially nostalgic and backward-looking, reflecting on a past age of national glory or triumph. This is evident in the widespread tendency to use ritual and commemoration to present past military victories as defining moments in a nation's history. It is also apparent in the use of traditional institutions as symbols of national identity. This occurs in the case of British, or, more accurately, English nationalism, which is closely linked to the institution of monarchy. Britain (plus Northern Ireland) is the United Kingdom, its national anthem is 'God Save the

Thatcherism: The free-market/strong state ideological stance associated with Margaret Thatcher; the UK version of the New Right political project.

Queen', and the royal family plays a prominent role in national celebrations such as Armistice Day, and on state occasions such as the opening of Parliament.

Conservative nationalism is particularly prominent when the sense of national identity is felt to be threatened or in danger of being lost. The issues of immigration and **supranationalism** have therefore helped to keep this form of nationalism alive in many modern states. Conservative reservations about immigration stem from the belief that cultural diversity leads to instability and conflict. As stable and successful societies must be based on shared values and a common culture, either immigration, particularly from societies with different religious and other traditions, should be firmly restricted or minority ethnic groups should be encouraged to assimilate into the culture of the 'host' society. This puts conservative nationalism clearly at odds with multiculturalism (as discussed in Chapter 9). Conservative nationalists are also concerned about the threat that supranational bodies, such as the EU, pose to national identity and so to the cultural bonds of society. This is expressed in the UK in the form of 'Euroscepticism', particularly strong within the Conservative Party, with similar views being expressed in continental Europe by a variety of far-right groups such as the French National Front. Eurosceptics not only defend sovereign national institutions and a distinctive national currency on the grounds that they are vital symbols of national identity, but also warn that the 'European project' is fatally misconceived because a stable political union cannot be forged out of such national, linguistic and cultural diversity.

Although conservative politicians and parties have derived considerable political benefit from their appeal to nationalism, opponents have sometimes pointed out that their ideas are based on misguided assumptions. In the first place, conservative nationalism can be seen as a form of elite manipulation. The 'nation' is invented and certainly defined by political leaders who may use it for their own purposes. This is most evident in times of war or international crisis, when the nation is mobilised to fight for the 'fatherland' by emotional appeals to patriotic duty. Furthermore, conservative nationalism may also serve to promote intolerance and bigotry. By insisting on the maintenance of cultural purity and established traditions, conservatives may portray immigrants, or foreigners in general, as a threat, and in the process promote, or at least legitimise, racist and xenophobic fears. The revival of national conservatism in the twenty-first century is discussed on pp. 57–8.

EXPANSIONIST NATIONALISM

In many countries the dominant image of nationalism is one of aggression and **militarism**, quite the opposite of a principled belief in national self-determination. The aggressive face of nationalism became apparent in the late nineteenth century as European powers indulged in a 'scramble for Africa' in the name of national glory and their 'place in the sun'. The imperialism of the late nineteenth century differed from that of earlier periods of colonial expansion in that it was supported by a climate of popular nationalism: national prestige was linked increasingly to the possession of an empire and each colonial victory

Supranationalism: The ability of bodies with transnational or global jurisdictions to impose their will on nation-states.

Militarism: The achievement of ends by military means, or the extension of military ideas, values and practices to civilian society.

was greeted by demonstrations of public approval. In the UK, a new word, **jingoism**, was coined to describe this mood of popular nationalism. In the early twentieth century, the growing rivalry of the European powers divided the continent into two armed camps, the Triple Entente, comprising the UK, France and Russia, and the Triple Alliance, containing Germany, Austria and Italy. When world war eventually broke out in August 1914, after a prolonged arms race and a succession of international crises, it provoked public rejoicing in all the major cities of Europe. Aggressive and expansionist nationalism reached its high point in the inter-war period when the authoritarian or fascist regimes of Japan, Italy and Germany embarked on policies of imperial expansion and world domination, eventually leading to war in 1939.

What distinguished this form of nationalism from earlier liberal nationalism was its chauvinism, a term derived from the name of Nicolas Chauvin, a French soldier who had been fanatically devoted to Napoleon I. Nations were not thought to be equal in their right to self-determination; rather, some nations were believed to possess characteristics or qualities that made them superior to others. Such ideas were clearly evident in European imperialism, which was justified by an ideology of racial and cultural superiority. In nineteenth-century Europe it was widely believed that the 'white' peoples of Europe and America were intellectually and morally superior to the 'black', 'brown' and 'yellow' peoples of Africa and Asia. Indeed, Europeans portrayed imperialism as a moral duty: colonial peoples were the 'white man's burden'. Imperialism supposedly brought the benefits of civilisation, and in particular Christianity, to the less fortunate and less sophisticated peoples of the world.

More particular varieties of national chauvinism have developed in the form of **pan-nationalism**. In Russia this took the form of pan-Slavism, sometimes called 'Slavophile nationalism', which was particularly strong in the late nineteenth and early twentieth centuries. The Russians are Slavs, and enjoy linguistic and cultural links with other Slavic peoples in eastern and south-eastern Europe. Pan-Slavism was defined by the goal of Slavic unity, which many Russian nationalists believed to be their country's historic mission. In the years before

Jingoism: A mood of nationalist enthusiasm and public celebration provoked by military expansion or imperial conquest.

Pan-nationalism: A style of nationalism that is dedicated to unifying a disparate people through either expansionism or political solidarity ('pan' means all or every).

Key concept ... FASCISM

Fascism is a political ideology whose core theme is the idea of an organically unified national community, embodied in a belief in 'strength through unity'. The individual, in a literal sense, is nothing; individual identity must be entirely absorbed into the community or social group. The fascist ideal is that of the 'new man', a hero, motivated by duty, honour and a willingness to sacrifice his life for the glory of his nation or race, and to give unquestioning obedience to a supreme leader. While Italian fascism was essentially an extreme form of statism, based on absolute loyalty towards a 'totalitarian; state', German fascism, or Nazism, was founded on racial theories, which portrayed the Aryan people as a 'master race' and advanced a virulent form of anti-Semitism (see p. 132).

1914, such ideas brought Russia into growing conflict with Austria–Hungary for control of the Balkans. The chauvinistic character of pan-Slavism derived from the belief that the Russians are the natural leaders of the Slavic people, and that the Slavs are culturally and spiritually superior to the peoples of central or western Europe. Pan-Slavism is therefore both anti-western and anti-liberal. Forms of pan-Slavism have been re-awakened since 1991 and the collapse of communist rule in Russia.

Traditional German nationalism also exhibited a marked chauvinism, which was born out of defeat in the Napoleonic Wars. Figures such as Johann Fichte and Friedrich Jahn reacted strongly against France and the ideals of its revolution, emphasising instead the uniqueness of German culture and its language, and the racial purity of its people. After unification in 1871, German nationalism developed a pronounced chauvinistic character with the emergence of pressure groups such as the Pan-German League and the Navy League, which campaigned for closer ties with German-speaking Austria and for a German empire, Germany's 'place in the sun'. Pan-Germanism was an expansionist and aggressive form of nationalism that envisaged the creation of a German-dominated Europe. German chauvinism found its highest expression in the racialist and anti-Semitic doctrines developed by the Nazis. The Nazis adopted the expansionist goals of pan-Germanism with enthusiasm, but justified them in the language of biology rather than politics.

National chauvinism breeds from a feeling of intense, even hysterical nationalist enthusiasm. The individual as a separate, rational being is swept away on a tide of patriotic emotion, expressed in the desire for aggression, expansion and war. Charles Maurras (see below) called such intense patriotism '**integral nationalism**'. Such militant nationalism is often accompanied by militarism. Military glory and conquest are the ultimate evidence of national greatness and have been capable of generating intense feelings of nationalist commitment.

Integral nationalism: A form of nationalism which emphasises the overriding importance of the nation, seen as possessing an existence and meaning beyond the life of any single individual.

KEY FIGURE

Charles Maurras (1868–1952)

A French writer, journalist and leading figure within the political movement *Action Française*, Maurras was a key exponent of right-wing nationalism and an influence on fascism (see p. 130). His idea of 'integral nationalism' emphasised the organic unity of the nation, fusing a clearly illiberal rejection of individualism and democracy with a stress on hierarchy and traditional institutions (in his case, the French monarchy and the Roman Catholic Church). Believing 'goddess France' to be a marvel unequalled in the entire world, Maurras conceived of the nation as having a pronounced aesthetic and metaphysical character. He nevertheless warned that France needed to be protected from its enemies within and without, including Protestants, Jews, Freemasons and foreigners in general. Maurras' nationalism resembled fascism most clearly in its emphasis on militarism. In his view, the mission of the nation was intrinsically linked to expansionism and war, grounded in the belief that, while some nations are destined for conquest and glory, others are weak and subordinate. For more on Maurras, see above and p. 132.

The civilian population is, in effect, militarised: it is infected by the martial values of absolute loyalty, complete dedication and willing self-sacrifice. When the honour or integrity of the nation is in question, the lives of ordinary citizens become unimportant. Such emotional intensity was amply demonstrated in August 1914, and perhaps also underlies the emotional power of jihad (crudely defined as 'holy war') from the viewpoint of militant Islamist groups.

National chauvinism has a particularly strong appeal for the isolated and powerless, for whom nationalism offers the prospect of security, self-respect and pride. Militant or integral nationalism requires a heightened sense of belonging to a distinct national group. Such intense nationalist feeling is often stimulated by 'negative integration', the portrayal of another nation or race as a threat or an enemy. In the face of the enemy, the nation draws together and experiences an intensified sense of its own identity and importance. National chauvinism therefore breeds from a clear distinction between 'them' and 'us'. There has to be a 'them' to deride or hate in order to forge a sense of 'us'. In politics, national chauvinism has commonly been reflected in racist ideologies, which divide the world into an 'in group' and an 'out group', in which the 'out group' becomes a scapegoat for all the misfortunes and frustrations suffered by the 'in group'. It is therefore no coincidence that chauvinistic political creeds are a breeding ground for racist ideas. Both pan-Slavism and pan-Germanism, for example, have been characterised by virulent anti-Semitism (see below).

ANTI-COLONIAL AND POSTCOLONIAL NATIONALISM

Nationalism may have been born in Europe, but it became a worldwide phenomenon thanks to imperialism. The experience of colonial rule helped to forge a sense of nationhood and a desire for 'national liberation' among the peoples of Asia and Africa, and gave rise to a specifically anti-colonial form of nationalism. During the twentieth century, the political geography of much of the world was transformed by anti-colonialism. Although the Treaty of Versailles applied the principle of self-determination to Europe, it was conveniently ignored in other parts of the world, where German colonies were simply

Key concept … ANTI-SEMITISM

By tradition, Semites are descendants of Shem, son of Noah, and include most of the peoples of the Middle East. Anti-Semitism refers specifically to prejudice against or hatred towards the Jews. In its earliest systematic form, anti-Semitism had a religious character, reflecting the hostility of Christians towards the Jews, based on their complicity in the murder of Jesus and their refusal to acknowledge him as the Son of God. Economic anti-Semitism developed from the Middle Ages onwards, expressing a distaste for the Jews as moneylenders and traders. The nineteenth century saw the birth of racial anti-Semitism in the works of Richard Wagner and H. S. Chamberlain, who condemned the Jewish peoples as fundamentally evil and destructive. Such ideas provided the ideological basis for German Nazism and found their most grotesque expression in the Holocaust.

transferred to UK and French control. However, during the inter-war period, independence movements increasingly threatened the overstretched empires of the UK and France. The final collapse of the European empires came after World War II. In some cases, a combination of mounting nationalist pressure and declining domestic economic performance persuaded colonial powers to depart relatively peacefully, as occurred in India and Pakistan in 1947 and in Malaysia in 1957. However, decolonisation in the post-1945 period was often characterised by revolution, and sometimes periods of armed struggle. This occurred, for instance, in the case of China, 1937–45 (against Japan), Algeria, 1954–62 (against France), and Vietnam, 1946–54 (against France) and 1964–75 (against the USA).

In a sense, the colonising Europeans had taken with them the seed of their own destruction: the doctrine of nationalism. For example, it is notable that many of the leaders of independence or liberation movements were western-educated. It is therefore not surprising that anti-colonial movements sometimes articulated their goals in the language of liberal nationalism, reminiscent of Mazzini or Woodrow Wilson. However, emergent African and Asian nations were in a very different position from that of the newly created European states of the nineteenth and early twentieth centuries. For these African and Asian nations, the quest for political independence was closely related to their awareness of economic under-development and their subordination to the industrialised states of Europe and North America. Anti-colonialism thus came to express the desire for national liberation in both political and economic terms, and this has left its mark on the form of nationalism practised in the developing world.

Some forms of anti-colonial nationalism nevertheless distanced themselves more clearly from western political traditions by constructing non-European models of national liberation. This had a range of implications, however. For example, the Indian spiritual and religious leader Mahatma Gandhi (1869–1948) advanced a political philosophy that fused Indian nationalism with an ethic of non-violence and self-sacrifice that was ultimately rooted in Hinduism. 'Home rule' for India was thus a spiritual condition, and not merely a political one, a stance underpinned by Gandhi's anti-industrialism, famously embodied in his wearing of home-spun clothes. In contrast, the Martinique-born French revolutionary theorist Frantz Fanon (1925–61) emphasised links between the anti-colonial struggle and violence. His theory of imperialism stressed the psychological dimension of colonial subjugation. For Fanon (1965), colonisation was not simply a political process, but also one through which a new 'species' of human is created. He argued that only the cathartic experience of violence is powerful enough to bring about this psycho-political regeneration.

However, most of the leaders of Asian and African anti-colonial movements were attracted to some form of socialism, ranging from the moderate and peaceful ideas represented by Gandhi and Nehru in India, to the revolutionary Marxism espoused by Mao Zedong (1893–1976) in China, Ho Chi Minh (1890–1969) in Vietnam and Fidel Castro (1926–2016) in Cuba. On the surface, socialism is more clearly related to internationalism than to nationalism. This reflects the stress within socialism, first, on social class, class loyalties having an intrinsically transnational character, and, at a deeper level, on the idea of a common humanity. Marx (see p. 67) thus declared in *The Communist Manifesto* that 'working men have no country'.

Socialist ideas nevertheless appealed powerfully to nationalists in the developing world. This was partly because socialism embodies values such as community and cooperation that are deeply entrenched in traditional, pre-industrial societies. More important, socialism, and in particular Marxism, provided an analysis of inequality and exploitation through which the colonial experience could be understood and colonial rule challenged. During the 1960s and 1970s, in particular, developing-world nationalists were drawn to revolutionary Marxism, influenced by the belief that colonialism is in practice an extended form of class oppression.

The Russian Bolshevik leader V. I. Lenin (1870– 1924) had earlier provided the basis for such a view by portraying imperialism as essentially an economic phenomenon, a quest for profit by capitalist countries seeking investment opportunities, cheap labour and raw materials, and secure markets (Lenin, [1916] 1970). The class struggle thus became a struggle against colonial exploitation and oppression. As a result, the overthrow of colonial rule implied not only political independence, but also a social revolution which would bring about economic as well as political emancipation.

In some cases, developing-world regimes have openly embraced Marxist–Leninist principles. On achieving independence, China, North Korea, Vietnam and Cambodia moved swiftly to seize foreign assets and nationalise economic resources. They founded one-party states and centrally planned economies, closely following the Soviet model. In other cases, states in Africa and the Middle East have developed a less ideological form of nationalistic socialism, as has been evident in Algeria, Libya, Zambia, Iraq and South Yemen. The 'socialism' proclaimed in such countries usually took the form of an appeal to a unifying national cause or interest, in most cases economic or social development, as in the case of so-called 'African socialism', embraced, for instance, by Tanzania, Zimbabwe and Angola.

The postcolonial period has thrown up quite different forms of nationalism, however. With the authority of socialism, and especially the attraction of Marxism–Leninism, declining significantly since the 1970s, nation building in the postcolonial period has been shaped increasingly by the rejection of western ideas and culture more than by the attempt to reapply them. If the West is regarded as the source of oppression and exploitation, postcolonial nationalism must seek an anti-western voice. In part, this has been a reaction against the dominance of western, and particularly US, culture and economic power in much of the developing world.

The principal vehicle for expressing such views has been religious fundamentalism. Although Islam in particular has thrown up a comprehensive programme of

Key concept ... **RELIGIOUS FUNDAMENTALISM**

Religious fundamentalism is defined by the belief that religion cannot and should not be confined to the private sphere, but finds its highest and proper expression in the politics of popular mobilisation and social regeneration. Although often related, religious fundamentalism should not be equated with scriptural literalism, as the 'fundamentals' of a creed are often extracted through a process of 'dynamic' interpretation by a charismatic leader. Religious fundamentalism also differs from ultra-orthodoxy, in that it advances a programme of moral and political regeneration of society in line with religious principles, as opposed to a retreat from a corrupt secular society into the purity of faith-based communal living. Ruthven (2007) associated religious fundamentalism with a 'search for meaning' in a world of growing doubt and uncertainty.

political renewal, in the form of Islamism, most fundamentalist religious movements have been more narrowly concerned with helping to clarify or redefine national or ethnic identity, examples being associated with Hinduism, Sikhism, Judaism and Buddhism. Hindu fundamentalism has been expressed in calls for the 'Hinduisation' of Muslim, Sikh and other communities in India. The Bharatiya Janata Party (BJP) has been the largest party in the Indian parliament since 1996, articulating, as it does, the newly prosperous middle classes' ambivalence towards modernity and, particularly, its concerns about a weakening of national identity. The more radical World Hindu Council preaches 'India for the Hindus', while its parent body, the RSS (Rashtriya Swayamsevak Sangh), aims to create a 'Greater India', stretching from Burma to Iraq. Sikh fundamentalism is associated with the struggle to found an independent nation-state, 'Khalistan', located in the present-day Punjab, with Sikhism as the state religion and its government obliged to ensure its unhindered flourishing. Jewish fundamentalists have transformed Zionism into a defence of the 'Greater Land of Israel', characterised by territorial aggressiveness. In the case of Israel's best-known fundamentalist group, Gushmun Emunim (Bloc of the Faithful), this has been expressed in a campaign to build Jewish settlements in territory occupied in the Six-Day War of 1967. Buddhist nationalism has been evident in both Sri Lanka and Burma, in the former case being associated with the 'Sinhalisation' of national identity and the war waged against Tamil separatism, finally crushed in 2009.

(?) QUESTIONS FOR DISCUSSION

- Do nations develop 'naturally', or are they, in some sense, invented?

- Why have nations and states often been confused?

- Is any group of people entitled to define itself as a 'nation'?

- How does nationalism differ from racism?

- To what extent is nationalism compatible with ethnic and cultural diversity?

- In what sense is liberal nationalism principled?

- Why have liberals viewed nationalism as the antidote to war?

- Are all conservatives nationalists? If so, why?

- Why has nationalism so often been associated with expansionism, conquest and war?

- To what extent is nationalism a backward-looking ideology?

- Why and how has developing-world nationalism differed from nationalism in the developed world?

(📖) FURTHER READING

Brown, D., *Contemporary Nationalism: Civic, Ethnocultural and Multicultural Politics* (2000). A clear and stimulating account of differing approaches to nationalism and of the contrasting forms of modern nationalist politics.

Hearn, J., *Rethinking Nationalism: A Critical Introduction* (2006). An innovative and wide-ranging study of nationalism that critically reviews approaches to the nature and origins of nationalism.

Özkirimli, U., *Theories of Nationalism*, 3rd edition (2017). A clear and genuinely international account of classical and modern contributions to debates about nationalism.

Spencer, P. and Wollman, H., *Nationalism: A Critical Introduction* (2002). A very useful survey of classical and contemporary approaches to nationalism that addresses all the key issues, theories and debates.

Feminism

PREVIEW

As a political term, 'feminism' was a twentieth-century invention and has only been a familiar part of everyday language since the 1960s. ('Feminist' was first used in the nineteenth century as a medical term to describe either the feminisation of men or the masculinisation of women.) In modern usage, feminism is invariably linked to the women's movement and the attempt to advance the social role of women.

Feminist ideology is defined by two basic beliefs: that women are disadvantaged because of their sex; and that this disadvantage can and should be overthrown. In this way, feminists have highlighted what they see as a political relationship between the sexes, the supremacy of men and the subjection of women in most, if not all, societies. In viewing gender divisions as 'political', feminists challenged a 'mobilisation of bias' that has traditionally operated within political thought, by which generations of male thinkers, unwilling to examine the privileges and power their sex had enjoyed, had succeeded in keeping the role of women off the political agenda.

Nevertheless, feminism has also been characterised by a diversity of views and political positions. The women's movement, for instance, has pursued goals that range from the achievement of female suffrage and an increase in the number of women in elite positions in public life, to the legalisation of abortion, and the ending of female circumcision. Similarly, feminists have embraced both revolutionary and reformist political strategies, and feminist theory has both drawn on established political traditions and values, notably liberalism and socialism, and, in the form of radical feminism, rejected conventional political ideas and concepts. However, feminist ideology has long since ceased to be confined to these 'core' traditions, with modern feminist thought focusing on new issues and characterised, generally, by a more radical engagement with the politics of difference.

CONTENTS

HISTORICAL OVERVIEW

Although the term 'feminism' may be of recent origin, feminist views have been expressed in many different cultures and can be traced back as far as the ancient civilisations of Greece and China. Christine de Pisan's *Book of the City of Ladies*, published in Italy in 1405, foreshadowed many of the ideas of modern feminism in recording the deeds of famous women of the past and advocating women's right to education and political influence. Nevertheless, it was not until the nineteenth century that an organised women's movement developed. The first text of modern feminism is usually taken to be Mary Wollstonecraft's (see p. 13) *A Vindication of the Rights of Woman* ([1792] 1967), written against the backdrop of the French Revolution. By the mid-nineteenth century, the women's movement had acquired a central focus: the campaign for female suffrage, the right to vote, which drew inspiration from the progressive extension of the franchise to men. This period is usually referred to as **first–wave feminism**, and was characterised by the essentially liberal demand that women should enjoy the same legal and political rights as men. Female suffrage was the principal goal of first-wave or **liberal feminism** because it was believed that if women could vote, all other forms of sexual discrimination or prejudice would quickly disappear.

The women's movement was strongest in those countries where political democracy was most advanced; women demanded rights that in many cases were already enjoyed by their husbands and sons. In the USA, a women's movement emerged during the 1840s, inspired in part by the campaign to abolish slavery. The famous Seneca Falls convention, held in 1848, marked the birth of the US women's rights movement. It adopted a Declaration of Sentiments, written by Elizabeth Cady Stanton (1815–1902), which deliberately drew on the language and principles of the Declaration of Independence and called, among other things, for female suffrage. The National Women's Suffrage Association, led by Stanton and Susan B. Anthony (1820–1906), was set up in 1869 and merged with the more conservative American Women's Suffrage Association in 1890. Similar movements developed in other western countries. In the UK, an organised movement developed during the 1850s and, in 1867, the House of Commons defeated the first attempt to introduce female suffrage, an amendment to the Second Reform Act, proposed by John Stuart Mill (see p. 27). The UK suffrage movement adopted increasingly militant tactics after the formation in 1903 of the Women's Social and Political Union, led by Emmeline Pankhurst (1858–1928) and her daughter Christabel (1880–1958). From their underground base in Paris, the Pankhursts coordinated a campaign of direct action in which 'suffragettes' carried out wholesale attacks on property and mounted a series of well-publicised public demonstrations.

'First-wave' feminism ended with the achievement of female suffrage, introduced first in New Zealand in 1893. The Nineteenth Amendment of the US Constitution granted the vote to American women in 1920. The franchise was extended to women in the UK in 1918, but they did not achieve equal voting rights with men for a further decade. Ironically, in many ways, winning the

First-wave feminism: The early form of feminism which developed in the mid-nineteenth century and was based on the pursuit of sexual equality in the areas of political and legal rights, particularly suffrage rights.

Liberal feminism: A form of feminism that is grounded in the belief that sexual differences are irrelevant to personal worth, and calls for equal rights for women and men in the public sphere.

right to vote weakened and undermined the women's movement. The struggle for female suffrage had united and inspired the movement, giving it a clear goal and a coherent structure. Furthermore, many activists naïvely believed that in winning suffrage rights, women had achieved full emancipation. It was not until the 1960s that the women's movement was regenerated, with the emergence of feminism's 'second wave'.

The publication in 1963 of Betty Friedan's *The Feminine Mystique* did much to relaunch feminist thought. Friedan (see p. 14) set out to explore what she called 'the problem with no name', the frustration and unhappiness many women experienced as a result of being confined to the roles of housewife and mother. **Second-wave feminism** acknowledged that the achievement of political and legal rights had not solved the 'women's question'. Indeed, feminist ideas and arguments became increasingly radical, and at times revolutionary. Books such as Kate Millett's *Sexual Politics* (1970) and Germaine Greer's *The Female Eunuch* (1970) pushed back the borders of what had previously been considered to be 'political' by focusing attention on the personal, psychological and sexual aspects of female oppression. The goal of second-wave feminism was not merely political emancipation but 'women's liberation', reflected in the ideas of the growing Women's Liberation Movement. Such a goal could not be achieved by political reforms or legal changes alone, but demanded, modern feminists argued, a more far-reaching and perhaps revolutionary process of social change.

Since the first flowering of radical feminist thought in the late 1960s and early 1970s, feminism has developed into a distinctive and established ideology, whose ideas and values challenge the most basic assumptions of conventional political thought. Feminism has succeeded in establishing **gender** perspectives as important themes in a range of academic disciplines, and in raising consciousness about gender issues in public life in general. By the 1990s, feminist organisations existed in all western countries and most parts of the developing world. However, three processes have accompanied these developments. The first is a process of de-radicalisation, whereby there has been a retreat from the sometimes uncompromising positions that characterised feminism in the early 1970s. This has led to the popularity of the idea of 'postfeminism', which suggests that, as feminist goals have been largely achieved, the women's movement has moved 'beyond feminism'. The second process is one of fragmentation. Instead of simply losing its radical or critical edge, feminist thinking has gone through a process of radical diversification, making it difficult, and perhaps impossible, any longer to identify 'common ground' within feminism. In addition to the 'core' feminist traditions – liberal feminism, **socialist feminism** and **radical feminism** – we must now add postmodern feminism, psychoanalytical feminism, black feminism, lesbian feminism, **transfeminism** and so on. The third, and related, process is the growing recognition of **intersectionality** and the tendency for women to have multiple social identities. Women, thus, do not just have a straightforward gender-based identity but one in which, for instance, race, social class, ethnicity, age, religion, nationality and sexual orientation can overlap or 'intersect' with gender. This implies that women may

Second-wave feminism: The form of feminism that emerged in the 1960s and 1970s, and was characterised by a more radical concern with 'women's liberation', including, and perhaps especially, in the private sphere.

Gender: A social and cultural distinction between males and females, as opposed to sex, which refers to biological and therefore ineradicable differences between women and men.

Socialist feminism: A form of feminism that links the subordination of women to the dynamics of the capitalist economic system, emphasising that women's liberation requires a process of radical social change.

Radical feminism: A form of feminism that holds gender divisions to be the most politically significant of social cleavages, and believes that they are rooted in the structures of domestic life.

Transfeminism: A form of feminism that rejects the idea of fixed identities and specifically avows sexual and gender ambiguity.

Intersectionality: A framework for the analysis of injustice and social inequality that emphasises the multidimensional or multi-faceted nature of personal identity and of related systems of domination.

be subject to interlocking systems of oppression and discrimination, as sexism becomes entangled with racism, xenophobia, homophobia and the like.

CORE IDEAS AND PRINCIPLES

SEX AND GENDER

Feminist thinking about human nature focuses primarily on the issues of sex and gender. The most common of all anti-feminist arguments, often associated with conservatives, asserts that gender divisions in society are 'natural': women and men merely fulfil the social roles for which nature designed them. A woman's physical and anatomical make-up thus suits her to a subordinate and domestic role in society; in short, 'biology is destiny'. The biological factor that is most frequently linked to women's social position is their capacity to bear children. Without doubt, childbearing is unique to the female sex, together with the fact that women menstruate and have the capacity to suckle babies. However, feminists insist that in no way do such biological facts necessarily disadvantage women nor determine their social destiny. Women may be mothers, but they need not accept the responsibilities of motherhood: nurturing, educating and raising children by devoting themselves to home and family. The link between childbearing and child-rearing is cultural rather than biological: women are *expected* to stay at home, bring up their children and look after the house because of the structure of traditional family life. Domestic responsibilities could be undertaken by the husband, or they could be shared equally between husband and wife in so-called 'symmetrical families'. Moreover, child-rearing could be carried out by the community or the state, or it could be undertaken by relatives, as in 'extended' families.

Feminists have traditionally challenged the idea that biology is destiny by drawing a sharp distinction between sex and gender. 'Sex', in this sense, refers to biological differences between females and males; these differences are natural and therefore are unalterable. The most important sex differences are those that are linked to reproduction. 'Gender', on the other hand, is a cultural term; it refers to the different roles that society ascribes to women and men. Gender differences are typically imposed through contrasting stereotypes of 'masculinity' and 'femininity'. As Simone de Beauvoir (see p. 151) pointed out, 'One is not born, but rather becomes, a woman.' Ideas that support or legitimise male domination typically blur the distinction between sex and gender, and assume that all social distinctions between women and men are rooted in biology or anatomy. Feminists, in contrast, usually deny that there is a necessary or logical link between sex and gender, and emphasise that gender differences are socially, or even politically, constructed.

Androgyny: The possession of both male and female characteristics; used to imply that human beings are sexless 'persons' in the sense that sex is irrelevant to their social role or political status.

Most feminists believe that sex differences between women and men are relatively minor and neither explain nor justify gender distinctions. As a result, human nature is thought to be **androgynous**. All human beings, regardless of sex, possess the genetic inheritance of a mother and a father, and therefore embody a blend of both female and male attributes or traits. Such a view accepts

PERSPECTIVES ON …
GENDER

LIBERALS have traditionally regarded differences between women and men as being of entirely private or personal significance. In public and political life, all people are considered as individuals, gender being as irrelevant as ethnicity or social class. In this sense, individualism is 'gender-blind'.

CONSERVATIVES have traditionally emphasised the social and political significance of gender divisions, arguing that they imply that the sexual division of labour between women and men is natural and inevitable. Gender is thus one of the factors that give society its organic and hierarchical character.

SOCIALISTS, like liberals, have rarely treated gender as a politically significant category. When gender divisions are significant it is usually because they reflect and are sustained by deeper economic and class inequalities.

FEMINISTS usually see gender as a cultural or political distinction, in contrast to biological and ineradicable sexual differences. Gender divisions are therefore a manifestation of male power. Difference feminists may nevertheless believe that gender differences reflect a psycho-biological gulf between female and male attributes and sensibilities.

that sex differences are biological facts of life but insists that they have no social, political or economic significance. Women and men should not be judged by their sex, but as individuals, as 'persons'. The goal of feminism is therefore the achievement of genderless 'personhood'. Establishing a concept of gender that is divorced from biological sex had crucial significance for feminist theory. Not only did it highlight the possibility of social change – socially constructed identities can be reconstructed or even demolished – but it also drew attention to the processes through which women had been 'engendered' and therefore oppressed.

Although most feminists have regarded the sex/gender distinction as empowering, others have attacked it. These attacks have been launched from two main directions. The first, advanced by so-called '**difference feminists**', suggests that there are profound and perhaps ineradicable differences between women and men. From this '**essentialist**' perspective, accepted by some but by no means all difference feminists, social and cultural characteristics are seen to reflect deeper biological differences. The second attack on the sex/gender distinction challenges the categories themselves. Postmodern feminists have questioned whether 'sex' is as clear-cut a biological distinction as is usually assumed. For example, the features of 'biological womanhood' do not apply to many who are classified as women: some women cannot bear children, some women are not sexually attracted to men, and so on. If there is a biology–culture continuum rather than a fixed biological/cultural divide, the categories 'female' and 'male' become more or less arbitrary, and the concepts of sex and gender become hopelessly entangled. An alternative approach to gender has been advanced by the trans movement, which seeks to explode the dualistic conception of gender, in which the human world is tidily divided into female and male parts. Such thinking is examined later in the chapter, in connection with *transfeminism*.

Difference feminism: A form of feminism which holds that there are deep and possibly ineradicable differences between women and men, whether these are rooted in biology, culture or material experience.

Essentialism: The belief that things have a core or fundamental nature, or 'essence'; the term is often used to suggest that biological factors are crucial in determining psychological and behavioural traits.

PATRIARCHY

Feminists use the concept of '**patriarchy**' to describe the power relationship between women and men. The term literally means 'rule by the father' (*pater* meaning father in Latin). Some feminists employ 'patriarchy' only in this specific and limited sense, to describe the structure of the family and the dominance of the husband/father within it, preferring to use broader terms such as 'male supremacy' or 'male dominance' to describe gender relations in society at large. However, feminists believe that the dominance of the father within the family symbolises male supremacy in all other institutions. Many would argue, moreover, that the patriarchal family lies at the heart of a systematic process of male domination, in that it reproduces male dominance in all other walks of life, including society, the state and, for socialist feminists in particular, the economy. Patriarchy is therefore commonly used in a broader sense to mean quite simply 'rule by men', both within the family and outside. Kate Millett (see below), for instance, described 'patriarchal government' as an institution whereby 'that half of the populace which is female is controlled by that half which is male'. She suggested that patriarchy contains two principles: 'male shall dominate female, elder male shall dominate younger'. A patriarchy is therefore a hierarchic society, characterised by both sexual and generational oppression.

The concept of patriarchy is, nevertheless, broad. Feminists may believe that men have dominated women in all societies, but accept that the forms and degree of oppression have varied considerably in different cultures and at different times. At least in western countries, the social position of women improved significantly during the twentieth century as a result of the achievement of the vote and broader access to education, changes in marriage and divorce law, the legalisation of abortion, and so on. However, in parts of the developing world, patriarchy still assumes a cruel, even gruesome, form: 80 million women, mainly in Africa, are subjected to the practice of circumcision; bride murders still occur in India; and the persistence of the dowry system ensures that female children are often unwanted and sometimes allowed to die.

Patriarchy: Literally, rule by the father; often used more generally to describe the dominance of men and subordination of women in society at large.

KEY FIGURE

Kate Millett (born 1934)

A US feminist writer, political activist and artist, Millett had a profound impact on radical feminism. Setting out to prove that 'sex is a status category with political implications', she argued that the origins of female oppression can be traced back to the structure of the traditional family. The overthrow of the patriarchal family is therefore the key to women's liberation. Millett based such thinking on the belief that profound psycho-social differences between males and females are essentially a product, not of biology, but of early socialisation within the family, the basic elements of gender identity being established before the age of eighteen months. In *Sexual Politics* (1970), Millett analysed the work of male writers, from D. H. Lawrence to Norman Mailer, highlighting their use of sex to degrade and undermine women. In her view, such literature reflects deeply patriarchal attitudes that pervade culture and society at large, providing evidence that patriarchy is a historical and social constant. For more on Millett, see above, pp. 139, 143, 151 and 152.

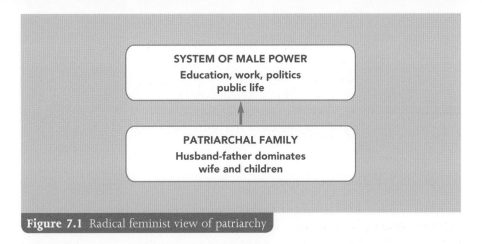

Figure 7.1 Radical feminist view of patriarchy

Feminists do not have a single or simple analysis of patriarchy, however. Liberal feminists, to the extent that they use the term, use it to draw attention to the unequal distribution of rights and entitlements in society at large. The face of patriarchy they highlight is therefore the under-representation of women in senior positions in politics, business, the professions and public life generally. Socialist feminists tend to emphasise the economic aspects of patriarchy. In their view, patriarchy operates in tandem with capitalism, gender subordination and class inequality being interlinked systems of oppression. Some socialist feminists, indeed, reject the term altogether, on the grounds that gender inequality is merely a consequence of the class system: capitalism, not patriarchy, is the issue. Radical feminists, on the other hand, place considerable stress on patriarchy. They see it as a systematic, institutionalised and pervasive form of male power that is rooted in the family. Patriarchy thus expresses the belief that the pattern of male domination and female subordination that characterises society at large is, essentially, a reflection of the power structures that operate within domestic life, as illustrated in Figure 7.1.

THE PERSONAL IS POLITICAL

Traditional notions of what is 'political' locate politics in the arena of public rather than private life. Politics has usually been understood as an activity that takes place within a 'public sphere' of government institutions, political parties, pressure groups and public debate. Family life and personal relationships have normally been thought to be part of a 'private sphere', and therefore to be 'non-political'. Modern feminists, on the other hand, insist that politics is an activity that takes place within all social groups and is not merely confined to the affairs of government or other public bodies. Politics exists whenever and wherever social conflict is found. Kate Millett (1970), for example, defined politics as 'power-structured relationships, arrangements whereby one group of persons is controlled by another'. The relationship between government and its citizens is therefore clearly political, but so is the relationship between employers and workers within a firm, and also relationships in the family, between husbands and wives, and between parents and children.

The definition of what is 'political' is not merely of academic interest. Feminists argue that sexual inequality has been preserved precisely because the sexual division of labour that runs through society has been thought of as 'natural' rather than 'political'. Traditionally, the public sphere of life, encompassing politics, work, art and literature, has been the preserve of men, while women have been confined to an essentially private existence, centred on the family and domestic responsibilities, as illustrated in Figure 7.2. If politics takes place only within the public sphere, the role of women and the question of sexual equality are issues of little or no political importance. Women, restricted to the private role of housewife and mother, are in effect excluded from politics.

Feminists have therefore sought to challenge the divide between 'public man' and 'private woman' (Elshtain, 1993). However, they have not always agreed about what it means to break down the public/private divide, about how it can be achieved, or about how far it is desirable. Radical feminists have been the keenest opponents of the idea that politics stops at the front door, proclaiming instead that 'the personal is the political'. Female oppression is thus thought to operate in all walks of life, and in many respects originates in the family itself. Radical feminists have therefore been concerned to analyse what can be called 'the politics of everyday life'. This includes the process of conditioning in the family, the distribution of housework and other domestic responsibilities, and the politics of personal and sexual conduct. For some feminists, breaking down the public/private divide implies transferring the responsibilities of private life to the state or other public bodies. For example, the burden of child rearing on women could be relieved by more generous welfare support for families or the provision of nursery schools or crèches at work. Socialist feminists have also viewed the private sphere as political, in that they have linked women's roles within the conventional family to the maintenance of the capitalist economic system. However, although liberal feminists object to restrictions on women's access to the public sphere of education, work and political life, they also warn against the dangers of politicising the private sphere, which, according to liberal theory, is a realm of personal choice and individual freedom.

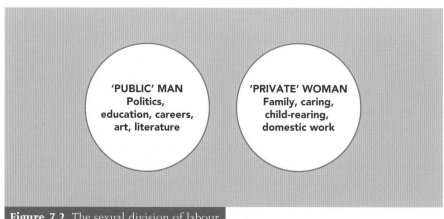

'PUBLIC' MAN
Politics,
education, careers,
art, literature

'PRIVATE' WOMAN
Family, caring,
child-rearing,
domestic work

Figure 7.2 The sexual division of labour

EQUALITY AND DIFFERENCE

Although the goal of feminism is the overthrow of patriarchy and the ending of sexist oppression, feminists have sometimes been uncertain about what this means in practice and how it can be brought about. Traditionally, women have demanded equality with men, even to the extent that feminism is often characterised as a movement for the achievement of sexual equality. However, the issue of equality has also exposed major fault lines within feminism: feminists have embraced contrasting notions of equality and some have entirely rejected equality in favour of the idea of difference. Liberal feminists champion legal and political equality with men. They have supported an equal rights agenda which would enable women to compete in public life on equal terms with men, regardless of sex. Equality thus means equal access to the public realm. Socialist feminists, in contrast, argue that equal rights may be meaningless unless women also enjoy social equality. Equality, in this sense, has to apply in terms of economic power, and so must address issues such as the ownership of wealth, pay differentials and the distinction between waged and unwaged labour. Radical feminists, for their part, are primarily concerned about equality in family and personal life. Equality must therefore operate, for example, in terms of child care and other domestic responsibilities, the control of one's own body, and sexual expression and fulfilment.

Despite tensions between them, these egalitarian positions are united in viewing gender differences in a negative light. **Equality feminism** links 'difference' to patriarchy, seeing it as a manifestation of oppression or subordination. From this viewpoint, the feminist project is defined by the desire to liberate women from 'difference'. However, other feminists champion difference rather than equality. Difference feminists regard the very notion of equality as either misguided or simply undesirable. To want to be equal to a man implies that women are 'male identified', in that they define their goals in terms of what men are or what men have. The demand for equality therefore embodies a desire to be 'like men'. Although feminists seek to overthrow patriarchy, many warn against the danger of modelling themselves on men, which would require them, for example, to adopt the competitive and aggressive behaviour that characterises male society. For many feminists, liberation means achieving fulfilment as women; in other words, being 'female identified'.

Difference feminists are thus often said to subscribe to a '**pro-woman**' position, which accepts that sex differences have political and social importance. This is based on the essentialist belief that women and men are fundamentally different at a psycho-biological level. The aggressive and competitive nature of men and the creative and empathetic character of women are thought to reflect deeper hormonal and other genetic differences, rather than simply the structure of society. To idealise androgyny or personhood and ignore sex differences is therefore a mistake. Women should recognise and celebrate the distinctive characteristics of the female sex; they should seek liberation *through* difference, as developed and fulfilled women, not as sexless 'persons'. In the form of **cultural feminism**, this has led to an emphasis on women's crafts, art and literature, and

Equality feminism: A form of feminism that aspires to the goal of sexual equality, whether this is defined in terms of formal rights, the control of resources, or personal power.

'Pro-woman' feminism: A form of feminism that advances a positive image of women's attributes and propensities, usually stressing creativity, caring and human sympathy, and cooperation.

Cultural feminism: A form of feminism that emphasises an engagement with a woman-centred culture and lifestyle, and is typically repelled by the corrupting and aggressive male world of political activism.

on experiences that are unique to women and promote a sense of 'sisterhood', such as childbirth, motherhood and menstruation.

TYPES OF FEMINISM

LIBERAL FEMINISM

Early feminism, particularly the 'first wave' of the women's movement, was deeply influenced by the ideas and values of liberalism. The first major feminist text, Wollstonecraft's *A Vindication of the Rights of Woman* ([1792] 1967), argued that women should be entitled to the same rights and privileges as men on the grounds that they are 'human beings'. She claimed that the 'distinction of sex' would become unimportant in political and social life if women gained access to education and were regarded as rational creatures in their own right. John Stuart Mill's *On the Subjection of Women* ([1869] 1970), written in collaboration with Harriet Taylor, proposed that society should be organised according to the principle of 'reason', and that 'accidents of birth' such as sex should be irrelevant. Women would therefore be entitled to the rights and liberties enjoyed by men and, in particular, the right to vote.

'Second-wave' feminism also has a significant liberal component. Liberal feminism has dominated the women's movement in the USA; for instance, the publication of Betty Friedan's *The Feminine Mystique* marked the resurgence of feminist thought in the 1960s. The 'feminine mystique' to which Friedan referred is the cultural myth that women seek security and fulfilment in domestic life and 'feminine' behaviour, a myth that serves to discourage women from entering employment, politics and public life in general. She highlighted what she called 'the problem with no name', by which she meant the sense of despair and deep unhappiness many women experience because they are confined to a domestic existence and are thus unable to gain fulfilment in a career or through political life. In 1966, Friedan helped to found and became the first leader of the

---

Differences between ...

EQUALITY AND DIFFERENCE FEMINISM

EQUALITY FEMINISM	DIFFERENCE FEMINISM
• androgyny	• essentialism
• personhood	• sisterhood
• human rights	• women's rights
• gender equality	• sexual liberation
• abolish difference	• celebrate difference
• sex/gender divide	• sex equals gender
• transcend biology	• embrace biology
• pro-human	• pro-woman
• men are redeemable	• men are 'the problem'
• engagement with men	• feminist separatism

National Organization for Women (NOW), which has developed into a powerful pressure group and the largest women's organisation in the world.

The philosophical basis of liberal feminism lies in the principle of individualism (see p. 12), the belief that the human individual is all-important and therefore that all individuals are of equal moral worth. Individuals are entitled to equal treatment, regardless of their sex, race, colour, creed or religion. If individuals are to be judged, it should be on rational grounds, on the content of their character, their talents, or their personal worth. Liberals express this belief in the demand for equal rights: all individuals are entitled to participate in, or gain access to, public or political life. Any form of discrimination against women in this respect should therefore be prohibited. Wollstonecraft, for example, insisted that education, in her day the province of men, should be opened up to women. J. S. Mill argued in favour of equal citizenship and political rights. Indeed, the entire suffrage movement was based on liberal individualism and the conviction that female emancipation would be brought about once women enjoyed equal voting rights with men. Liberal feminist groups therefore aim to break down the remaining legal and social pressures that restrict women from pursuing careers and being politically active. They seek, in particular, to increase the representation of women in senior positions in public and political life.

Liberal feminism is essentially reformist: it seeks to open up public life to equal competition between women and men, rather than to challenge what many other feminists see as the patriarchal structure of society itself. In particular, liberal feminists generally do not wish to abolish the distinction between the public and private spheres of life. Reform is necessary, they argue, but only to ensure the establishment of equal rights in the public sphere: the right to education, the right to vote, the right to pursue a career and so on. Significant reforms have undoubtedly been achieved in the industrialised West, notably the extension of the franchise, the 'liberalisation' of divorce law and abortion, equal pay and so on. Nevertheless, far less attention has been paid by liberal feminists to the private sphere, specifically to the sexual division of labour and distribution of power within the family.

Liberal feminists have usually assumed that women and men have different natures and inclinations, and therefore accept that, at least in part, women's leaning towards family and domestic life is influenced by natural impulses and so reflects a willing choice. This certainly applied in the case of nineteenth-century feminists, who regarded the traditional structure of family life as 'natural', but it is also evident in the work of modern liberal feminists such as Friedan. In The Second Stage (1983) Friedan discussed the problem of reconciling the achievement of 'personhood', made possible by opening up broader opportunities for women in work and public life, with the need for love, represented by children, home and the family. Friedan's emphasis on the continuing and central importance of the family in women's lives has been criticised by more radical feminists for contributing to a 'mystique of motherhood'. Others have condemned it for suggesting that women can 'have it all', being successful in terms of career advancement as well as in terms of motherhood and homemaking.

Finally, the demand for equal rights, which lies at the core of liberal feminism, has principally attracted those women whose education and social backgrounds equip them to take advantage of wider educational and career opportunities. For example, nineteenth-century feminists and the leaders of the suffrage movement were usually educated, middle-class women who had the opportunity to benefit from the right to vote, pursue a career or enter public life. The demand for equal rights assumes that all women would have the opportunity to take advantage of, for example, better educational and economic opportunities. In reality, women are judged not only by their talents and abilities, but also by social and economic factors. If emancipation simply means the achievement of equal rights and opportunities for women and men, other forms of social disadvantage – for example, those linked to social class and race – are ignored. Liberal feminism may therefore reflect the interests of white, middle-class women in developed societies but fail to address the problems of working-class women, black women and women in the developing world.

SOCIALIST FEMINISM

Although some early feminists subscribed to socialist ideas, socialist feminism only became prominent in the second half of the twentieth century. In contrast to their liberal counterparts, socialist feminists have not believed that women simply face political or legal disadvantages that can be remedied by equal legal rights or the achievement of equal opportunities. Rather, they argue that the relationship between the sexes is rooted in the social and economic structure itself, and that nothing short of profound social change, some would say a social revolution, can offer women the prospect of genuine emancipation.

The central theme of socialist feminism is that patriarchy can only be understood in the light of social and economic factors. The classic statement of this argument was developed in Friedrich Engels' *The Origins of the Family, Private Property and the State* ([1884] 1976). Engels (see p. 72) suggested that the position of women in society had changed fundamentally with the development of capitalism and the institution of private property. In pre-capitalist societies, family life had been communistic, and 'mother right' – the inheritance of property and social position through the female line – was widely observed. Capitalism, however, being based on the ownership of private property by men, had overthrown 'mother right' and brought about what Engels called 'the world historical defeat of the female sex'. Like many subsequent socialist feminists, Engels believed that female oppression operates through the institution of the family. The 'bourgeois family' is patriarchal and oppressive because men wish to ensure that their property will be passed on only to their sons. Men achieve undisputed paternity by insisting on monogamous marriage, a restriction that is rigorously applied to wives, depriving them of other sexual partners but, as Engels noted, is routinely ignored by their husbands. Women are compensated for this repression by the development of a 'cult of femininity', which extols the attractions of romantic love but, in reality, is an organised hypocrisy designed to protect male privileges and property. Other socialist feminists have proposed that the traditional, patriarchal family should be replaced by a system of communal living and 'free love', as advocated by

KEY FIGURE

Charlotte Perkins Gilman (1860–1935)

 A US writer, lecturer and campaigner for social reform, Gilman was a prominent early socialist feminist. In *Women and Economics* (1898), she analysed gender relations within a social Darwinian framework. Arguing that women's subjugation derives essentially from their economic dependence on men, seen as 'sex slavery', Gilman called for an expansion of women's access to paid employment made possible by a sharing of housework between husbands and wives and the increasing use of centralised nurseries and community kitchens. She also anticipated aspects of radical feminism in drawing attention to the ways in which androcentric culture prepares girls and women for a life of domesticity and subordination, and in championing the idea of the mother-centric world. Gilman thus highlighted the pressures on young girls to conform to social expectations about their future role that stem from, for example, the toys they play with and the clothes they wear. However, like most feminists of her era, she also accepted the existence of inherited sex-linked behaviours. For more on Gilman, see below.

early utopian socialists such as Charles Fourier (1772–1837) and Robert Owen (1771–1858). Figures such as Charlotte Perkins Gilman (see above) nevertheless argued that women's subjugation could be overcome through the reform, rather than the abolition, of the institution of monogamous marriage.

Most socialist feminists agree that the confinement of women to a domestic sphere of housework and motherhood serves the economic interests of capitalism. As Sheila Rowbotham (see p. 150) has thus argued, the struggle for women's liberation is essentially bound up with the struggle against capitalism. Some socialist feminists have argued that women constitute a 'reserve army of labour', which can be recruited into the workforce when there is a need to increase production, but easily shed and returned to domestic life during a recession, without imposing a burden on employers or the state. At the same time, women's domestic labour is vital to the health and efficiency of the economy. In bearing and rearing children, women are producing the next generation of capitalism's workers. Similarly, in their role as housewives, women relieve men of the burden of housework and child-rearing, allowing them to concentrate their time and energy on paid and productive employment. The traditional family provides the worker with a powerful incentive to find and keep a job because he has a wife and children to support. However, as Rowbotham has pointed out, the family is also a place where men take refuge from the alienation and frustrations of life as a 'wage slave'. In contrast to their role as capitalist workers, men within the family enjoy the status and power that comes from being 'breadwinners', and are also relieved of the burden of 'trivial' domestic labour.

Although socialist feminists agree that the 'women's question' cannot be separated from social and economic life, they are profoundly divided about the nature of that link. Gender divisions clearly cut across class cleavages, creating tension within socialist feminist analysis about the relative importance of gender and social class, and raising particularly difficult questions for Marxist feminists. Orthodox Marxists insist on the primacy of class politics over sexual

KEY FIGURE

Sheila Rowbotham (born 1943)

A British feminist, socialist and historian, Rowbotham has been active within the UK women's movement since its origins in the 1960s, advocating a participatory, decentralised approach to social change that links the needs and struggles of all oppressed groups. In works such as *Women, Resistance and Revolution* (1972) and *Hidden from History* (1973), she sought to reclaim the past for women as a source of knowledge and strength that has the potential to contribute to present campaigns. Attempting to combine Marxist and feminist perspectives, a key theme in Rowbotham's work has been to explore the complex links between class exploitation and the subjection of women, helping to explain the dual oppression to which capitalism subjects women. This can be seen, for instance, both in the pressure that women in a capitalism system are under to sell their labour in order to support their family, and in the extent to which the family operates not just as a mechanism for controlling women but also serves as a refuge for alienated male workers. For more on Rowbotham, see p. 149.

politics. This suggests that class exploitation is a deeper and more significant process than sexual oppression. It also suggests that women's emancipation will be a by-product of a social revolution in which capitalism is overthrown and replaced by socialism. Women seeking liberation should therefore recognise that the 'class war' is more important than the 'sex war'. Such an analysis suggests that feminists should devote their energies to the labour movement rather than support a separate and divisive women's movement.

However, modern socialist feminists have found it increasingly difficult to accept the primacy of class politics over sexual politics. In part, this was a consequence of the disappointing progress that had been made by women in state-socialist societies such as the Soviet Union, suggesting that socialism does not, in itself, end patriarchy. For modern socialist feminists, sexual oppression is every bit as important as class exploitation. Many of them subscribe to a form of neo-Marxism, which accepts the interplay of economic, social, political and cultural forces in society. They therefore refuse to analyse the position of women in simple economic terms and have, instead, given attention to the cultural and ideological roots of patriarchy. For example, Juliet Mitchell (1971), suggested that women fulfil four social functions: (1) they are members of the workforce and are active in production; (2) they bear children and thus reproduce the human species; (3) they are responsible for socialising children; and (4) they are sex objects. From this perspective, liberation requires that women achieve emancipation in each of these areas, and not merely that the capitalist class system is replaced by socialism.

RADICAL FEMINISM

One of the distinctive features of second-wave feminism is that many feminist writers moved beyond the perspectives of existing political ideologies. Gender differences in society were regarded for the first time as important in

KEY FIGURE

Simone de Beauvoir (1908–86)

 A French novelist, playwright and social critic, de Beauvoir, in her work, reopened the issue of gender politics and foreshadowed the ideas of later radical feminists. Addressing the question 'What is a woman?' she rejected the idea that women can be understood in terms either of their biological function or of the idea of the eternal feminine. In *The Second Sex* (1949), she developed a complex critique of patriarchal culture, in which the masculine is represented as the positive or the norm, while the feminine is portrayed as the 'other' – fundamentally limiting women's freedom and denying them their full humanity. 'Otherness' thus explains the imbalances and inequalities that exist between men and women in terms of the fact that while men are defined independently of women, as free and autonomous beings, women are always defined in relation to men; they are man's 'other'. De Beauvoir placed her faith in rationality and critical analysis as the means of exposing this process. For more on de Beauvoir, see pp. 140 and 151.

themselves, needing to be understood in their own terms. Liberal and socialist ideas had already been adapted to throw light on the position of women in society, but neither acknowledged that gender is the most fundamental of all social divisions. During the 1960s and 1970s, however, the feminist movement sought to uncover the influence of patriarchy not only in politics, public life and the economy, but in all aspects of social, personal and sexual existence. This trend was evident in the pioneering work of Simone de Beauvoir, and was developed by early radical feminists such as Eva Figes, Germaine Greer and Kate Millett.

Figes' *Patriarchal Attitudes* (1970) drew attention not to the more familiar legal or social disadvantages suffered by women, but to the fact that patriarchal values and beliefs pervade the culture, philosophy, morality and religion of society. In all walks of life and learning, women are portrayed as inferior and

Differences between …
LIBERAL AND RADICAL FEMINISM

LIBERAL FEMINISM
- female emancipation
- gender inequality
- individualism
- conventional politics
- public/private divide
- access to public realm
- equal rights/opportunities
- reform/gradualism
- political activism

RADICAL FEMINISM
- women's liberation
- patriarchy
- sisterhood
- the personal is political
- transform private realm
- gender equality
- sexual politics
- revolutionary change
- consciousness-raising

subordinate to men, a stereotype of 'femininity' being imposed on women by men. In *The Female Eunuch* (1970), Greer suggested that women are conditioned to a passive sexual role, which has repressed their true sexuality as well as the more active and adventurous side of their personalities. In effect, women have been 'castrated' and turned into sexless objects by the cultural stereotype of the 'eternal feminine'. In *Sexual Politics* (1970), Millett described patriarchy as a 'social constant' running through all political, social and economic structures and found in every historical and contemporary society, as well as in all major religions. The different roles of women and men have their origin in a process of 'conditioning': from a very early age boys and girls are encouraged to conform to very specific gender identities. This process takes place largely within the family – 'patriarchy's chief institution' – but it is also evident in literature, art, public life and the economy. Millett proposed that patriarchy should be challenged through a process of '**consciousness–raising**', an idea influenced by the Black Power movement of the 1960s and early 1970s.

The central feature of radical feminism is the belief that sexual oppression is the most fundamental feature of society and that other forms of injustice – class exploitation, racial hatred and so on – are merely secondary. Gender is thought to be the deepest social cleavage and the most politically significant; more important, for example, than social class, race or nation. Radical feminists have therefore insisted that society be understood as 'patriarchal' to highlight the central role of sex oppression. Patriarchy thus refers to a systematic, institutionalised and pervasive process of gender oppression.

For most radical feminists, patriarchy is a system of politico-cultural oppression, whose origins lie in the structure of family, domestic and personal life. Female liberation thus requires a sexual revolution in which these structures are overthrown and replaced. Such a goal is based on the assumption that human nature is essentially androgynous. However, radical feminism encompasses a number of divergent elements, some of which emphasise the fundamental and unalterable difference between women and men. An example of this is the 'pro-woman' position, particularly strong in France and the USA. This position extols the positive virtues of fertility and motherhood. Women should not try to be 'more like men'. Instead, they should recognise and embrace their sisterhood, the bonds that link them to all other women. The pro-woman position therefore accepts that women's attitudes and values are different from men's, but implies that in certain respects women are superior, possessing the qualities of creativity, sensitivity and caring, which men can never fully appreciate or develop. Such ideas have been associated in particular with ecofeminism, which is examined in Chapter 8.

Consciousness-raising: Strategies to remodel social identity and challenge cultural inferiority by an emphasis on pride, self-worth and self-assertion.

The acceptance of deep and possibly unalterable differences between women and men has led some feminists towards cultural feminism, a retreat from the corrupting and aggressive male world of political activism into an apolitical, woman-centred culture and lifestyle. Conversely, other feminists have become politically assertive and even revolutionary. If sex differences are natural, then

	LIBERAL FEMINISM	RADICAL FEMINISM	SOCIALIST FEMINISM	BLACK FEMINISM	POSTMODERN FEMINISM
KEY THEMES	• INDIVIDUALISM • RIGHTS • LEGAL AND POLITICAL EQUALITY	• PATRIARCHY • PERSONAL IS POLITICAL • SISTERHOOD	• CLASS OPPRESSION • BOURGEOIS FAMILY • CAPITALISM AND PATRIARCHY LINKED	• RACISM • MULTIPLE OPPRESSIONS • DIFFERENCES BETWEEN WOMEN	• ANTI-FOUNDATIONALISM • DISCOURSE • DECONSTRUCT GENDER IDENTITIES
CORE GOAL	EQUAL ACCESS FOR WOMEN AND MEN TO THE PUBLIC REALM	RADICAL TRANSFORMATION OF ALL SPHERES OF LIFE	RESTRUCTURE ECONOMIC LIFE TO ACHIEVE GENDER EQUALITY	COUNTER INTERCONNECTED RACIAL, GENDER AND CLASS STRUCTURES	EMBRACE FLUID, FREE-FLOATING GENDER IDENTITIES

Figure 7.3 Types of feminism

the roots of patriarchy lie within the male sex itself. 'All men' are physically and psychologically disposed to oppress 'all women'; in other words, 'men are the enemy'. This clearly leads in the direction of feminist separatism. Men constitute an oppressive 'sex-class' dedicated to aggression, domination and destruction; so the female 'sex-class' is therefore the 'universal victim'. For example, Susan Brownmiller's *Against Our Will* (1975) emphasised that men dominate women through a process of physical and sexual abuse. Men have created an 'ideology of rape', which amounts to a 'conscious process of intimidation by which all men keep all women in a state of fear'. Brownmiller argued that men rape because they can, because they have the 'biological capacity to rape', and that even men who do not rape nevertheless benefit from the fear and anxiety that rape provokes among all women.

Feminists who have pursued this line of argument also believe that it has profound implications for women's personal and sexual conduct. Sexual equality and harmony is impossible because all relationships between women and men must involve oppression. Heterosexual women are therefore thought to be 'male identified', incapable of fully realising their true nature and becoming 'female identified'. This has led to the development of political lesbianism, which holds that sexual preferences are an issue of crucial political importance for women. Only women who remain celibate or choose lesbianism can regard themselves as 'woman-identified women'. In the slogan attributed to Ti-Grace Atkinson: 'feminism is the theory; lesbianism is the practice' (Charvet, 1982). However, the issues of separatism and lesbianism have deeply divided the women's movement. The majority of feminists see such uncompromising positions as a distorted reflection of the misogyny, or woman-hating, that pervades traditional male society. Instead, they remain faithful to the goal of sexual equality and the belief that it is possible to establish harmony between women and men in a non-sexist society. Hence, they believe that sexual preferences are strictly a matter of personal choice and not a question of political commitment.

DEVELOPMENTS IN MODERN FEMINISM

Since the 1970s, it has become increasingly difficult to analyse feminism simply in terms of the three-fold division into liberal, socialist and radical traditions. Tensions within the 'core' traditions have sometimes deepened, and, on other occasions, boundaries between the traditions have been blurred. New forms of feminism have also emerged, including third-wave feminism, transfeminism and postfeminism.

Third-wave feminism

The term 'third-wave feminism' has been adopted increasingly since the 1990s by a younger generation of feminist theorists for whom the campaigns and demands of the 1960s and 1970s women's movement have seemed to be of limited relevance to their own lives. This was both because of the emergence of new issues in feminist politics and because of the political and social transformations that second-wave feminism has brought about (Heywood and Drake, 1997). If there is a unifying theme within third-wave feminism it is a more radical engagement with the politics of difference, especially going beyond those strands within radical feminism that emphasise that women are different from men by showing a greater concern with differences *between* women. In so doing, third-wave feminists have tried to rectify an over-emphasis within earlier forms of feminism on the aspirations and experiences of middle-class, white women in developed societies, thereby illustrating the extent to which the contemporary women's movement is characterised by diversity, hybridity and a greater awareness of intersectionality.

This has allowed the voices of, among others, low-income women, women in the developing world and 'women of colour' to be heard more effectively. Black feminism has been particularly effective in this respect, challenging the tendency within conventional forms of feminism to ignore racial differences and to suggest that women endure a common oppression by virtue of their sex. Especially strong in the USA, and developed in the writings of theorists such as bell hooks (see p. 155), black feminism portrays sexism and racism as linked systems of oppression, and highlights the particular and complex range of gender, racial and economic disadvantages that confront women of colour.

Poststructuralism:
An intellectual tradition, related to postmodernism, that emphasises that all ideas and concepts are expressed in language that itself is enmeshed in complex relations of power.

Discourse: Human interaction, especially communication: discourse may disclose or illustrate power relations.

In being concerned about issues of 'identity', and the processes through which women's identities are constructed (and can be reconstructed), third-wave feminism also reflects the influence of **poststructuralism**. Influenced particularly by the ideas of the French philosopher Michel Foucault (1926–84), poststructuralism has drawn attention to the link between power and systems of thought using the idea of **discourse**, or 'discourses of power'. In crude terms, this implies that knowledge is power. Poststructuralist or postmodernist feminists question the idea of a fixed female identity, also rejecting the notion that insights can be drawn from a distinctive set of women's experiences. From the poststructural perspective, even the idea of 'woman' may be nothing more than a fiction, as supposedly indisputable biological differences between women and men are, in significant ways, shaped by gendered discourses (not all women are

KEY FIGURE

bell hooks (born 1952)

A cultural critic, feminist and writer, Gloria Jean Watkins (better known by her pen name, bell hooks) has emphasised that feminist theorising must take account of intersectionality and be approached from the lenses of gender, race and social class. In her classic *Ain't I a Woman* (1985), hooks examined the history of black women in the USA. Arguing that in the USA racism takes precedence over sexism, she advanced a powerful critique of the implicit racism of the mainstream women's movement. This has not only focused primarily on the concerns of white, college-educated and middle/upper class women, but also portrayed feminism as a lifestyle choice rather than a political commitment. Her other books include *Feminism is for Everyone* (2000). This critique focused not only on the tendency of the feminist movement to be dominated by the concerns of white, college-educated and middle/upper class women but also on the limitations of viewing feminism as a lifestyle choice. Hooks has claimed that women of colour tend to be ignored by both the feminist and black liberation movements. Since the former mainly articulates the needs of white women, while the latter primarily addresses the needs of black men, black women end up being invisible in political terms. For more on hooks, see p. 154.

capable of bearing children, for example). However, it is questionable whether the consistent application of poststructural or postmodern analysis is compatible with the maintenance of a distinctively feminist political orientation.

Transfeminism

Transfeminism (also written as 'trans feminism') emerged out of feminism's encounters, from the early 1990s onwards, with the concerns of people who identify themselves as **transgender** or **transsexual**. Although what is called 'trans politics' is not associated with a single or simple theory of gender, its central theme is a rejection of the binary conception of gender, with a stress, instead, on gender and sexual ambiguity, sometimes based on the idea of a gender continuum. People are thus seen as neither women nor men (Beasley, 2005). From the trans perspective, gender is not something ascribed to individuals by society, or imposed on them by cultural stereotypes; instead it is a matter of self-definition based on inner feelings. In this vein, Butler (2006) proposed a concept of gender as a reiterated social performance, rather than the expression of a prior reality.

Such thinking has nevertheless been viewed as deeply problematic by traditional feminists, not least because of the importance they placed on culturally defined gender in explaining the oppression of women. However, over time, there has been a greater willingness by feminists to take on board issues raised by the trans movement, while supporters of trans politics have increasingly recognised the extent to which its thinking may be applicable to all women (Scott-Dixon, 2006). Not only does this reflect widening support within feminism for a more personalised and nuanced approach to gender, but it also demonstrates a growing awareness of the parallels and overlaps that exist between sexism and **transphobia**.

Transgender: A term denoting or relating to people who do not conform to prevailing expectations about gender, usually by crossing over or moving between gender identities.

Transsexual: A term denoting or relating to people who do not conform to the sex they were assigned at birth, and who may seek to realign their gender and their sex through medical intervention.

Transphobia: Prejudice against or dislike of people who do not conform to prevailing expectations about gender identity.

Postfeminism

The process of de-radicalisation within feminism has nevertheless been most marked in relation to so-called 'postfeminism', which is defined by a rejection of second-wave feminist issues and themes, rather than by an attempt to update or remodel them. For instance, Camille Paglia (1990) attacked the tendency of feminism to portray women as 'victims', and insisted on the need for women to take greater responsibility for their own sexual and personal conduct. Similarly, in *Fire with Fire* (1994), Naomi Wolf called on women to use the 'new female power', based on the belief that the principal impediments to women's social advancement are psychological rather than political. Confronted by such tendencies, established feminists have sometimes protested against the rise of what they see as 'lifestyle feminism'. In *The Whole Woman* (1999), Germaine Greer attacked the notion that women are 'having it all', arguing that they have abandoned the goal of liberation and settled for a phoney equality that amounts to assimilation, aping male behaviour and male values. This, perhaps, highlights the capacity of patriarchy to reproduce itself generation after generation, in part by subordinating women through creating bogus forms of emancipation.

⑦ QUESTIONS FOR DISCUSSION

● Why and how have feminists challenged conventional notions of politics?

● Why has the distinction between sex and gender been so important to feminist analysis?

● What role does patriarchy play in feminist theory?

● Why do some feminists reject the goal of gender equality?

● To what extent is feminism compatible with liberalism?

● In what sense is radical feminism revolutionary?

● Is socialist feminism a contradiction in terms?

● Are the differences within feminism greater than the similarities?

● Have the core liberal, socialist and radical feminist traditions been exhausted?

● To what extent can feminism engage with the politics of difference?

● Is feminism compatible with trans theory?

● Have the objectives of feminism largely been achieved?

📖 FURTHER READING

Bryson, V., *Feminist Political Theory: An Introduction*, 3rd edn (2016). A thorough and accessible introduction to the development and range of feminist theories.

Butler, J., *Gender Trouble* (2006). A stimulating book that challenges traditional feminism's 'essentialist' notion of the female, and proposes a concept of gender as reiterated social performance.

Schneir, M., *The Vintage Book of Feminism: The Essential Writings of the Contemporary Women's Movement* (1995). A useful and comprehensive collection of writings from major feminist theorists.

Walters, M., *Feminism: A Very Short Introduction* (2005). A historical account of feminism that explores its earliest roots as well as the issues that have concerned feminism at different points in its development.

8 Ecologism

PREVIEW

The term 'ecology' was coined by the German zoologist Ernst Haeckel (1834–1919) in 1866, derived from the Greek *oikos*, meaning household or habitat. He used it to refer to 'the investigations of the total relations of the animal both in its organic and its inorganic environment'. Since the early years of the twentieth century, ecology has been recognised as a branch of biology that studies relationships among living organisms and their environment. It has, however, increasingly been converted into a political term by the use made of it, especially since the 1960s, by the growing green movement.

As a political ideology, ecologism (also known as 'green ideology' or 'green politics') is based on the belief that nature is an interconnected whole, embracing humans and non-humans, as well as the inanimate world. This has encouraged green thinkers to question (but not necessarily reject) the anthropocentric, or human-centred, assumptions of conventional political ideologies, allowing them to come up with new ideas about, among other things, economics, morality and social organisation. Nevertheless, there are different strains and tendencies within green ideology. Some greens are committed to 'shallow' ecology (sometimes viewed as environmentalism, as opposed to ecologism), which attempts to harness the lessons of ecology to human ends and needs, and embraces a 'modernist' or reformist approach to environmental change. 'Deep' ecologists, on the other hand, completely reject any lingering belief that the human species is in some way superior to, or more important than, any other species. Moreover, green ideology has drawn from a variety of other ideologies, notably socialism, anarchism and feminism, thereby acknowledging that the relationship between humankind and nature has an important social dimension. Each of these approaches to the environment offers a different model of the ecologically viable society of the future.

HISTORICAL OVERVIEW

Although modern environmental politics did not emerge until the 1960s and 1970s, ecological ideas can be traced back to much earlier times. Many have suggested that the principles of contemporary ecologism, or green ideology, owe much to ancient pagan religions, which stressed the concept of an Earth Mother, and to eastern religions such as Hinduism, Buddhism and Daoism. However, to a large extent, green ideology was, and remains, a reaction against the process of industrialisation. This was evident in the nineteenth century, when the spread of urban and industrial life created a profound nostalgia for an idealised rural existence, as conveyed by novelists such as Thomas Hardy (1840–1928) and political thinkers such as the UK libertarian socialist William Morris (1834–96) and Peter Kropotkin (see p. 104). This reaction was often strongest in those countries that had experienced the most rapid and dramatic process of industrialisation. For example, Germany's rapid industrialisation in the nineteenth century deeply scarred its political culture, creating powerful myths about the purity and dignity of peasant life, and giving rise to a strong 'back to nature' movement among German youth. Such romantic **pastoralism** was most likely to surface during the twentieth century in right-wing political doctrines, not least the 'Blood and Soil' ideas of the German Nazis.

The growth of green ideology since the 1960s has been provoked by the further and more intense advance of industrialisation and urbanisation, linked to the emergence of post-material sensibilities among young people in particular. Environmental concern has become more acute because of the fear that economic growth is endangering both the survival of the human race and the very planet it lives on. Such anxieties have been expressed in a growing body of literature. Rachel Carson's *The Silent Spring* (1962), a critique of the damage done to wildlife and the human world by the increased use of pesticides and other agricultural chemicals, is often considered to have been the first book to draw attention to a developing ecological crisis. Other important early works included

Pastoralism: A belief in the virtues of rural existence: simplicity, community and a closeness to nature, in contrast to the allegedly corrupting influence of urban and industrialised life.

KEY FIGURE

Rachel Carson (1907–64)

A US marine biologist and conservationist, Carson did much through her writings to stimulate interest in scientific and environmental topics, contributing to the growth of the green movement. In her best-selling *The Silent Spring* (1962), she highlighted the malign consequences to humans, birds, fish and plant life of the widespread use of powerful toxic agents, especially chemical pesticides, within US agriculture, reflecting the extent to which agri-business and state sponsorship threaten ecological balance and therefore sustainability. Carson's writings are suffused by a sense wonder at the integrity, stability and beauty of nature, especially as found in the sea; she viewed life as a 'miracle beyond comprehension', insisting that all forms of life deserve respect. However, although Carson condemned the idea of the 'control of nature', seeing it as a form of human arrogance, she adopted an essentially anthropocentric approach that emphasised that respect for ecology ultimately serves human interests. Her other books include *The Sea Around Us* (1951). For more on Carson, see above.

Ehrlich and Harriman's *How to Be a Survivor* (1971), Goldsmith et al.'s *Blueprint for Survival* (1972), the unofficial UN report *Only One Earth* (Ward and Dubois, 1972) and the Club of Rome's *The Limits to Growth* (Meadows et al., 1972).

A new generation of activist pressure groups have also developed – ranging from Greenpeace and Friends of the Earth to animal liberation activists and so-called 'eco-warrior' groups – campaigning on issues such as the dangers of pollution, the dwindling reserves of fossil fuels, deforestation and animal experimentation. Together with established and much larger groups, such as the Worldwide Fund for Nature, this has led to the emergence of a high profile and increasingly influential green movement. From the 1980s onwards, environmental questions have been kept high on the political agenda by green parties, which now exist in most industrialised countries, often modelling themselves on the pioneering efforts of the German Greens. Environmental issues have also become an increasingly major focus of international concern and activity. Indeed, as discussed in the final section of the chapter, the environment could arguably be regarded as *the* global political issue. The UN Conference on the Human Environment, held in Stockholm in 1972, was the first attempt to establish an international framework to promote a coordinated approach to environmental problems. The idea of 'sustainable development' (see p. 168) was advanced in the 1987 Brundtland Report, a product of the work of the UN World Commission on Environment and Development, and by the Rio 'Earth Summit' in 1992.

CORE IDEAS AND PRINCIPLES

ECOLOGY

The central principle of all forms of green thought is **ecology**. Ecology developed as a distinct branch of biology through a growing recognition that plants and animals are sustained by self-regulating natural systems – ecosystems – composed of both living and non-living elements. Simple examples of an ecosystem are a field, a forest or, as illustrated in Figure 8.1, a pond. All ecosystems tend towards a state of harmony or equilibrium through a system of self-regulation. Biologists refer to this as **homeostasis**. Food and other resources are recycled, and the population size of animals, insects and plants adjusts naturally to the available food supply. However, such ecosystems are not 'closed' or entirely self-sustaining: each interreacts with other ecosystems. A lake may constitute an ecosystem, but it also needs to be fed with fresh water from tributaries, and receive warmth and energy from the sun. In turn, the lake provides water and food for species living along its shores, including human communities. The natural world is therefore made up of a complex web of ecosystems, the largest of which is the global ecosystem, commonly called the 'ecosphere' or 'biosphere'.

The development of scientific ecology radically altered our understanding of the natural world and of the place of human beings within it. Ecology conflicts quite dramatically with the notion of humankind as 'the master' of nature, and instead suggests that a delicate network of interrelationships that had hitherto been ignored sustains each human community, indeed the entire human

Ecology: The study of the relationship between living organisms and the environment; ecology stresses the network of relationships that sustains all forms of life.

Homeostasis: The tendency of a system, especially the physiological systems of higher animals, to maintain internal equilibrium.

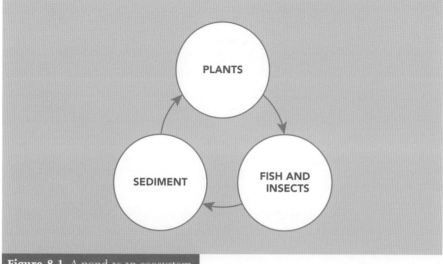

Figure 8.1 A pond as an ecosystem

species. Green thinkers argue that humankind currently faces the prospect of environmental disaster precisely because, in its passionate but blinkered pursuit of material wealth, it has upset the 'balance of nature' and endangered the very ecosystems that make human life possible. This has happened in a broad variety of ways. These include the exponential growth in the world's human population; the depletion of finite and irreplaceable fuel resources such as coal, oil and natural gas; the eradication of tropical rain forests that help clean the air and regulate the Earth's climate; the pollution of rivers, lakes and forests and the air itself; the use of chemical, hormonal and other additives to foodstuffs; and the threat to biodiversity that has resulted from the thousand-fold increase in species extinction that has coincided with the dominance of the human species.

Ecologism provides a radically different vision of nature and the place of human beings within it, one that favours **ecocentrism** and challenges **anthropocentrism**. Human nature is viewed not as an entity in its own right, but as part of a larger and more significant entity, nature or the world itself. Human nature is thus inseparable from what can be called 'non-human nature'. However, green or environmental thinkers have applied ecological ideas in different ways, and sometimes drawn quite different conclusions. The most important distinction in the environmental movement is between what the Norwegian philosopher and mountaineer Arne Naess (1912–2008) termed '**shallow ecology**' and '**deep ecology**'. The 'shallow' or 'humanist' perspective accepts the lessons of ecology but uses them essentially to further human needs and ends. In other words, it preaches that if we conserve and cherish the natural world, it will continue to sustain human life. This amounts to a form of 'light' or 'enlightened' anthropocentrism, and is reflected in a concern with issues such as cutting back on the use of finite, non-renewable resources and reducing pollution. While some regard such a stance as a form of 'weak' ecologism, others classify it as a means to distinguish it more clearly from ecologism. The 'deep' perspective, however, advances a form of 'strong' ecologism that completely rejects any lingering belief

Ecocentrism:
A theoretical orientation that gives priority to the maintenance of ecological balance rather than the achievement of human ends.

Anthropocentrism:
A belief that human needs and interests are of overriding moral and philosophical importance; the opposite of ecocentrism.

Shallow ecology: A green ideological perspective that harnesses the lessons of ecology to human needs and ends, and is associated with values such as sustainability and conservation.

Deep ecology: A green ideological perspective that rejects anthropocentrism and gives priority to the maintenance of nature, and is associated with values such as biocentric equality, diversity and decentralisation.

PERSPECTIVES ON ...
NATURE

LIBERALS see nature as a resource to satisfy human needs, and thus rarely question human dominion over it. Lacking value in itself, nature is invested with value only when it is transformed by human labour, or when it is harnessed to human ends.

CONSERVATIVES often portray nature as threatening, even cruel, characterised by an amoral struggle and harshness that also shapes human existence. Humans may be seen as part of nature within a 'great chain of being', their superiority nevertheless being enshrined in their status as custodians of nature.

SOCIALISTS, like liberals, have viewed and treated nature as merely a resource. However, a romantic or pastoral tradition within socialism has also extolled the beauty, harmony and richness of nature, and looks to human fulfilment through a closeness to nature.

ANARCHISTS have often embraced a view of nature that stresses unregulated harmony and growth. Nature therefore offers a model of simplicity and balance, which humans would be wise to apply to social organisation in the form of social ecology.

FEMINISTS generally hold nature to be creative and benign. By virtue of their fertility and disposition to nurture, women are often thought to be close to nature and in tune with natural forces, while men, creatures of culture, are out of step or in conflict with nature.

ECOLOGISTS, particularly deep ecologists, regard nature as an interconnected whole, embracing humans and non-humans as well as the inanimate world. Nature is sometimes seen as a source of knowledge and 'right living', human fulfilment coming from a closeness to and respect for nature, not from the attempt to dominate it.

that the human species is in some way superior to, or more important than, any other species, or indeed nature itself. It is based on the more challenging idea that the purpose of human life is to help sustain nature, and not the other way around. (Deep ecology is discussed in greater detail on pp. 177–80.)

Differences between ...
SHALLOW AND DEEP ECOLOGY

'SHALLOW' ECOLOGY	'DEEP' ECOLOGY
• environmentalism	• ecologism
• 'light' anthropocentricism	• ecocentrism
• science	• mysticism
• humankind	• nature
• limited holism	• radical holism
• instrumental value	• value-in-nature
• modified humanism	• biocentric equality
• animal welfare	• animal rights
• sustainable growth	• anti-growth
• personal development	• ecological consciousness

HOLISM

Traditional political ideologies have typically assumed that human beings are the masters of the natural world, and have therefore regarded nature as little more than an economic resource. In that sense, they have been part of the problem and not part of the solution. In *The Turning Point* (1982), Fritjof Capra traced the origin of such ideas to the scientists and philosophers, such as René Descartes (1596–1650) and Isaac Newton (1642–1727). The world had previously been seen as organic; however, these seventeenth-century philosophers portrayed it as a machine, whose parts could be analysed and understood through the newly discovered scientific method. Science enabled remarkable advances to be made in human knowledge and provided the basis for the development of modern industry and technology. So impressive were the fruits of science, that intellectual inquiry in the modern world has come to be dominated by **scientism**. However, Capra argued that orthodox science, what he referred to as the 'Cartesian–Newtonian paradigm', amounts to the philosophical basis of the contemporary environmental crisis. Science treats nature as a machine, implying that, like any other machine, it can be tinkered with, repaired, improved on or even replaced. If human beings are to learn that they are part of the natural world rather than its masters, Capra suggested that this fixation with the 'Newtonian world-machine' must be overthrown and replaced by a new paradigm.

In searching for this new paradigm, ecological thinkers have been attracted to a variety of ideas and theories, drawn from both modern science and ancient myths and religions. However, the unifying theme among these ideas is the notion of **holism**. The term 'holism' was coined in 1926 by Jan Smuts (1870–1950), a Boer general and twice prime minister of South Africa. He used it to describe the idea that the natural world could only be understood as a whole and not through its individual parts. Smuts believed that science commits the sin of reductionism: it reduces everything it studies to separate parts and tries to understand each part in itself. In contrast, holism suggests that each part only has meaning in relation to other parts, and ultimately in relation to the whole. For example, a holistic approach to medicine would not just consider physical ailments but would see these as a manifestation of imbalances within the patient as a whole, taking account of psychological, emotional, social and environmental factors.

Although many green thinkers criticise science, others have suggested that modern science may offer a new paradigm for human thought. Capra, for example, argued that the Cartesian–Newtonian world-view has now been abandoned by many scientists, particularly by physicists like himself. During the twentieth century, with the development of so-called 'new physics', physics moved a long way beyond the mechanistic and reductionist ideas of Newton. The breakthrough was achieved at the beginning of the twentieth century by the German-born US physicist Albert Einstein (1879–1955), whose theory of relativity fundamentally challenged the traditional concepts of time and space. Einstein's work was taken further by quantum theory, developed by physicists such as Niels Bohr (1885–1952) and Verner Heisenberg (1901–76). In quantum theory the physical world is understood not as a collection of individual

Scientism: The belief that scientific method is the only value-free and objective means of establishing truth, and is applicable to all fields of learning.

Holism: A belief that the whole is more important than its parts; holism implies that understanding is gained by studying relationships among the parts.

molecules, atoms or even particles, but as a **system**, or, more accurately, a network of systems. A systems view of the world concentrates not on individual building blocks, but on the principles of organisation within the system. It therefore stresses the relationships within the system and the integration of its various elements within the whole.

An alternative and particularly fertile source of new concepts and theories has been religion. In *The Tao of Physics* (1975), Capra drew attention to important parallels between the ideas of modern physics and those of eastern mysticism. He argued that religions such as Hinduism, Daoism and Buddhism, particularly Zen Buddhism, have long preached the unity or oneness of all things, a discovery that western science only made in the twentieth century. Many in the green movement have been attracted by eastern mysticism, seeing in it both a philosophy that gives expression to ecological wisdom and a way of life that encourages compassion for fellow human beings, other species and the natural world. Other writers believe that ecological principles are embodied in monotheistic religions such as Christianity, Judaism and Islam, which regard both humankind and nature as products of divine creation. In such circumstances, human beings are viewed as God's stewards on Earth, being invested thereby with a duty to cherish and preserve the planet.

However, perhaps the most influential concepts for modern greens have been developed by looking back to pre-Christian spiritual ideas. Primitive religions often drew no distinction between human and other forms of life, and, for that matter, little distinction between living and non-living objects. All things are alive: stones, rivers, mountains and even the Earth itself, often conceived of as 'Mother Earth'. The idea of an Earth Mother has been particularly important for green thinkers trying to articulate a new relationship between human beings and the natural world, especially so for those sympathetic to ecofeminism, examined later in the chapter.

In a similar vein, the British independent scientist and environmental thinker James Lovelock (born 1919) developed the idea of the Gaia hypothesis (see p. 165). The idea of Gaia has developed into an 'ecological ideology' that conveys the powerful message that human beings must respect the health of the planet, and act to conserve its beauty and resources. It also contains a revolutionary vision of the relationship between the animate and inanimate world. However, Gaia philosophy does not always correspond to the concerns of the green movement. Humanist ecologists have typically wished to change policies and attitudes in order to ensure the continued survival of the human species. Gaia, on the other hand, is non-human, and Gaia theory suggests that the health of the planet matters more than that of any individual species living on it at present. Lovelock has suggested that those species that have prospered have been ones that have helped Gaia to regulate its own existence, while any species that poses a threat to the delicate balance of Gaia, as green thinkers argue humans currently do, is likely to be extinguished. Lovelock has nevertheless been strongly committed to science, and, contrary to the views of many in the

System: A collection of parts that operate through a network of reciprocal interactions and thereby constitute a complex whole.

Key concept ... GAIA HYPOTHESIS

The Gaia hypothesis advances the idea that the Earth is best understood as a living entity that acts to maintain its own existence (Gaia is the name of the Greek goddess of the Earth). The basis for the Gaia hypothesis is that the Earth's biosphere, atmosphere, oceans and soil exhibit precisely the same kind of self-regulating behaviour that characterises other forms of life. Gaia has maintained 'homeostasis', a state of dynamic balance, despite the major changes that have taken place in the solar system. The most dramatic evidence of this is the fact that although the sun has warmed up by more than 25 per cent since life began, the temperature on Earth and the composition of its atmosphere have remained virtually unchanged.

environmental movement, has stressed the importance of nuclear power in providing a solution to environmental problems.

SUSTAINABILITY

Ecological thinkers argue that the ingrained assumption of conventional political creeds, articulated by virtually all mainstream political parties (so-called 'grey' parties), is that human life has unlimited possibilities for material growth and prosperity. Indeed, green thinkers commonly lump capitalism and socialism together, and portray them both as examples of 'industrialism'. A particularly influential metaphor for the environmental movement has been the idea of 'spaceship Earth', because this emphasises the notion of limited and exhaustible wealth. The idea that Earth should be thought of as a spaceship was first suggested by Kenneth Boulding (1966). Boulding argued that human beings have traditionally acted as though they live in a 'cowboy economy', an economy with unlimited opportunities, like the American West during the frontier period. He suggested that this encourages, as it did in the American West, 'reckless, exploitative, and violent behaviour'. However, as a spaceship is a capsule, it is a 'closed' system. 'Open' systems receive energy or inputs from outside; for example, all ecosystems on Earth – ponds, forests, lakes and seas – are sustained by the sun. However, 'closed' systems, as the Earth itself becomes when it is thought of as a spaceship, show evidence of '**entropy**'. All 'closed' systems tend to decay or disintegrate because they are not sustained by external inputs. Ultimately, however wisely and carefully human beings behave, the Earth, the sun, and indeed all planets and stars, will be exhausted and die. When the 'entropy law' is applied to social and economic issues it produces very radical conclusions.

Entropy: A tendency towards decay or disintegration, exhibited by all 'closed' systems.

Fossil fuels: Fuels that are formed from the decomposition of buried dead organisms, making them rich in carbon; examples include oil, natural gas and coal.

No issue reflects the law of entropy more clearly than the 'energy crisis'. Industrialisation and mass affluence have been made possible by the exploitation of coal, gas and oil reserves, providing fuel for power stations, factories, motor cars, aeroplanes and so on. These fuels are **fossil fuels**. They are also non-renewable: once used up they cannot be replaced. In *Small Is Beautiful* (1973), E. F. Schumacher (see p. 167) argued that human beings have made the mistake

Key concept ... INDUSTRIALISM

The term 'industrialism', as used by environmental theorists, relates to a 'super-ideology' that encompasses capitalism and socialism, left-wing and right-wing thought. As an economic system, industrialism is characterised by large-scale production, the accumulation of capital and relentless growth. As a philosophy, it is dedicated to materialism, utilitarian values, absolute faith in science and a worship of technology. Many green thinkers thus see industrialism as 'the problem'. Ecosocialists, however, blame capitalism rather than industrialism (which ignores important issues such as the role of ownership, profit and the market), while ecofeminists argue that industrialism has its origins in patriarchy.

of regarding energy as an 'income' that is being constantly topped-up each week or each month, rather than as 'natural capital' that they are forced to live off. This mistake has allowed energy demands to soar, especially in the industrialised West, at a time when finite fuel resources are, green thinkers warn, close to depletion and unlikely to last to the end of the twenty-first century. As the spaceship draws towards the close of the 'fossil-fuel age', it approaches disintegration because, as yet, there are insufficient alternative sources of energy to compensate for the loss of coal, oil and gas.

Not only have humans failed to recognise that they live within the constraints of a 'closed' ecosystem, but they have also been unwisely cavalier in plundering its resources. Garrett Hardin (1968) developed a particularly influential model to explain why over-exploitation of environmental resources has occurred, in the form of the 'tragedy of the commons'. The parable of the 'tragedy of the commons' sheds light on the behaviour of individuals within the community, the actions of groups within society, and the strategies adopted by states within the international system. However, the parable also highlights why it is often so difficult to tackle environmental problems at any level. Any viable solution to the environmental crisis must offer a means of dealing with the 'tragedy of the commons'.

Nevertheless, green economics is not only about warnings and threats; it is also about solutions. Entropy may be an inevitable process; however, its effects can be slowed down or delayed considerably if governments and private citizens respect ecological principles. Green thinkers argue that the human species will only survive and prosper if it recognises that it is merely one element of a complex biosphere, and that only a healthy, balanced biosphere will sustain human life. Policies and actions must therefore be judged by the principle of '**sustainability**'. Sustainability sets clear limits on human ambitions and material dreams because it requires that production does as little damage as possible to the fragile global ecosystem. For example, a sustainable energy policy must be based on a dramatic reduction in the use of fossil fuels and a search for alternative, renewable energy sources such as solar energy, wind power and wave power. These are by their very nature sustainable and can be treated as 'income' rather than 'natural capital'.

Sustainability: The capacity of a system to maintain its health and continue in existence over a period of time.

Key concept ... TRAGEDY OF THE COMMONS

The idea of the 'tragedy of the commons' draws parallels between global environmental degradation and the fate of common land before the introduction of enclosures. Common land or common fisheries stocks encourage individuals to act in rationally self-interested ways, each exploiting the resources available to satisfy their needs and the needs of their families and communities. However, the collective impact of such behaviour may be devastating, as the vital resources on which all depend become depleted or despoiled. Thus, as Hardin (1968) put it, 'Freedom in a commons brings ruin to all.' The parable of the 'tragedy of the commons' is usually used to justify tackling environmental problems either by strengthening political authority or by restricting population growth.

Sustainability, however, requires not merely the implementation of government controls or tax regimes to ensure a more enlightened use of natural resources, but, at a deeper level, the adoption of an alternative approach to economic activity. This is precisely what Schumacher (1973) sought to offer in his idea of 'Buddhist economics'. For Schumacher, Buddhist economics is based on the principle of 'right livelihood' and stands in stark contrast to conventional economic theories, which assume that individuals are nothing more than 'utility maximisers'. Buddhists believe that, in addition to generating goods and services, production facilitates personal growth by developing skills and talents, and helps to overcome egocentredness by forging social bonds and encouraging people to work together. Such a view moves economics a long way from its conventional obsession with wealth creation, creating what Schumacher called economics 'as if people mattered'.

There is nevertheless considerable debate about what sustainability implies in practice. Reformist or **modernist ecologists** support 'weak' sustainability,

Modernist ecology:
A reformist tendency within green politics that seeks to reconcile ecology with the key features of capitalist modernity.

KEY FIGURE

Ernst Friedrich ('Fritz') Schumacher (1911–77)

A German-born UK economist, statistician and environmental thinker, Schumacher championed the cause of human-scale production, intermediate technology and what he called 'Buddhist economics'. The latter was defined as 'economics as if people mattered', and stressed the importance of 'right livelihood'. Schumacher's seminal work, *Small Is Beautiful* (1973), was imbued with a deep spiritual vision and reflected a rejection of western materialism and economic exploitation. In it, he advanced a critique of traditional economics' obsession with growth for growth's sake, and condemned the value system on which it is based, particularly the fact that it is divorced from nature. Crucial to his work was the belief that an infinite growth of material consumption is impossible in a finite world. For Schumacher, size was a critical question. His championing of 'the small' reflected not only deep reservations about the value of the traditional theory of economies of scale (or what he called 'rationalism by giantism'), but also the belief that small scale organisation promotes compassion, morality and a sense of common purpose. For more on Schumacher, see pp. 165, 167, and 170.

which tries to reconcile ecology with economic growth through getting richer but at a slower pace. One way in which this could be achieved would be through changes to the tax system, either to penalise and discourage pollution or to reduce the use of finite resources. However, radical ecologists, who include both **social ecologists** and deep ecologists, support (if to different degrees) 'strong' sustainability, which places far greater stress on preserving 'natural capital' and is more critical of economic growth. If, as some radical ecologists argue, the origin of the ecological crisis lies in materialism, consumerism and a fixation with economic growth, the solution lies in 'zero growth' and the construction of a 'post-industrial age' in which people live in small, rural communities and rely on craft skills. This could mean a fundamental and comprehensive rejection of industry and modern technology – literally a 'return to nature'.

ENVIRONMENTAL ETHICS

Ecological politics, in all its forms, is concerned with extending moral thinking in a number of novel directions. This is because conventional ethical systems are clearly anthropocentric, orientated around the pleasure, needs and interests of human beings. In such philosophies, the non-human world is invested with value only to the extent that it satisfies human ends. One ethical issue that even humanist or 'shallow' ecologists grapple with extensively is the question of our moral obligations towards future generations (see p. 169). However, the notion of cross-generational justice has also been criticised. Conventional moral thinkers have sometimes argued that, as all rights depend on reciprocity, it is absurd to endow people who have yet to be born with rights that impose duties on people currently alive, since the unborn cannot discharge any duties towards the living. Moreover, in view of the potentially unlimited size of future generations, the burdens imposed by 'futurity' are, in practical terms, incalculable. The present generation may, therefore, either be making sacrifices for the benefit of future generations who may prove to be much better off than themselves, or their sacrifices may be entirely inadequate to meet future needs.

An alternative approach to environmental ethics involves applying moral standards and values developed in relation to human beings to other species and

Social ecology: A broad tendency within green politics that links ecological sustainability to radical social change, or the eco-anarchist principle that human communities should be structured according to ecological principles.

Key concept ... SUSTAINABLE DEVELOPMENT

Sustainable development refers to 'development that meets the needs of the present without compromising the ability of future generations to meet their own needs' (Brundtland Report, 1987). It therefore embodies two concepts: (1) the concept of need, particularly the essential needs of the world's poor; and (2) the concept of limitations, especially related to the environment's ability to meet future as well as present needs. So-called *weak* sustainability takes economic growth to be desirable but simply insists that growth must be limited to ensure that ecological costs do not threaten its long-term sustainability, allowing 'human capital' to be substituted for 'natural capital'. *Strong* sustainability rejects the pro-growth implications of weak sustainability, and focuses just on the need to preserve and sustain 'natural capital'.

organisms. The most familiar attempt to do this is in the form of '**animal rights**'. Peter Singer's (1976) case for animal welfare had a considerable impact on the growing animal liberation movement. Singer argued that an altruistic concern for the well-being of other species derives from the fact that, as sentient beings, they are capable of suffering. Drawing on utilitarianism, he pointed out that animals, like humans, have an interest in avoiding physical pain, and he therefore condemned any attempt to place the interests of humans above those of animals as '**speciesism**'. However, altruistic concern for other species does not imply equal treatment. Singer's argument does not apply to non-sentient life forms such as trees, rocks and rivers. Moreover, the moral imperative is the avoidance of suffering, with special consideration being given to more developed and self-aware animals, notably to the great apes. On the other hand, Singer's argument implies that a reduced moral consideration should be given to human foetuses and mentally impaired people who have no capacity for suffering (Singer, 1993).

Nevertheless, the moral stance of deep ecology goes much further, in particular by suggesting that nature has value in its own right; that is, intrinsic value. From this perspective, environmental ethics have nothing to do with human instrumentality and cannot be articulated simply through the extension of human values to the non-human world. Goodin (1992), for instance, attempted to develop a 'green theory of value', which holds that resources should be valued precisely because they result from natural processes rather than human activity. However, since this value stems from the fact that the natural landscape helps people to see 'some sense and pattern in their lives' and to appreciate 'something larger' than themselves, it embodies a residual **humanism** that fails to satisfy some deep ecologists. The distinctive ethical stance of deep ecology is discussed at greater length later in the chapter.

POST-MATERIALISM AND ECOLOGICAL CONSCIOUSNESS

Ecologist ideology seeks not only to revise conventional moral thinking, but also to reshape our understanding of happiness and human well-being. In particular, green thinkers have advanced a critique of **materialism** and consumerism.

> ### Key concept ... FUTURE GENERATIONS
>
> The idea that the needs and interests of 'future generations', those yet to be born, should be taken into account in ethical reasoning is deeply rooted in green thought because the ecological impact of present actions may not be felt for decades or even centuries. What can be called cross-generational justice can be seen as a 'natural duty', an extension of a moral concern for our children and, by extension, their children, and so on. Concern for future generations has also been linked to the idea of 'ecological stewardship'. This is the notion that the present generation is merely the custodian of the wealth that has been generated by past generations and so is obliged to conserve it for the benefit of future generations.

Animal rights: Moral entitlements that are based on the belief that as animals are non-human 'persons', they deserve the same consideration (at least in certain areas) as human beings.

Speciesism: A belief in the superiority of one species over other species, through the denial of their moral significance.

Humanism: A philosophy that gives moral priority to the achievement of human needs and ends.

Materialism: An emphasis on material needs and their satisfaction, usually implying a link between pleasure or happiness and the level of material consumption.

Consumerism is a psycho-cultural phenomenon whereby personal happiness is equated with the consumption of material possessions, giving rise to what the German psychoanalyst and social philosopher Erich Fromm (1979) called a 'having' attitude of mind. For green theorists, 'having' – the disposition to seek fulfilment in acquisition and control – is deficient in at least two respects. First, it tends to undermine, rather than enhance, psychological and emotional well-being. As modern advertising and marketing techniques tend to create ever-greater material desires, they leave consumers in a constant state of dissatisfaction because, however much they acquire and consume, they always want more. Consumerism thus works not through the satisfaction of desires, but through the generation of new desires, keeping people in an unending state of neediness, want and aspiration. Such thinking is sustained by the emerging discipline of 'happiness economics', which suggests that once citizens enjoy fairly comfortable living standards it is not absolute wealth but relative wealth that affects subjective well-being (Layard, 2011).

Second, materialism and consumerism provide the cultural basis for environmental degradation. This occurs as the 'consumer society' encourages people to place short-term economic considerations ahead of longer-term ecological concerns, in which case nature is nothing other than a commodity or resource. In this light, green ideology can be seen to be associated with the ideas of post-materialism and anti-consumerism.

In line with green ideology's post-material orientation, green thinkers have tended to view human development as dangerously unbalanced: human beings are blessed with massive know-how and material wealth, but possess precious little 'know-why'. Humankind has acquired the ability to fulfil its material ambitions, but not the wisdom to question whether these ambitions are sensible, or even sane. As Schumacher (1973) warned, 'Man is now too clever to survive without wisdom.' However, some 'shallow' or humanistic ecologists have serious misgivings when this quest for wisdom draws green ideology into the realms of religious mysticism or New Age ideas. Many ecologists, particularly those who subscribe to deep ecology, have nevertheless embraced world-views

Key concept ... POST-MATERIALISM

Post-materialism is a theory that explains the nature of political concerns and values in terms of levels of economic development. It is based loosely on Abraham Maslow's (1908–70) 'hierarchy of needs', which places self-esteem and self-actualisation above material or economic needs. Post-materialism assumes that conditions of material scarcity breed egoistical and acquisitive values, meaning that politics is dominated by economic issues (who gets what). However, in conditions of widespread prosperity, individuals tend to express more interest in 'post-material' or 'quality of life' issues. These are typically concerned with morality, political justice and personal fulfilment, and include gender equality, world peace, racial harmony, ecology and animal rights.

that are quite different from those that have traditionally dominated political thought in the developed West. This, they argue, is the basis of the 'paradigm shift' that green ideology aims to bring about, and without which it is doomed to repeat the mistakes of the 'old' politics because it cannot move beyond its concepts and assumptions.

In their search for an alternative model of human well-being, green theorists have generally emphasised the importance of 'quality of life' issues and concerns, thereby divorcing happiness from a simple link to material acquisition. Such thinking is taken most seriously by eco-anarchists, ecofeminists and especially deep ecologists. In line with Fromm, they have been more willing to contrast 'having' with 'being', the latter representing satisfaction that is derived from experience and sharing, leading to personal growth, even spiritual awareness. The key feature of 'being' as an attitude of mind is that it seeks to transcend the self, or individual ego, and to recognise that each person is intrinsically linked to all other living things, and, indeed, to the universe itself. This is sometimes known as '**ecological consciousness**'. The Australian philosopher Warwick Fox (1990) claimed to go beyond deep ecology in embracing 'transpersonal ecology', the essence of which is the realisation that 'things are', that human beings and all other entities are part of a single unfolding reality. For Naess, self-realisation is attained through a broader and deeper 'identification with others' (Naess, 1973). Such ideas have often been shaped by eastern religions, most profoundly by Buddhism, which has been portrayed as an ecological philosophy in its own right. One of the key doctrines of Buddhism is the idea of 'no self', the notion that the individual ego is a myth or delusion, and that awakening or enlightenment involves transcending the self and recognising the oneness of life.

TYPES OF ECOLOGISM

MODERNIST ECOLOGY

'Modernist' or 'reformist ecology' refers to the form of green ideology that is practised by most environmental pressure groups and by a growing range of mainstream political parties. Modernist ecology is reformist in that it seeks to advance ecological principles and promote 'environmentally sound' practices, but without rejecting the central features of capitalist modernity – individual self-seeking, materialism, economic growth and so on. It is thus very clearly a form of 'shallow' or humanist ecology. The key feature of modernist ecology is the recognition that there are environmental 'limits to growth', in the sense that pollution, increased CO_2 emissions, the exhaustion of non-renewable energy sources and other forms of environmental degradation ultimately threaten prosperity and economic performance. The watchword of this form of green ideology is therefore sustainable development (in the sense of 'weak' sustainability) or, more specifically, environmentally sustainable capitalism. As, in economic terms, this means 'getting richer more slowly', modernist ecology extends moral and philosophical sensibilities only in modest directions. Indeed, it is often condemned by more radical ecologists as hopelessly compromised: part of

Ecological consciousness: An awareness of the oneness or interconnectedness of all things, allowing people to move beyond narcissistic selfishness and egoism.

the problem rather than part of the solution. The two main ideological influences on modernist ecology are liberalism and conservatism.

Ecoliberalism

Liberalism has, at best, an ambivalent relationship with green ideology. Radical ecologists criticise individualism (see p. 12) as a stark example of anthropocentrism, and condemn utilitarianism (see p. 23), the moral philosophy that underpins much of classical liberalism, on the grounds that it equates happiness with material consumption. On a larger scale, liberalism's atomistic view of society has been seen as the political expression of the 'Cartesian–Newtonian paradigm' (Capra, 1982). However, the stress found within modern liberalism on self-realisation and developmental individualism can be said to sustain a form of 'enlightened' anthropocentrism, which encourages people to take into account long-term, and not merely short-term, interests, and to favour 'higher' pleasures (including an appreciation of the natural world) over 'lower' pleasures (such as material consumption). This can be seen, for example, in John Stuart Mill's (see p. 27) criticism of rampant industrialisation and his defence of a stationary population level and a steady-state economy, on the grounds that the contemplation of nature is an indispensable aspect of human fulfilment.

Ecoconservatism

Conservatives, for their part, have evinced a sympathy for environmental issues, on two main grounds. First, ecoconservatism has drawn on a romantic and nostalgic attachment to a rural way of life threatened by the growth of towns and cities. It is clearly a reaction against industrialisation and the idea of 'progress'. It does not envisage the construction of a post-industrial society, founded on the principles of cooperation and ecology, but rather a return to, or the maintenance of, a more familiar pre-industrial one. Such environmental sensibilities typically focus on the issue of conservation and on attempts to protect the natural heritage – woodlands, forests and so on – as well as the architectural and social heritage. The conservation of nature is therefore linked to a defence of traditional values and institutions.

Green capitalism: The idea that a reliance on the capitalist market mechanism will deliver ecologically sustainable outcomes, usually linked to assumptions about capitalism's consumer responsiveness.

Consumer sovereignty: The notion, based on the theory of competitive capitalism, that consumer choice is the ultimately determining factor within a market economy.

Second, conservatives have advocated market-based solutions to environmental problems, even espousing the idea of '**green capitalism**'. Market-based environmental solutions include the adoption of tax structures that incentivise 'eco-friendly' individual and corporate behaviour, and emissions trading schemes such as that proposed by the 1997 Kyoto Protocol on climate change. The theory of green capitalism has two features. The first is the assumption that the market mechanism can and will respond to pressure from more ecologically aware consumers by forcing firms to produce 'environmentally sound' goods and adopt 'green' technologies. Such thinking relies on the idea of **consumer sovereignty** and acknowledges the impact of the trend towards so-called 'responsible consumption'.

The second way in which capitalism is supposedly 'green' is linked to the idea that long-term corporate profitability can only be achieved in a context of sustainable development. Capitalism, in short, has no interest in destroying the planet. However, there are important differences within modernist ecology over the proper balance between the state and capitalism. Although some supporters of green capitalism favour unregulated market competition, most modernist ecologists support a managed capitalist system in which environmental degradation is treated as an externality, or 'social cost', that can only be dealt with effectively by government.

SOCIAL ECOLOGY

'Social ecology' is a term coined by Murray Bookchin (see p. 175) to refer to the idea that ecological principles can and should be applied to social organisation, in which case an anarchist commune can be thought of as an ecosystem. However, the term can also be used more broadly to refer to a range of ideas, each of which recognises that environmental degradation is, in some way, linked to existing social structures. The advance of ecological principles therefore requires a process of radical social change. Social ecology, thus defined, encompasses three distinct traditions:

▶ ecosocialism

▶ eco-anarchism

▶ ecofeminism.

Ecosocialism

There is a distinct socialist strand within the green movement, which has been particularly pronounced among the German Greens, many of whose leaders have been former members of far-left groups. Ecosocialism has drawn from the pastoral socialism of thinkers such as William Morris, who extolled the virtues of small-scale craft communities living close to nature. However, it has more usually been associated with Marxism. For example, Rudolph Bahro (1982) argued that the root cause of the environmental crisis is capitalism. The natural world has been despoiled by industrialisation, but this is merely a consequence of capitalism's relentless search for profit. In this view, capitalism's anti-ecological bias derives from a number of sources. These include that private property encourages the belief that humans are dominant over nature; that the market economy 'commodifies' nature, in the sense that it turns it into something that only has exchange-value and so can be bought and sold; and that the capitalist system breeds materialism and consumerism, and so leads to relentless growth. From this perspective, the idea of 'green capitalism' is a contradiction in terms. Any attempt to improve the environment must therefore involve a process of radical social change, some would say a social revolution.

The core theme of ecosocialism is the idea that capitalism is the enemy of the environment, while socialism is its friend. However, as with socialist feminism, such a formula embodies tension between two elements, this time between 'red' and 'green' priorities. If environmental catastrophe is nothing more than a by-product of capitalism, environmental problems are best tackled by abolishing capitalism, or at least taming it. Therefore, ecologists should not form separate green parties or set up narrow environmental organisations, but work within the larger socialist movement and address the real issue: the economic system. On the other hand, socialism has also been seen as another 'pro-production' political creed: it espouses exploiting the wealth of the planet, albeit for the good of humanity rather than just the capitalist class. Socialist parties have been slow to adopt environmental policies because they, like other 'grey' parties, continue to base their electoral appeal on the promise of economic growth. As a result, ecologists have often been reluctant to subordinate the green to the red, hence the proclamation by the German Greens that they are 'neither left nor right'.

Ecosocialists argue that socialism is naturally ecological. If wealth is owned in common it will be used in the interests of all, which means in the long-term interests of humanity. However, it is unlikely that ecological problems can be solved simply by a change in the ownership of wealth. This was abundantly demonstrated by the experience of state socialism in the Soviet Union and eastern Europe, which produced some of the world's most intractable environmental problems. Examples include the Aral Sea in Central Asia, once the fourth biggest lake in the world, which has shrunk to 10 per cent of its original size as a result of the re-routing of two rivers; and the Chernobyl nuclear explosion in the Ukraine in 1986.

Eco-anarchism

Perhaps the ideology that has the best claim to being environmentally sensitive is anarchism. Some months before the publication of Rachel Carson's *The Silent Spring*, Murray Bookchin brought out *Our Synthetic Environment* ([1962] 1975). Many in the green movement also acknowledge a debt to nineteenth-century anarcho-communists, particularly Peter Kropotkin. Bookchin (1977) suggested that there is a clear correspondence between the ideas of anarchism and the principles of ecology, articulated in the idea of 'social ecology', which is based on the belief that ecological balance is the surest foundation for social stability. Anarchists believe in a stateless society, in which harmony develops out of mutual respect and social solidarity among human beings. The richness of such a society is founded on its variety and diversity. Green thinkers also believe that balance or harmony develops spontaneously within nature, in the form of ecosystems, and that these, like anarchist communities, require no external authority or control. The anarchist rejection of government within human society thus parallels the green thinkers' warnings about human 'rule' within the natural world. Bookchin therefore likened an anarchist community to an ecosystem, and suggested that both are distinguished by respect for the principles of diversity, balance and harmony.

Anarchists have also advocated the construction of decentralised societies, organised as a collection of communes or villages, a social vision to which many deep ecologists are also attracted. Life in such communities would be lived close to nature, each community attempting to achieve a high degree of self-sufficiency. Such communities would be economically diverse; they would produce food

and a wide range of goods and services, and therefore contain agriculture, craft work and small-scale industry. Self-sufficiency would make each community dependent on its natural environment, spontaneously generating an understanding of organic relationships and ecology. In Bookchin's view, decentralisation would lead to 'a more intelligent and more loving use of the environment'.

Without doubt, the conception that many green theorists have of a post-industrial society has been influenced by the writings of Kropotkin and William Morris. The green movement has also adopted ideas such as decentralisation, participatory democracy and direct action, from anarchist thought. However, even when anarchism is embraced as providing a vision of an ecologically sound future, it is seldom accepted as a means of getting there. Anarchists believe that progress will only be possible when government and all forms of political authority are overthrown. In contrast, many in the green movement see government as an agency through which collective action can be organised, and therefore as the most likely means through which the environmental crisis can be addressed, at least in the short term. They fear that dismantling or even weakening government may simply give free rein to those forces that generated industrialisation and blighted the natural environment in the first place.

Ecofeminism

The idea that feminism offers a distinctive and valuable approach to green issues has grown to such a point that ecofeminism has developed into one of the major philosophical schools of environmentalist thought, its key practitioners including Ynestra King, Carolyn Merchant (see p. 176) and Mary Daly. The basic theme of ecofeminism is that ecological destruction has its origins in patriarchy: nature is under threat not from humankind but from men and the institutions of male power. Feminists who adopt an androgynous or sexless view of human nature argue that patriarchy has distorted the instincts and sensibilities of men by divorcing them from the 'private' world of nurturing, home-making

Carolyn Merchant (born 1936)

A US ecofeminist philosopher and historian of science, Merchant has highlighted in her work the links between gender oppression and the 'death of nature'. Merchant developed a feminist critique of the way in which the scientific revolution that began in the seventeenth century had subverted the mothering image of the natural world dominant in the Middle Ages. Environmental degradation could therefore be explained ultimately in terms of the application by men of a mechanistic view of nature. This meant that respect for the wonder and organic character of nature was displaced by a disposition to seize, bind and exploit nature, with similar implications for gender relations. Merchant thus drew parallels between the violation of women and the 'rape' of 'virgin' land. In this light, she argued that a global environmental revolution had to be underpinned by a radical, societal restructuring of gender relations. Merchant's chief works include *The Death of Nature* (1983) and *Radical Ecology* (1992). For more on Merchant, see p. 175.

and personal relationships. The sexual division of labour thus inclines men to subordinate both women and nature, seeing themselves as 'masters' of both. From this point of view, ecofeminism can be classified as a particular form of social ecology. However, many ecofeminists subscribe to essentialism, in that their theories are based on the belief that there are fundamental and ineradicable differences between women and men.

Such a position is adopted, for instance, by Mary Daly in *Gyn/Ecology* (1979). Daly argued that women would liberate themselves from patriarchal culture if they aligned themselves with 'female nature'. The notion of an intrinsic link between women and nature is not a new one. Pre-Christian religions and 'primitive' cultures often portrayed the Earth or natural forces as a goddess, an idea resurrected

			SOCIAL ECOLOGY			
		MODERNIST ECOLOGY	ECOSOCIALISM	ECO-ANARCHISM	ECOFEMINISM	DEEP ECOLOGY
KEY THEMES		• ENLIGHTENED ANTHROPO-CENTRISM • LIMITS TO GROWTH • 'WEAK' SUSTAINABILITY • FUTURE GENERATIONS	• END OF COMMODIFI-CATION • COLLECTIVISE WEALTH • PRODUCTION FOR USE	• DECENTRALIS-ATION • SELF-MANAGEMENT • CRITIQUE OF CONSUMERISM	• ESSENTIAL DIFFERENCE BETWEEN WOMEN AND MEN • WOMEN LINKED TO 'NATURE' • MEN LINKED TO 'CULTURE'	• RADICAL HOLISM • VALUE-IN-NATURE • BIOCENTRIC EQUALITY • 'STRONG' SUSTAINABILITY
CORE GOAL		BALANCE BETWEEN ECOLOGY AND CAPITALIST MODERNITY	SOCIAL REVOLUTION: REPLACE CAPITALISM WITH SOCIALISM	DISMANTLE STRUCTURES OF POLITICAL AUTHORITY	OVERTHROW PATRIARCHY AND ESTABLISH MATRIARCHY	PARADIGM SHIFT: CAST OFF MECHANISTIC/ ATOMISTIC WORLD-VIEW

ANTHROPOCENTRISM ← → ECOCENTRISM

Figure 8.2 Types of green ideology

in the Gaia hypothesis. Modern ecofeminists, however, highlight the biological basis for women's closeness to nature, in particular the fact that they bear children and suckle babies. The fact that women cannot live separately from natural rhythms and processes in turn structures their politico-cultural orientation. Traditional 'female' values therefore include reciprocity, cooperation and nurturing, values that have a 'soft' or ecological character. The idea that nature is a resource to be exploited or a force to be subdued is more abhorrent to women than men, because they recognise that nature operates in and through them, and intuitively sense that personal fulfilment stems from acting with nature rather than against it. The overthrow of patriarchy therefore promises to bring with it an entirely new relationship between human society and the natural world, meaning that ecofeminism shares with deep ecology a firm commitment to ecocentrism.

If there is an essential or 'natural' bond between women and nature, the relationship between men and nature is quite different. While women are creatures of nature, men are creatures of culture: their world is synthetic or (literally) man-made, a product of human ingenuity rather than natural creativity. In the male world, then, intellect is ranked above intuition, materialism is valued over spirituality, and mechanical relationships are emphasised over holistic ones. In politico-cultural terms, this is reflected in a belief in self-striving, competition and hierarchy. The implications of this for the natural world are clear. Patriarchy, in this view, establishes the supremacy of culture over nature, the latter being nothing more than a force to be subdued, exploited or risen above. Ecological destruction and gender inequality are therefore part of the same process in which 'cultured' men rule over 'natural' women.

DEEP ECOLOGY

The term 'deep ecology' (sometimes called 'ecocentrism', 'ecosophy' or 'ecophilosophy') was coined in 1973 by Arne Naess. For Naess, deep ecology is 'deep' because it persists in asking deeper questions concerning 'why' and 'how', and is thus concerned with fundamental philosophical questions about the impact of the human species on the biosphere. The key belief of deep ecology is that ecology and anthropocentrism (in all its forms, including 'enlightened' anthropocentrism) are simply irreconcilable; indeed, anthropocentrism is an offence against the principle of ecology.

This rejection of anthropocentrism has had profound moral and political implications. Deep ecologists have viewed nature as the source of moral goodness. Nature thus has 'intrinsic' or inherent value, not just 'instrumental' value deriving from the benefits it brings to human beings. A classic statement of the ethical framework of deep ecology is articulated in Aldo Leopold's *A Sand County Almanac* ([1948] 1968) in the form of the 'land ethic': 'A thing is right when it tends to preserve the integrity, stability and beauty of the biotic community. It is wrong when it tends otherwise.' Such a moral stance implies '**biocentric equality**'. Naess (1989) expressed this in the idea that all species have an 'equal right to live and bloom', reflecting the benefits of **biodiversity**. Such ecocentric ethical thinking has been accompanied by a deeper and more

Biocentric equality: The principle that all organisms and entities in the biosphere are of equal moral worth, each being an expression of the goodness of nature.

Biodiversity: The range of species within a biotic community, often thought to be linked to its health and stability.

challenging philosophical approach that amounts to nothing less than a new **metaphysics**, a new way of thinking about and understanding the world. In addressing metaphysical issues, deep ecology is radical in a way and to a degree that does not apply elsewhere in ideological thought. Deep ecology calls for a change in consciousness, specifically the adoption of 'ecological consciousness', or 'cosmological consciousness'. At the heart of this is an 'inter-subjective' model of selfhood that allows for no distinction between the self and the 'other', thereby collapsing the distinction between humankind and nature.

Deep ecology is also associated with a distinctive analysis of environmental degradation and how it should be tackled. Instead of linking the environmental crisis to particular policies or a specific political, social or economic system (be it industrialisation, capitalism, patriarchy or whatever), deep ecologists argue that it has more profound cultural and intellectual roots. The problem lies in the mechanistic world-view that has dominated the thinking of western societies since about the seventeenth century, and which subsequently came to affect most of the globe. Above all, this dominant paradigm is dualistic: it understands the world in terms of distinctions (self/other, humankind/nature, individual/society, mind/matter, reason/emotion and so on) and thus allows nature to be thought of as inert and valueless in itself, a mere resource for satisfying human ends. In this light, nothing less than a paradigm change – a change in how we approach and think about the world – will properly address the challenge of environmental degradation. Deep ecologists have looked to a wide range of ideas and theories to bring about this paradigm change, including, as discussed earlier, modern physics, eastern mysticism and primitive religion. Each of these is attractive because it offers a vision of radical holism. In emphasising that the whole is more important than its individual parts, they are clearly non-dualistic and provide a basis for an ecocentrism that prioritises the maintenance of ecological balance over the achievement of narrowly human ends.

Metaphysics: The branch of philosophy that is concerned with explaining the fundamental nature of existence, or being.

KEY FIGURE

Aldo Leopold (1887–1948)

A US philosopher, woodsman and environmentalist, Leopold is sometimes seen as the father of wildlife conservation in the USA. Originally a forester and keen on hunting, Leopold later rejected the distinction between 'bad' predators and 'good' animals on the grounds that both are necessary to a healthy ecosystem. His main contribution to environmental thinking was the idea of the 'land ethic', developed in *A Sand County Almanac* (1948). This portrayed human beings as plain members and citizens of the land-community, imposing major restraints on how they could deal with nature. Although commonly associated with deep ecology, Leopold did not envisage a 'hands-off' approach to human–environmental relations, as effective conservation requires a balance between ecological sustainability and economic expediency. He thus did not accept that non-human nature has an intrinsic value. Rather than rejecting outright economic valuations of the natural world, his concern was to prevent economic valuations of nature from 'crowding out' alternative valuations, based, for example, on ethical, aesthetics and social considerations. For more on Leopold, see p. 177.

In addition to its moral and philosophical orientation, deep ecology has been associated with a wider set of goals and concerns. These include:

▶ *Wilderness preservation*. Deep ecologists seek to preserve nature 'wild and free', based on the belief that the natural world, unspoilt by human intervention, is a repository of wisdom and morality. **Preservationism** is nevertheless different from conservationism, in that the latter is usually taken to imply protecting nature in order to satisfy long-term human ends. The 'wilderness ethic' of deep ecology is often linked to the ideas of Henry David Thoreau (1817–62), who left Concord, Massachusetts, in 1845 to live in solitude in the woods by Walden Pond, an experience described in *Walden* ([1854] 1983).

▶ *Population control*. Although greens from many traditions have shown a concern about the exponential rise in the human population, deep ecologists have placed a particular emphasis on this issue, often arguing that a substantial decrease in the human population is the only way of ensuring the flourishing of non-human life. To this end, some deep ecologists have rejected aid to the developing world; called for a reduction in birth rates, especially in the developing world; or argued that immigration from the developing world to the developed world should be stopped.

▶ *Simple living*. Deep ecologists believe that humans have no right to reduce the richness and diversity of nature except, as Naess put it, to satisfy vital needs. This is a philosophy of 'walking lighter on the Earth'. It certainly implies an emphasis on promoting the quality of life ('being') rather than the quantity of possessions ('having'), and is often linked to a post-material model of self-realisation, commonly understood as **self–actualisation**. This implies being 'inwardly rich but outwardly poor'.

▶ *Bioregionalism*. This is the idea that human society should be reconfigured in line with naturally defined regions, each 'bioregion', in effect, being an ecosystem. **Bioregionalism** is clearly at odds with established territorial divisions, based on national or state borders. Although deep ecologists seldom look to prescribe how humans should organise themselves within such bioregions, there is general support for self-reliant, self-supporting, autonomous communities.

Nevertheless, the role and importance of deep ecology within larger green political thought has been a matter of considerable controversy. Not only has the significance of deep ecology, in terms of the philosophical and ethical debates it has stimulated, greatly outweighed its practical importance within the green movement, but it has also attracted sometimes passionate criticism from fellow green thinkers. Humanist ecologists roundly reject the idea that their views are merely a 'shallow' version of deep ecology, arguing instead that deep ecology is philosophically and morally flawed. The philosophical flaw of deep ecology is the belief that anthropocentrism and ecology are mutually exclusive. From this perspective, a concern with human well-being, or at least long-term and sustainable human well-being, requires respect for ecology rather than its

Preservationism: The disposition to protect natural systems, often implying keeping things 'just as they are' and restricting the impact of humans on the environment.

Self-actualisation: An 'inner', even quasi-spiritual, fulfilment that is achieved by transcending egoism and materialism.

Bioregionalism: The belief that the territorial organisation of economic, social and political life should take into account the ecological integrity of bioregions.

betrayal. The moral flaws of deep ecology stem from the idea of the 'intrinsic' value of nature. In the humanist view, environmental ethics cannot be non-anthropocentric because morality is a human construct: 'good' and 'bad' are only meaningful when they are applied to human beings and their living conditions. Deep ecology has also come under attack from social ecologists, notably Murray Bookchin. For Bookchin, deep ecology is not only socially conservative (because it ignores the radical social change that needs to accompany any 'inner' revolution) but, in turning its back on rationalist thought and embracing mysticism, it is also guilty of succumbing to what Bookchin called 'vulgar Californian spiritualism' or 'Eco-la-la'.

? QUESTIONS FOR DISCUSSION

- How does an ecocentric perspective challenge conventional approaches to politics?
- Is 'enlightened' anthropocentrism a contradiction in terms?
- Why have green thinkers been ambivalent about science?
- Should all thinking strive to be holistic?
- What are the features of a sustainable economy?
- How has green ideology extended conventional moral thinking?
- Do we have obligations to future generations, and if so, how far do they extend?
- Why and how have green theorists rethought the nature of human fulfilment?
- Which political ideologies are most compatible with ecological thinking, and why?
- To what extent can the goals of green ideology only be achieved through radical social change?
- Does deep ecology constitute the philosophical core of green political thought?
- Can ecologism ever be electorally and politically viable?

📖 FURTHER READING

Baxter, B., *Ecologism: An Introduction* (1999). A clear and comprehensive survey of the main components of ecologism that considers its moral, political and economic implications.

Dobson, A., *Green Political Thought* (2007). An accessible and very useful account of the ideas behind green politics; sometimes seen as the classic text on the subject.

Eckersley, R., *Environmentalism and Political Theory: Towards an Ecocentric Approach* (1992). A detailed and comprehensive examination of the impact of environmentalist ideas on contemporary political thought.

Marshall, P., *Nature's Web: Rethinking Our Place on Earth* (1995). A history of ecological ideas that serves as a compendium of the various approaches to nature in different periods and from different cultures.

9 Multiculturalism

PREVIEW

Although multicultural societies have long existed – examples include the Ottoman empire, which reached its peak in the late sixteenth and early seventeenth centuries, and the USA from the early nineteenth century onwards – the term 'multiculturalism' is of relatively recent origin. It was first used in 1965 in Canada to describe a distinctive approach to tackling the issue of cultural diversity. In 1971, multiculturalism, or 'multiculturalism within a bilingual framework', was formally adopted as public policy in Canada, providing the basis for the introduction of the Multiculturalism Act in 1988. Australia also officially declared itself multicultural and committed itself to multiculturalism in the early 1970s. However, the term 'multiculturalism' has only been prominent in wider political debate since the 1990s.

Multiculturalism is more an arena for ideological debate than an ideology in its own right. As an arena for debate, it encompasses a range of views about the implications of growing cultural diversity and, in particular, about how cultural difference can be reconciled with civic unity. Its key theme is therefore diversity within unity. A multiculturalist stance implies a positive endorsement of communal diversity, based on the right of different cultural groups to recognition and respect. In this sense, it acknowledges the importance of beliefs, values and ways of life in establishing a sense of self-worth for individuals and groups alike. Distinctive cultures thus deserve to be protected and strengthened, particularly when they belong to minority or vulnerable groups. However, there are a number of competing models of a multicultural society, which draw on, variously, the ideas of liberalism, pluralism and cosmopolitanism. On the other hand, the multiculturalist stance has also been deeply controversial, and has given rise to a range of objections and criticisms.

CONTENTS

HISTORICAL OVERVIEW

Multiculturalism first emerged as a theoretical stance through the activities of the black consciousness movement of the 1960s, primarily in the USA. The origins of black nationalism date back to the early twentieth century and the emergence of a 'back to Africa' movement inspired by figures such as Marcus Garvey (see p. 122). Black politics, however, gained greater prominence in the 1960s with an upsurge in both the reformist and revolutionary wings of the movement. In its reformist guise, the movement took the form of a struggle for civil rights that reached national prominence in the USA under the leadership of Martin Luther King (1929–68). The strategy of non-violent civil disobedience was nevertheless rejected by the Black Power movement, which supported black separatism and, under the leadership of the Black Panther Party, founded in 1966, promoted the use of armed confrontation. Of more enduring significance, however, have been the Black Muslims (now the Nation of Islam), who advocate a separatist creed based on the idea that black Americans are descended from an ancient Muslim tribe.

The late 1960s and early 1970s witnessed growing political assertiveness among minority groups, sometimes expressed through **ethnocultural nationalism**, in many parts of western Europe and elsewhere in North America. This was most evident among the French-speaking people of Quebec in Canada, but it was also apparent in the rise of Scottish and Welsh nationalism in the UK, and the growth of separatist movements in Catalonia and the Basque area in Spain, Corsica in France, and Flanders in Belgium. A trend towards ethnic assertiveness was also found among the Native Americans in Canada and the USA, the aboriginal peoples in Australia, and the Maoris in New Zealand. In response to these pressures, a growing number of countries adopted official multiculturalism policies, the Canadian Multiculturalism Act (1988) being perhaps the classic example.

The common theme among these emergent forms of ethnic politics was a desire to challenge economic and social marginalisation, and sometimes racial oppression. In this sense, ethnic politics was a vehicle for political liberation, its enemy being structural disadvantage and ingrained inequality. For blacks in North America and western Europe, for example, the establishment of an ethnic identity provided a means of confronting a dominant white culture that had traditionally emphasised their inferiority and demanded subservience.

Apart from growing assertiveness among established minority groups, multicultural politics has also been strengthened by trends in international migration since 1945 that have significantly widened cultural diversity in many societies. Migration rates rose steeply in the early post-1945 period, as western states sought to recruit workers from abroad to help in the process of post-war reconstruction. In many cases, migration routes were shaped by links between European states and their former colonies. Thus, immigrants to the UK in the 1950s and 1960s came mainly from the West Indies and the Indian subcontinent, while immigration in France came largely from Algeria, Morocco and Tunisia.

Ethnocultural nationalism: A form of nationalism that is fuelled primarily by a keen sense of ethnic and cultural distinctiveness and the desire to preserve it.

In the case of West Germany, immigrants were *Gastarbeiter* (guest workers), usually recruited from Turkey or Yugoslavia. Immigration into the USA since the 1970s has come mainly from Mexico and other Latin American countries. For instance, the Latino or Hispanic community in the USA has exceeded the number of African-Americans, and it is estimated that by 2050 about a quarter of the US population will be Latinos.

However, during the 1990s there was a marked intensification of cross-border migration across the globe, creating what some have seen as a 'hyper-mobile planet'. There are two main reasons for this. First, there has been a growing number of refugees, reaching a peak of about 18 million in 1993. This resulted from an upsurge in war, ethnic conflict and political upheaval in the post-Cold War era, in areas ranging from Algeria, Rwanda and Uganda to Bangladesh, Indochina and Afghanistan. The collapse of communism in eastern Europe in 1989–91 contributed to this by creating, almost overnight, a new group of migrants as well as by sparking a series of ethnic conflicts, especially in the former Yugoslavia. Second, economic globalisation intensified pressures for international migration in a variety of ways, as discussed in the final section of this chapter.

By the early 2000s, a growing number of western states, including virtually all the member states of the European Union, had responded to such developments by incorporating multiculturalism in some way into public policy. This was in recognition of the fact that multi-ethnic, multi-religious and multicultural trends within modern societies have become irreversible. In short, despite the continuing and sometimes increasing prominence of issues such as immigration and asylum, a return to monoculturalism, based on a unifying national culture, is no longer feasible. Indeed, arguably the most pressing ideological issue such societies now confront is how to reconcile cultural diversity with the maintenance of civic and political cohesion. Nevertheless, the advent of global terrorism and the launch of the so-called 'war on terror' pushed multicultural politics further up the political agenda. The spread of religious fundamentalism (see p. 135), and particularly Islamism, to western states encouraged some to speculate on whether Samuel Huntington's famous 'clash of civilisations' is happening not just between societies but also *within* them. Whereas supporters of multiculturalism have argued that cultural recognition and minority rights help to keep political extremism at bay, opponents warn that multicultural politics may provide a cloak for, or even legitimise, political extremism.

CORE IDEAS AND PRINCIPLES

POLITICS OF RECOGNITION

Multiculturalists argue that minority cultural groups are disadvantaged in relation to majority groups, and that remedying this involves significant changes in society's rules and institutions. As such, multiculturalism, in common with many other ideological traditions (not least socialism and feminism), is associated with the advancement of marginalised, disadvantaged or oppressed groups. However, multiculturalism draws from a novel approach to such matters, one that departs from conventional approaches to social advancement. Three contrasting approaches can be adopted, based, respectively, on the ideas of rights, redistribution and recognition (see Figure 9.1).

The notion of the 'politics of rights' is rooted in the ideas of republicanism (see p. 186), which are associated by many (but by no means all) with liberalism. Republicanism is concerned primarily with the problem of legal and political exclusion, the denial to certain groups of rights that are enjoyed by their fellow citizens. Republican thinking was, for example, reflected in first-wave feminism, in that its campaign for female emancipation focused on the struggle for votes for women and equal access for women and men to education, careers and public life in general. The republican stance can, in this sense, be said to be 'difference-blind': it views difference as 'the problem' (because it leads to discriminatory or unfair treatment) and proposes that difference be banished or transcended in the name of equality. Republicans therefore believe that social advancement can be brought about largely through the establishment of **formal equality**.

The contrasting idea of the 'politics of redistribution' is rooted in a social reformist stance that embraces, among other traditions, modern liberalism and social democracy. It arose out of the belief that universal **citizenship** and formal equality are not sufficient, in themselves, to tackle the problems of subordination and marginalisation. People are held back not merely by legal and political exclusion, but also, and more importantly, by social disadvantage – poverty, unemployment, poor housing, lack of education and so on. The key idea of social reformism is the principle of equal opportunities, the belief in a 'level playing field' that allows people to rise or fall in society strictly on the basis of personal ability and their willingness to work. This implies a shift from legal egalitarianism to social egalitarianism, the latter involving a system of social

APPROACH	MAIN OBSTACLE TO ADVANCEMENT	KEY THEME	REFORMS AND POLICIES
POLITICS OF RIGHTS (REPUBLICANISM)	LEGAL AND POLITICAL EXCLUSION	UNIVERSAL CITIZENSHIP	• FORMAL EQUALITY (LEGAL AND POLITICAL RIGHTS) • BAN DISCRIMINATION • PROHIBIT ETHICAL/ CULTURAL/RACIAL PROFILING
POLITICS OF REDISTRIBUTION (SOCIAL REFORMISM)	SOCIAL DISADVANTAGE	EQUALITY OF OPPORTUNITY	• SOCIAL RIGHTS • WELFARE AND REDISTRIBUTION • POSITIVE DISCRIMINATION
POLITICS OF RECOGNITION (MULTICULTURALISM)	CULTURAL-BASED MARGINALISATION	GROUP SELF-ASSERTION	• RIGHT TO RESPECT AND RECOGNITION • MINORITY RIGHTS • GROUP SELF- DETERMINATION

Figure 9.1 Contrasting approaches to social advancement

Formal equality: Equality based on people's status in society, especially their legal and political rights (legal and political equality).

Citizenship: Membership of a state: a relationship between the individual and the state based on reciprocal rights and responsibilities.

> ## Key concept ... **REPUBLICANISM**
>
> Republicanism refers, most simply, to a preference for a republic over a monarchy. However, the term 'republic' suggests not merely the absence of a monarch but, in the light of its Latin root, *res publica* (meaning common or collective affairs), it implies that the people should have a decisive say in the organisation of the public realm. The central theme of republican political theory is a concern with a particular form of freedom, sometimes seen as 'freedom as non-domination' (Pettit, 1999). This combines liberty, in the sense of protection against arbitrary or tyrannical rule, with active participation in public and political life. The moral core of republicanism is expressed in a belief in civic virtue, understood to include public spiritedness, honour and patriotism (see p. 112).

engineering that redistributes wealth so as to alleviate poverty and overcome disadvantage. In such an approach, difference is acknowledged as it highlights the existence of social injustice. Nevertheless, this amounts to no more than a provisional or temporary acknowledgement of difference, in that different groups are identified only in order to expose unfair practices and structures, which can then be reformed or removed.

Multiculturalism, for its part, developed out of the belief that group marginalisation often has even deeper origins. It is not merely a legal, political or social phenomenon but is, rather, a cultural phenomenon, one that operates through stereotypes and values that structure how people see themselves and are seen by others. In other words, universal citizenship and equality of opportunity do not go far enough. Egalitarianism has limited value, in both its legal and social forms, and may even be part of the problem (in that it conceals deeper structures of cultural marginalisation). In this light, multiculturalists have been inclined to emphasise difference rather than equality. This is reflected in the 'politics of recognition', which involves a positive endorsement, even a celebration, of cultural difference, allowing marginalised groups to assert themselves by reclaiming an authentic sense of cultural identity.

The foundations for such a politics of recognition were laid by the postcolonial theories that developed out of the collapse of the European empires in the early post-World War II period. Black nationalism and multiculturalism can, indeed, both be viewed as offshoots of postcolonialism (see p. 187). The significance of postcolonialism was that it sought to challenge and overturn the cultural dimensions of imperial rule by establishing the legitimacy of non-western, and sometimes anti-western, political ideas and traditions. Edward Said's *Orientalism* ([1978] 2003) is sometimes seen as the most influential text of postcolonialism, developing, as it does, a critique of **Eurocentrism**. Orientalism highlights the extent to which western cultural and political hegemony over the rest of the world, but over the Orient in particular, had been maintained through elaborate stereotypical fictions that belittled and demeaned non-western peoples and

Eurocentrism: The application of values and theories drawn from European culture to other groups and peoples, implying a biased or distorted world-view.

Key concept ... POSTCOLONIALISM

Postcolonialism originated as a trend in literary and cultural studies that sought to address the cultural conditions characteristic of newly independent societies. Its purpose has been primarily to expose and overturn the cultural and psychological dimensions of colonial rule, recognising that 'inner' subjugation can persist long after the political structures of colonialism have been removed. A major thrust of postcolonialism has thus been to establish the legitimacy of non-western, and sometimes anti-western, political ideas and traditions. Postcolonialism has thus sought to give the developing world a distinctive political voice, separate from the universalist pretensions of liberalism and socialism. However, critics of postcolonialism have argued that, all too often, it has been used as a justification for traditional values and authority structures.

cultures. Examples of such stereotypes include ideas such as the 'mysterious East', 'inscrutable Chinese' and 'lustful Turks'.

CULTURE AND IDENTITY

Multiculturalism's politics of recognition is shaped by a larger body of thought which holds that **culture** is basic to political and social identity. Multiculturalism, in that sense, is an example of the politics of cultural self-assertion. In this view, a pride in one's culture, and especially a public acknowledgement of one's cultural identity, gives people a sense of social and historical rootedness. In contrast, a weak or fractured sense of cultural identity leaves people feeling isolated and confused. In its extreme form, this can result in what has been called 'culturalism' – as practised by writers such as the French political philosopher Montesquieu (1689–1775), and the pioneer of cultural nationalism, Herder (see p. 121) – which portrays human beings as culturally defined creatures. In its modern form, cultural politics has been shaped by two main forces: communitarianism and identity politics (see p. 189).

Communitarianism advances a *philosophical* critique of liberal universalism – the idea that, as individuals, people in all societies and all cultures have essentially the same 'inner' identity. In contrast, communitarians champion a shift away from universalism to particularism, reflecting an emphasis less on what people share or have in common and more on what is distinctive about the groups to which they belong. Identity, in this sense, links the personal to the social, and sees the individual as 'embedded' in a particular cultural, social, institutional or ideological context. Multiculturalists therefore accept an essentially communitarian view of human nature, which stresses that people cannot be understood 'outside' society but are intrinsically shaped by the social, cultural and other structures within which they live and develop. Communitarian philosophers such as Alasdair MacIntyre (1981) and Michael Sandel (1982) portrayed the idea of the abstract individual – the 'unencumbered self' – as a recipe for rootless atomism. Only groups and communities can give people a genuine sense

Culture: Beliefs, values and practices that are passed on from one generation to the next through learning; culture is distinct from nature.

of identity and moral purpose. During the 1980s and 1990s, a major debate raged in philosophy between liberals and communitarians. However, one of the consequences of this debate was a growing willingness among many liberal thinkers to acknowledge the importance of culture. This, in turn, made liberalism more open to the attractions of multiculturalism, helping to give rise to the tradition of **liberal multiculturalism**.

'Identity politics' is a broad term that encompasses a wide range of political trends and ideological developments, ranging from ethnocultural nationalism and religious fundamentalism to second-wave feminism and **pluralist multiculturalism**. What all forms of identity politics nevertheless have in common is that they advance a *political* critique of liberal universalism. Liberal universalism is a source of oppression, even a form of cultural imperialism, in that it tends to marginalise and demoralise subordinate groups and peoples. It does this because, behind a façade of universalism, the culture of liberal societies is constructed in line with the values and interests of its dominant groups: men, whites, the wealthy and so on. Subordinate groups and peoples are either

Liberal multiculturalism:
A form of multiculturalism that is committed to toleration and seeks to uphold freedom of choice and of moral sphere, especially in relation to culture and religion.

Pluralist multiculturalism:
A form of multiculturalism that is committed to 'deep' diversity, based on the benefits of cultural entrenchment and the need to resist cultural imperialism.

PERSPECTIVES ON ...
CULTURE

LIBERALS have sometimes been critical of traditional or 'popular' culture, seeing it as a source of conformism and a violation of individuality. 'High' culture, however, especially in the arts and literature, may nevertheless be viewed as a manifestation of, and stimulus to, individual self-development. Culture is thus valued only when it promotes intellectual development.

CONSERVATIVES place a strong emphasis on culture, emphasising its benefits in terms of strengthening social cohesion and political unity. Culture, from this perspective, is strongest when it overlaps with tradition and therefore binds one generation to the next. Conservatives support monocultural societies, believing that only a common culture can inculcate the shared values that bind society together.

SOCIALISTS, and particularly Marxists, have viewed culture as part of the ideological and political 'superstructure' that is conditioned by the economic 'base'. In this view, culture is a reflection of the interests of the ruling class, its role being primarily ideological. Culture thus helps to reconcile subordinate classes to their oppression within the capitalist class system.

FEMINISTS have often been critical of culture, believing that, in the form of patriarchal culture, it reflects male interests and values and serves to demean women, reconciling them to a system of gender oppression. Nevertheless, cultural feminists have used culture as a tool of feminism, arguing that, in strengthening distinctive female values and ways of life, it can safeguard the interests of women.

MULTICULTURALISTS view culture as the core feature of personal and social identity, giving people an orientation in the world and strengthening their sense of cultural belonging. They believe that different cultural groups can live peacefully and harmoniously within the same society because the recognition of cultural difference underpins, rather than threatens, social cohesion. However, cultural diversity must in some way, and at some level, be balanced against the need for common civic allegiances.

Key concept ... IDENTITY POLITICS

Identity politics is an orientation towards social or political theorising, rather than a coherent body of ideas with a settled political character. It seeks to challenge and overthrow oppression by reshaping a group's identity through what amounts to a process of politico-cultural self-assertion. This reflects two core beliefs. (1) Group marginalisation operates through stereotypes and values developed by dominant groups that structure how marginalised groups see themselves and are seen by others. These inculcate a sense of inferiority, even shame. (2) Subordination can be challenged by reshaping identity to give the group concerned a sense of pride and self-respect (e.g., 'black is beautiful' or 'gay pride'). Embracing or proclaiming a positive social identity is thus an act of defiance or liberation.

consigned an inferior or demeaning stereotype, or they are encouraged to identify with the values and interests of dominant groups (that is, their oppressors). However, identity politics does not only view culture as a source of oppression; it is also seen as a source of liberation and empowerment, particularly when it seeks to cultivate a 'pure' or 'authentic' sense of identity. Embracing such an identity is therefore a political act, a statement of intent, and a form of defiance. This is what gives identity politics its typically combative character and imbues it with psycho-emotional force. All forms of identity politics thus attempt to fuse the personal and the political.

MINORITY RIGHTS

The advance of multiculturalism has gone hand in hand with a willingness to recognise minority rights, sometimes called 'multicultural' rights. The most systematic attempt to identify such rights was undertaken by Will Kymlicka (see p. 190). Kymlicka ([1995] 2000) identified three kinds of minority rights:

► self-government rights

► polyethnic rights

► representation rights.

Self-government rights belong, Kymlicka argued, to what he called 'national minorities', indigenous peoples who are territorially concentrated, possess a shared language and are characterised by a 'meaningful way of life across the full range of human activities'. Examples include the Native Americans; the First Nations, Inuits and Metis peoples in Canada; the Maoris in New Zealand; the aboriginal peoples in Australia; and the Sami people in parts of northern Sweden, Norway and Finland. In these cases, the right to self-government involves the devolution of political power, usually through federalism, to political units that are substantially controlled by their members, although it may extend to the right of secession and, therefore, to sovereign independence. For example, the territory of Nunavut in Canada, formed in 1999, is largely self-governing and has its own territorial legislature.

Polyethnic rights are rights that help ethnic groups and religious minorities, which have developed through immigration, to express and maintain their cultural distinctiveness. This would, for instance, provide the basis for legal exemptions, such as the exemption of Jews and Muslims from animal slaughtering laws, and the exemption of Muslim girls from school dress codes. Special *representation* rights attempt to redress the under-representation of minority or disadvantaged groups in education and in senior positions in political and public life. Kymlicka justified 'reverse' or '**positive' discrimination** in such cases, on the grounds that it is the only way of ensuring the full and equal participation of all groups in the life of their society, thus ensuring that public policy reflects the interests of diverse groups and peoples, and not merely those of traditionally dominant groups.

Minority or multicultural rights are distinct from the traditional liberal conception of rights, in that they belong to groups rather than to individuals. This highlights the extent to which multiculturalists subscribe to collectivism (see p. 64) rather than individualism (see p. 12). Minority rights are also often thought of as 'special' rights. These are rights that are specific to the groups to which they belong, each cultural group having different needs for recognition based on the particular character of its religion, traditions and way of life. For instance, legal exemptions for Sikhs to ride motorcycles without wearing crash helmets, or perhaps to wear ceremonial daggers, would be meaningless to other groups.

Positive discrimination:
Preferential treatment towards a group designed to compensate its members for past disadvantage or structural inequality.

Minority rights have nevertheless been justified in a variety of ways. First, minority rights have been viewed, particularly by liberal multiculturalists, as a guarantee of individual freedom and personal autonomy. In this view, culture is a vital tool that enables people to live autonomous lives. Charles Taylor (see p. 191) thus argues that individual self-respect is intrinsically bound up with cultural membership. As people derive an important sense of who they are from their cultures, individual rights cannot but be entangled with minority rights.

KEY FIGURE

Will Kymlicka (born 1962)

A Canadian political philosopher, Kymlicka is often seen as the leading theorist of liberal multiculturalism. Influenced by the ideas of John Rawls (see p. 30), he sought to find ways in which people with diverse beliefs could live together without any imposing their values on the others. In works such as *Liberalism, Community and Culture* (1989) and *Multicultural Citizenship* ([1995] 2000), Kymlicka argued that certain 'collective rights' of minority cultures are consistent with liberal-democratic principles, but acknowledged that no single formula can be applied to all minority groups, particularly as the needs and aspirations of immigrants differ from those of indigenous peoples. For Kymlicka, cultural identity and minority rights are closely linked to personal autonomy. Seeing people as 'cultural creatures' but rejecting the communitarian assertion that identity is constituted through culture, Kymlicka argues that culture constitutes an inescapable context for freedom and autonomy by, for example, helping people make intelligent decisions about what is valuable. For more on Kymlicka, see pp. 189, 190 and 191.

Second, in many cases minority rights are seen as a way of countering oppression. In this view, societies can 'harm' their citizens by trivialising or ignoring their cultural identities – harm, in this case, being viewed as a 'failure of recognition' (Taylor, 1994). Minority groups are always threatened or vulnerable because the state, despite its pretence of neutrality, is inevitably aligned with a dominant culture, whose language is used, whose history is taught, and whose cultural and religious practices are observed in public life. Of particular importance in this respect is the issue of '**offence**' and the idea of a right not to be offended. This in particular concerns religious groups who consider certain beliefs to be sacred, and are therefore especially deserving of protection. To criticise, insult or even ridicule such beliefs is thus seen as an attack on the group itself – as was evident, for instance, in protests in 1989 against the publication of Salman Rushdie's *The Satanic Verses*, and against allegedly anti-Islamic cartoons published in Denmark in 2006. States such as the UK have, as a result, introduced laws banning expressions of religious hatred.

Third, minority rights have been supported on the grounds that they redress social injustice. In this view, minority rights are a compensation for unfair disadvantages and for under-representation, usually addressed through a programme of 'positive' discrimination. This has been particularly evident in the USA, where the political advancement of African-Americans has, since the 1960s, been associated with so-called '**affirmative action**'. For example, in the case of *Regents of the University of California v. Bakke* (1978), the Supreme Court upheld the principle of 'reverse' discrimination in educational admissions, allowing black students to gain admission to US universities with lower qualifications than white students.

Offence: (In this sense) to feel hurt, even humiliated; an injury against one's deepest beliefs.

Affirmative action: Policies or programmes that are designed to benefit disadvantaged minority groups (or, potentially, women) by affording them special assistance.

Finally, multiculturalists such as Kymlicka believe that indigenous peoples or national minorities are entitled to rights that go beyond those of groups that have formed as a result of immigration. In particular, the former are entitled to rights of self-government, on at least two grounds. First, indigenous peoples have been dispossessed and subordinated through a process of colonisation. In

KEY FIGURE

Charles Taylor (born 1931)

A Canadian academic and political philosopher, Taylor drew on communitarian thinking to construct a theory of multiculturalism as 'the politics of recognition'. Emphasising the twin ideas of equal dignity (rooted in an appeal to people's humanity) and equal respect (reflecting difference and the extent to which personal identity is culturally situated), Taylor's multiculturalism goes beyond classical liberalism, while also rejecting particularism and moral relativism. He argued that according respect and recognition to minority cultures is essential if dominant and minority cultures are to engage in sustained dialogue with a view to developing a shared understanding of the good life. For Taylor, identity is defined by the commitments and identifications which provide the frame or horizon within which people can try to determine what is good or valuable, or how they ought to behave. Taylor's most influential work in this field is *Multiculturalism and 'The Politics of Recognition'* (1994). For more on Taylor, see pp. 190 and 191.

no way did they choose to give up their culture or distinctive way of life; neither did they consent to the formation of a new state. In these circumstances, minority rights are, at least potentially, 'national' rights. In contrast, as migration involves some level of choice and voluntary action (even allowing for the possible impact of factors such as poverty and persecution), immigrant groups can be said to be under an obligation to accept the core values and governmental arrangements of their country of settlement. Migration and settlement can therefore be seen as a form of implicit consent. Second, indigenous peoples tend to be territorially concentrated, making the devolution of political authority practicable, something that very rarely applies in the same way, or to the same degree, to groups that have formed through immigration.

The issue of minority rights has nevertheless been highly controversial. These controversies have included, first, that because minority rights address the distinctive needs of particular groups, they have sometimes been criticised for blocking integration into the larger society. The issue of the veil, as worn by some Muslim women, has attracted particular attention in this respect. While supporters of the right of Muslim women to wear the veil have argued that it is basic to their cultural identity, critics have objected to it either because it discriminates against women or because the veil is a symbol of separateness. Second, 'positive' discrimination has been criticised, both by members of majority groups, who believe that it amounts to unfair discrimination, and by some members of minority groups, who argue that it is demeaning and possibly counter-productive (because it implies that such groups cannot gain advancement through their own efforts).

Third, the idea that 'offence' amounts to evidence of oppression has implications for traditional liberal rights, notably the right to freedom of expression. If freedom of expression means anything, it surely means the right to express views that others find objectionable or offensive, a stance that suggests that 'harm' must involve a physical threat, and not just a 'failure of recognition'. Finally, there is inevitable tension between minority rights and individual rights, in that cultural belonging, particularly when it is based on ethnicity or religion, is usually a product of family and social background, rather than personal choice. As most people do not 'join' an ethnic or religious group it is difficult to see why they should be *obliged* to accept its beliefs or follow its practices. Tensions between the individual and the group highlight the sometimes difficult relationship between liberalism and multiculturalism, discussed later in the chapter.

DIVERSITY

Multiculturalism has much in common with nationalism. Both emphasise the capacity of culture to generate social and political cohesion, and both seek to bring political arrangements into line with patterns of cultural differentiation. Nevertheless, whereas nationalists believe that stable and successful societies are ones in which nationality, in the sense of a shared cultural identity, coincides with citizenship, multiculturalists hold that cultural diversity is compatible with, and perhaps provides the best basis for, political cohesion. Multiculturalism is characterised by a steadfast refusal to link diversity to conflict or instability. All forms of multiculturalism are based on the assumption that diversity and unity can, and should, be blended with one another: they are not opposing forces (even though, as discussed in the next section, multiculturalists have different views about where the balance between them should be drawn).

In this sense, multiculturalists accept that people can have multiple identities and multiple loyalties; for instance, to their country of origin and their country of settlement. Indeed, multiculturalists argue that cultural recognition underpins political stability. People are willing and able to participate in society precisely because they have a firm and secure identity, rooted in their own culture. From this perspective, the denial of cultural recognition results in isolation and powerlessness, providing a breeding ground for extremism and the politics of hate. For instance, growing support for Islamism and other forms of religious fundamentalism has been interpreted in this light.

Multiculturalists do not just believe that diversity is possible; they believe it is also desirable and should be celebrated. Apart from its benefits to the individual in terms of a stronger sense of cultural identity and belonging, multiculturalists believe that diversity is of value to society at large. This can be seen, in particular, in terms of the vigour and vibrancy of a society in which there are a variety of lifestyles, cultural practices, traditions and beliefs. Multiculturalism, in this sense, parallels ecologism, in drawing links between diversity and systemic health. Cultural diversity is seen to benefit society in the same way that biodiversity benefits an ecosystem. An additional advantage of diversity is that, by promoting cultural exchange between groups that live side by side with one another, it fosters cross-cultural **toleration** and understanding, and therefore a willingness to respect 'difference'. Diversity, in this sense, is the antidote to social polarisation and prejudice.

Nevertheless, this may highlight internal tension within multiculturalism itself. On the one hand, multiculturalists emphasise the distinctive and particular nature of cultural groups and the need for individual identity to be firmly embedded in a cultural context. On the other hand, by encouraging cultural exchange and mutual understanding, they risk blurring the contours of group identity and creating a kind of 'pick-and-mix', melting-pot society in which individuals have a 'shallower' sense of social and historical identity. As people learn more about other cultures, the contours of their 'own' culture are, arguably, weakened.

TYPES OF MULTICULTURALISM

LIBERAL MULTICULTURALISM

There is a complex and, in many ways, ambivalent relationship between liberalism and multiculturalism. Some view liberalism and multiculturalism as rival political traditions, arguing either that multiculturalism threatens cherished liberal values or that liberalism, or, as Tariq Modood (see p. 194) has argued, some narrow forms of liberalism, serve as an inadequate basis for

Toleration: Forbearance; a willingness to accept views or actions with which one is in disagreement.

KEY FIGURE

Tariq Modood (born 1952)

A British Pakistani sociologist and political scientist, Modood has defended multiculturalism as a theory and as a series of policies. In works such as *Multicultural Politics* (2005) and *Multiculturalism* (2007), he has portrayed liberal or ideological secularism, which seeks to exclude religion from the state, as an obstacle to multicultural integration. Instead, he champions an accommodative secularism which aims to foster multi-faith inclusivity by recognising organised religion as a potential public good or national resource. Highlighting the benefits of strong cultural identities, Modood endorses a vision of multicultural citizenship that is compatible with multiple forms of contemporary groupness and does not treat the values and practices of one group as the model to which other groups must conform. He identifies four views of integration. *Assimilation* demands conformity on the part of minorities; *individualist-integration* leaves minorities free to cultivate their own identities in private and as individuals; *multiculturalism* involves a remaking of citizenship and national identity to include group identities; and *cosmopolitanism* fosters unity across cultural/national boundaries. For more on Modood, see p. 193.

multicultural politics. Since the 1970s, however, liberal thinkers have taken the issue of cultural diversity increasingly seriously, and have developed a form of liberal multiculturalism. Its cornerstone has been a commitment to toleration and a desire to uphold freedom of choice in the moral sphere, especially in relation to matters that are of central concern to particular cultural or religious traditions. This has contributed to the idea that liberalism is 'neutral' in relation to the moral, cultural and other choices that citizens make. John Rawls (see p. 30), for example, championed this belief in arguing that liberalism strives to establish conditions in which people can establish the good life as each defines it ('the right'), but it does not prescribe or try to promote any particular values or moral beliefs ('the good'). Liberalism, in this sense, is 'difference-blind': it treats factors such as culture, ethnicity, race, religion and gender as, in effect, irrelevant, because all people should be evaluated as morally autonomous individuals.

However, toleration is not morally neutral, and only provides a limited endorsement of cultural diversity. In particular, toleration extends only to views, values and social practices that are themselves tolerant; that is, ideas and actions that are compatible with personal freedom and autonomy. Liberals thus cannot accommodate '**deep**' **diversity**. For example, liberal multiculturalists may be unwilling to endorse practices such as female circumcision, forced (and possibly arranged) marriages and female dress codes, however much the groups concerned may argue that these are crucial to the maintenance of their cultural identity. The individual's rights, and particularly his or her freedom of choice, must therefore come before the rights of the cultural group in question.

Deep diversity: Diversity that rejects the idea of objective or 'absolute' standards and so is based on moral relativism.

The second feature of liberal multiculturalism is that it draws an important distinction between 'private' and 'public' life. It sees the former as a realm of freedom, in which people are, or should be, free to express their cultural, religious and language identity, whereas the latter must be characterised by at least a bedrock of shared civic allegiances. Citizenship is thus divorced from cultural identity, making the latter essentially a private matter. Such a stance implies that multiculturalism is compatible with civic nationalism. This can be seen in the so-called 'hyphenated nationality' that operates in the USA, through which people view themselves as African-Americans, Polish-Americans, German-Americans and so on. In this tradition, integration, rather than diversity, is emphasised in the public sphere. The USA, for instance, stresses proficiency in English and a knowledge of US political history as preconditions for gaining citizenship. In the more radical 'republican' multiculturalism that is practised in France, an emphasis on laïcité, or secularism, in public life has led to bans on the wearing of the hijab, or Muslim headscarf, in schools, and since 2003 to a ban on all forms of overt religious affiliation in French schools. In 2010, France passed legislation banning the full face veil (the niqab and burqa) in public, with Belgium following suit in 2011. Some multiculturalists, however, view such trends as an attack on multiculturalism itself.

The third and final aspect of liberal multiculturalism is that it regards liberal democracy (see p. 18) as the sole legitimate political system. The virtue of liberal democracy is that it alone ensures that government is based on the consent of the people, and, in providing guarantees for personal freedom and toleration, it helps to uphold diversity. Liberal multiculturalists would therefore oppose calls, for instance, for the establishment of an Islamic state based on the adoption of Shari'a law, and may even be willing to prohibit groups or movements that campaign for such a political end. Groups are therefore only entitled to toleration and respect if they, in turn, are prepared to tolerate and respect other groups.

PLURALIST MULTICULTURALISM

Pluralism (see p. 197) provides firmer foundations for a politics of difference than does liberalism. For liberals, as has been seen, diversity is endorsed but only when it is constructed within a framework of toleration and personal autonomy, amounting to a form of **'shallow' diversity**. This is the sense in which liberals 'absolutise' liberalism (Parekh, 2005). Isaiah Berlin (see p. 196) nevertheless went beyond liberal toleration in endorsing the idea of **value pluralism**. This holds, in short, that people are bound to disagree about the ultimate ends of life, as it is not possible to demonstrate the superiority of one moral system over another. As values clash, the human predicament is inevitably characterised by moral conflict. In this view, liberal or western beliefs, such as support for personal freedom, toleration and democracy, have no greater moral authority than illiberal or non-western beliefs. Berlin's ([1958] 1969) stance implies a form of live-and-let-live multiculturalism, or what has been called the 'politics of indifference'. However, as Berlin remained a liberal to the extent that he believed that only within a society that respects individual liberty can value pluralism be contained, he failed to demonstrate how liberal and illiberal cultural beliefs can co-exist harmoniously within the same society. Nevertheless, once liberalism accepts moral pluralism, it is difficult to contain it within a liberal framework. John Gray (1995), for instance, argued that pluralism implies a 'post-liberal' stance, in which liberal values, institutions and regimes are no longer seen to enjoy a monopoly of legitimacy (see Figure 9.2).

Shallow diversity: Diversity that is confined by the acceptance of certain values and beliefs as 'absolute' and therefore non-negotiable.

Value pluralism: The theory that there is no single, overriding conception of the 'good life', but rather a number of competing and equally legitimate conceptions.

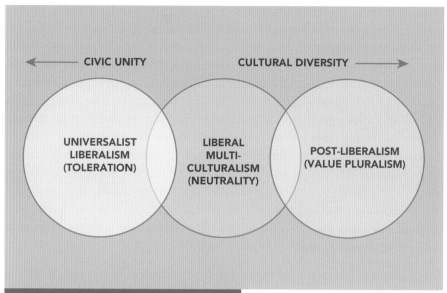

Figure 9.2 Liberalism and cultural diversity

An alternative basis for pluralist multiculturalism has been advanced by Bhikhu Parekh (2005). In Parekh's (see p. 197) view, cultural diversity is, at heart, a reflection of the dialectic or interplay between human nature and culture. Although human beings are natural creatures, who possess a common species-derived physical and mental structure, they are also culturally constituted in the sense that their attitudes, behaviour and ways of life are shaped by the groups to which they belong. A recognition of the complexity of human nature, and the fact that any culture expresses only part of what it means to be truly human, therefore provides the basis for a politics of recognition and thus for a viable form of multiculturalism. Such a stance goes beyond liberal multiculturalism in that it stresses that western liberalism gives expression only to certain aspects of human nature.

KEY FIGURE

Isaiah Berlin (1909–97)

A Riga-born British historian of ideas and a philosopher, Berlin developed a form of liberal pluralism that was grounded in a life-long commitment to reason and empirical knowledge. Basic to Berlin's philosophical stance was the idea that conflicts of values are intrinsic to human life, a position that has influenced 'post-liberal' thinking about multiculturalism. As he insisted that the values people live by must not conflict with the fundamental sense of what it is to be a human being, he held that value pluralism can only exist in a liberal society. A major implication of Berlin's belief that there is no higher rational standard capable of resolving moral conflicts, is the impossibility of utopia. Not only is the notion of a single path to perfection an illusion but it is also a recipe for political repression, making Plato, Marx and others enemies of the 'open society'. Berlin's best-known political work is *Four Essays on Liberty* ([1958] 1969), in which he extolled the virtues of 'negative' freedom over 'positive' freedom. For more on Berlin, see pp. 15–16 and 195.

KEY FIGURE

Bhikhu Parekh (born 1935)

An Indian-born political theorist and member of the House of Lords, Parekh has developed an influential defence of cultural diversity from a pluralist perspective. In *Rethinking Multiculturalism* (2005), he rejected universalist liberalism on the grounds that what is reasonable and moral is embedded in and mediated by culture, which, in turn, helps people to make sense of their lives and the world around them. 'Variegated' treatment, including exemptions from laws that apply to the wider society and policies such as affirmative action, is therefore required to put ethnic, cultural or religious minorities on an equal footing with the majority community. In this vein, Parekh has advocated the state funding in the UK of Muslim schools. In *A New Politics of Identity* (2008), he argued that ethnic, religious, national and other identities need, in a global age, to be integrated within a universal human identity that is both rooted and open, allowing people to belong to both a particular community and to humankind as a whole. For more on Parekh, see pp. 195 and 196.

Beyond pluralist multiculturalism, a form of 'particularist' multiculturalism can be identified. Particularist multiculturalists emphasise that cultural diversity takes place within a context of unequal power, in which certain groups have customarily enjoyed advantages and privileges that have been denied to other groups. Particularist multiculturalism is very clearly aligned to the needs and interests of marginalised or disadvantaged groups. The plight of such groups tends to be explained in terms of the corrupt and corrupting nature of western culture, values and lifestyles, which are either believed to be tainted by the inheritance of colonialism and racism (see p. 123) or associated with 'polluting' ideas such as materialism and permissiveness. In this context, an emphasis on cultural distinctiveness amounts to a form of political resistance, a refusal to succumb to repression or corruption. However, such an emphasis on cultural 'purity', which may extend to an unwillingness to engage in cultural exchange, raises concerns about the prospects for civic cohesion: diversity may be stressed at the expense of unity. Particularist multiculturalism may thus give rise to a form of 'plural monoculturalism' (Sen, 2006), in which each cultural group

Key concept ... PLURALISM

Pluralism, in its broadest sense, is a belief in or commitment to diversity or multiplicity, the existence of many things. As a descriptive term, 'pluralism' may denote the existence of party competition (*political* pluralism), a multiplicity of ethical values (*moral* or value pluralism), a variety of cultural beliefs (*cultural* pluralism) and so on. As a normative term it suggests that diversity is healthy and desirable, usually because it safeguards individual liberty and promotes debate, argument and understanding. More narrowly, pluralism is a theory of the distribution of political power. As such, it holds that power is widely and evenly dispersed in society, not concentrated in the hands of an elite or ruling class. In this form, pluralism is usually seen as a theory of 'group politics', implying that group access to government ensures broad democratic responsiveness.

gravitates towards an undifferentiated communal ideal, which has less and less in common with the ideals of other groups.

COSMOPOLITAN MULTICULTURALISM

Cosmopolitanism (see below) and multiculturalism can be seen as entirely distinct, even conflicting, ideological traditions. Whereas cosmopolitanism encourages people to adopt a global consciousness which emphasises that ethical responsibility should not be confined by national borders, multiculturalism appears to particularise moral sensibilities, focusing on the specific needs and interests of a distinctive cultural group. However, for theorists such as Jeremy Waldron (1995), multiculturalism can effectively be equated with cosmopolitanism. Cosmopolitan multiculturalists endorse cultural diversity and identity politics, but they view them as essentially transitional states in a larger reconstruction of political sensibilities and priorities. This position celebrates diversity on the grounds of what each culture can learn from other cultures, and because of the prospects for personal self-development that are offered by a world of wider cultural opportunities and options. This results in what has been called a 'pick-and-mix' multiculturalism, in which cultural exchange and cultural mixing are positively encouraged. People, for instance, may eat Italian food, practise yoga, enjoy African music and develop an interest in world religions.

Culture, from this perspective, is fluid and responsive to changing social circumstances and personal needs; it is not fixed and historically embedded, as pluralist or particularist multiculturalists would argue. A multicultural society is thus a 'melting pot' of different ideas, values and traditions, rather than a 'cultural mosaic' of separate ethnic and religious groups. In particular, the cosmopolitan stance positively embraces **hybridity**. This recognises that, in the modern world, individual identity cannot be explained in terms of a single cultural structure, but rather exists, in Waldron's (1995) words, as a 'melange' of commitments, affiliations and roles. Indeed, for Waldron, immersion in the traditions of a particular culture is like living in Disneyland and thinking

Hybridity: A condition of social and cultural mixing in which people develop multiple identities.

Key concept ... COSMOPOLITANISM

'Cosmopolitanism' literally means a belief in a *cosmopolis* or 'world state'. *Moral* cosmopolitanism is the belief that the world constitutes a single moral community, in that people have obligations (potentially) towards all other people in the world, regardless of nationality, religion, ethnicity and so on. All forms of moral cosmopolitanism are based on a belief that every individual is of equal moral worth, most commonly linked to the doctrine of human rights (see p. 12). *Political* cosmopolitanism (sometimes called 'legal' or 'institutional' cosmopolitanism) is the belief that there should be global political institutions, and possibly a world government. However, most modern political cosmopolitans favour a system in which authority is divided between global, national and local levels.

	LIBERAL MULTICULTURALISM	PLURALIST MULTICULTURALISM	COSMOPOLITAN MULTICULTURALISM
KEY THEMES	• COMMUNITARIANISM • MINORITY RIGHTS • DIVERSITY STRENGTHENS TOLERATION AND PERSONAL AUTONOMY	• IDENTITY POLITICS • CULTURAL EMBEDDEDNESS • DIVERSITY COUNTERS GROUP OPPRESSION	• COSMOPOLITANISM • CULTURAL MIXING • HYBRIDITY
CORE GOAL	CULTURAL DIVERSITY WITHIN A LIBERAL-DEMOCRATIC FRAMEWORK	'STRONG' DIVERSITY, RECOGNISING LEGITIMACY OF NON-LIBERAL AND LIBERAL VALUES	FLUID AND MULTIPLE IDENTITIES PROVIDE THE BASIS FOR GLOBAL CITIZENSHIP

Figure 9.3 Types of multiculturalism

that one's surroundings epitomise what it is for a culture to exist. If we are all now, to some degree, cultural 'mongrels', multiculturalism is as much an 'inner' condition as it is a feature of modern society. The benefit of this form of multiculturalism is that it broadens moral and political sensibilities, ultimately leading to the emergence of a 'one world' perspective. However, multiculturalists from rival traditions criticise the cosmopolitan stance for stressing unity at the expense of diversity. To treat cultural identity as a matter of self-definition, and to encourage hybridity and cultural mixing, is, arguably, to weaken any genuine sense of cultural belonging.

CRITIQUES OF MULTICULTURALISM

The advance of multicultural ideas and policies has stimulated considerable political controversy. Together with the conversion of liberal and other progressive thinkers to the cause of minority rights and cultural recognition, oppositional forces have also emerged. This has been expressed most clearly in the growing significance, since the 1980s, of anti-immigration parties and movements in many parts of the world. Examples of these include the Front National in France, the Freedom Party in Austria, Vlaams Blok in Belgium, Pim Fortuyn's List in the Netherlands and the One Nation party in Australia. Further evidence of a retreat from 'official' multiculturalism can be seen in bans on the wearing of veils by Muslim women in public places. Such bans have been introduced in France and Belgium, while at least four German states have banned the wearing of Muslim headscarves in schools. However, ideological opposition to multiculturalism has come from a variety of sources. The most significant of these have been:

▶ liberalism

▶ conservatism

▶ feminism

▶ social reformism.

The liberal critique

While some liberals have sought to embrace wider cultural diversity, others have remained critical of the ideas and implications of multiculturalism. The key theme in liberal criticisms is the threat that multiculturalism poses to individualism, reflected in the core multiculturalist assumption that personal identity is embedded in group or social identity. Multiculturalism is therefore, like nationalism and even racism (see p. 123), just another form of collectivism, and, like all forms of collectivism, it subordinates the rights and needs of the individual to those of the social group. In this sense, it threatens individual freedom and personal self-development, and so implies that cultural belonging is a form of captivity. Amartya Sen (2006) developed a particularly sustained attack on what he called the 'solitaristic' theory that underpins multiculturalism (particularly in its pluralist and particularist forms), which suggests that human identities are formed by membership of a *single* social group. This, Sen argued, not only leads to the 'miniaturisation' of humanity, but also makes violence more likely, as people identify only with their own monoculture and fail to recognise the rights and integrity of people from other cultural groups. Multiculturalism thus breeds a kind of 'ghettoisation' that diminishes, rather than broadens, cross-cultural understanding. According to Sen, solitaristic thinking is also evident in ideas that emphasise the incompatibility of cultural traditions, such as the 'clash of civilisations' thesis (Huntington, 1996). Even when liberals are sympathetic to multiculturalism they condemn pluralist, and especially particularist, multiculturalism for endorsing as legitimate, ideas which they view as anti-democratic and oppressive, such as the theories of militant Islam.

The conservative critique

Conservatism is the political tradition that contrasts most starkly with multiculturalism. Indeed, most of the anti-immigration nationalist backlash against multiculturalism draws from essentially conservative assumptions. In other cases, it more closely resembles the racial nationalism of fascism (see p. 130), or even Nazi race theory. The chief conservative objection to multiculturalism is that shared values and a common culture are a necessary precondition for a stable and successful society. As discussed in Chapter 5, conservatives therefore favour nationalism over multiculturalism. The basis for such a view is the belief that human beings are drawn to others who are similar to themselves. A fear or distrust of strangers or foreigners is therefore 'natural' and unavoidable. From this perspective, multiculturalism is inherently flawed: multicultural societies are inevitably fractured and conflict-ridden societies, in which suspicion, hostility and even violence come to be accepted as facts of life. The multiculturalist image of 'diversity within unity' is thus a myth, a sham exposed by the simple facts of social psychology.

The appropriate political responses to the threats embodied in multiculturalism therefore include restrictions on immigration (particularly from parts of the world whose culture is different from the 'host' society), pressures for

Differences between …
UNIVERSALIST AND PLURALIST LIBERALISM

UNIVERSALIST LIBERALISM	PLURALIST LIBERALISM
• universal reason	• scepticism
• search for truth	• pursuit of order
• fundamental values	• value pluralism
• liberal toleration	• politics of difference
• human rights	• cultural rights
• liberal-democratic culture	• multiculturalism
• liberal triumphalism	• plural political forms

assimilation to ensure that minority ethnic communities are absorbed into the larger 'national' culture, and, in the view of the far right, the repatriation of immigrants to their country of origin. A further aspect of the conservative critique of multiculturalism reflects concern about its implications for the majority or 'host' community. In this view, multiculturalism perpetrates a new, albeit 'reverse', set of injustices, by demeaning the culture of the majority group by associating it with colonialism and racism, while favouring the interests and culture of minority groups through 'positive' discrimination and the allocation of 'special' rights.

The feminist critique

The relationship between feminism and multiculturalism has sometimes been a difficult one. Although forms of Islamic feminism (considered in Chapter 8) have sought to fuse the two traditions, feminists have more commonly raised concerns about multiculturalism. This happens when minority rights and the politics of recognition serve to preserve and legitimise patriarchal and traditionalist beliefs that systematically disadvantage women, an argument that may equally be applied to gays and lesbians, and is sometimes seen as the 'minorities within minorities' problem. Cultural practices such as dress codes, family structures and access to elite positions have thus been seen to establish structural gender biases. Multiculturalism may therefore be little more than a concealed attempt to bolster male power, the politics of cultural recognition being used within minority communities to legitimise continued female subordination.

The social reformist critique

Social reformists have advanced a number of criticisms of multiculturalism, linked to its wider failure to address the interests of disadvantaged groups or sections of society adequately. Concerns, for instance, have been raised about the extent to which multiculturalism encourages groups to seek advancement through cultural or ethnic assertiveness, rather than through a more explicit

Assimilation: The process through which immigrant communities lose their cultural distinctiveness by adjusting to the values, allegiances and lifestyles of the 'host' society.

struggle for social justice. In that sense, the flaw of multiculturalism is its failure to address issues of class inequality: the 'real' issue confronting minority groups is not their lack of cultural recognition but their lack of economic power and social status. Indeed, as Brian Barry (2002) argued, by virtue of its emphasis on cultural distinctiveness, multiculturalism serves to divide, and therefore weaken, people who have a common economic interest in alleviating poverty and promoting social reform. Similarly, a more acute awareness of cultural difference may weaken support for welfarist and redistributive policies, as it may narrow people's sense of social responsibility (Goodhart, 2004). The existence of a unifying culture that transcends ethnic and cultural differences may therefore be a necessary precondition for the politics of social justice.

? QUESTIONS FOR DISCUSSION

- How and why is multiculturalism linked to the politics of recognition?
- Is multiculturalism a form of communitarianism?
- What is the justification for minority or multicultural rights?
- Is multiculturalism compatible with the idea of individual rights?
- Why do multiculturalists believe that diversity provides the basis for a politically stable society?
- Why have liberals supported diversity, and when do they believe that diversity is 'excessive'?
- How does pluralism go 'beyond' liberalism?
- Are western cultures tainted by the inheritance of colonialism and racism?
- Can multiculturalism be reconciled with any form of nationalism?
- To what extent is there tension between cultural rights and women's rights?
- What impact does multiculturalism have on the politics of redistribution?
- Could multiculturalism lead to cosmopolitanism?

📖 FURTHER READING

Kymlicka, W., *Multicultural Citizenship* (2000). A highly influential attempt to reconcile multiculturalism with liberalism by advancing a model of citizenship that is based on the recognition of minority or multicultural rights.

Modood, T., *Multiculturalism* (2013). A distinctive contribution to the debate about multiculturalism that highlights the urgent need to include Muslims in contemporary conceptions of democratic citizenship.

Parekh, B., *Rethinking Multiculturalism: Cultural Diversity and Political Theory*, 2nd edn (2005). A comprehensive defence of the pluralist perspective on cultural diversity that also discusses the practical problems confronting multicultural societies.

Taylor, C., *Multiculturalism: Examining the Politics of Recognition* (1995). A wide-ranging and authoritative set of essays on various aspects of multicultural politics.

Bibliography

Acton, Lord (1956) *Essays on Freedom and Power*. London: Meridian.

Adorno, T., Frenkel-Brunswik, E., Levinson, D. and Sandford, R. (1950) *The Authoritarian Personality*. New York: Harper.

Anderson, B. (1983) *Imagined Communities: Reflections on the Origins and Spread of Nationalism*. London: Verso.

Aughey, A., Jones, G. and Riches, W. T. M. (1992) *The Conservative Political Tradition in Britain and the United States*. London: Pinter.

Bahro, R. (1982) *Socialism and Survival*. London: Heretic Books.

Bakunin, M. (1973) *Selected Writings*, ed. A. Lehning. London: Cape.

Bakunin, M. (1977) 'Church and State', in G. Woodcock (ed.), *The Anarchist Reader*. London: Fontana.

Barry, B. (2002) *Culture and Equality*. Cambridge and New York: Polity Press.

Baxter, B. (1999) *Ecologism: An Introduction*. Edinburgh: Edinburgh University Press.

Beasley, C. (2005) *Gender and Sexuality: Critical Theories and Critical Thinkers*. London and Thousand Oaks, CA: Sage Publications.

Beauvoir, S. de (1968) *The Second Sex*, trans. H. M. Parshley. New York: Bantam.

Bellamy, R. (1992) *Liberalism and Modern Society: An Historical Argument*. Cambridge: Polity Press.

Berlin, I. ([1958] 1969) 'Two Concepts of Liberty', in *Four Essays on Liberty*. London: Oxford University Press.

Bernstein, E. ([1898] 1962) *Evolutionary Socialism*. New York: Schocken.

Bobbio, N. (1996) *Left and Right: The Significance of a Political Distinction*. Oxford: Polity Press.

Bookchin, M. ([1962] 1975) *Our Synthetic Environment*. London: Harper & Row.

Bookchin, M. (1977) 'Anarchism and Ecology', in G. Woodcock (ed.), *The Anarchist Reader*. London: Fontana.

Boulding, K. (1966) 'The Economics of the Coming Spaceship Earth', in H. Jarrett (ed.), *Environmental Quality in a Growing Economy*. Baltimore, MD: Johns Hopkins Press.

Bourne, R. (1977) 'War Is the Health of the State', in G. Woodcock (ed.), *The Anarchist Reader*. London: Fontana.

Brown, D. (2000) *Contemporary Nationalism: Civic, Ethnocultural and Multicultural Politics*. London: Routledge.

Brownmiller, S. (1975) *Against Our Will: Men, Women and Rape*. New York: Simon & Schuster.

Brundtland Report (Our Common Future) (1987). Oxford: Oxford University Press.

Bryson, V. (2016) *Feminist Political Theory: An Introduction*, 3rd edn. London and New York: Palgrave Macmillan.

Burke, E. ([1790] 1968) *Reflections on the Revolution in France*. Harmondsworth: Penguin.

Butler, J. (2006) *Gender Trouble*. Abingdon and New York: Routledge.

Capra, F. (1975) *The Tao of Physics*. London: Fontana.

Capra, F. (1982) *The Turning Point*. London: Fontana (Boston, MA: Shambhala, 1983).

Carson, R. (1962) *The Silent Spring*. Boston, MA: Houghton Mifflin.

Charvet, J. (1982) *Feminism*. London: Dent.

Christoyannopoulos, A. (2011) *Religious Anarchism: New Perspectives*. Newcastle upon Tyne: Cambridge Scholars Publishing.

Club of Rome. See Meadows et al. (1972).

Crosland, C. A. R. (1956) *The Future of Socialism*. London: Cape (Des Plaines, IL: Greenwood, 1977).

Daly, M. (1979) *Gyn/Ecology: The Meta-Ethics of Radical Feminism*. Boston, MA: Beacon Press.

Darwin, C. ([1859] 1972) *On the Origin of Species*. London: Dent.

Dobson, A. (2007) *Green Political Thought*, 4th edn. London: Routledge.

Eckersley, R. (1992) *Environmentalism and Political Theory: Towards an Ecocentric Approach*. London: UCL Press.

Egoumenides, M. (2014) *Philosophical Anarchism and Political Obligation*. London: Bloomsbury.

Ehrlich, P. and Harriman, R. (1971) *How to Be a Survivor*. London: Pan.

Elshtain, J. B. (1993) *Public Man, Private Woman: Women in Social and Political Thought*. Oxford: Martin Robertson, and Princeton, NJ: Princeton University Press.

Engels, F. ([1884] 1976) *The Origins of the Family, Private Property and the State*. London: Lawrence & Wishart (New York: Pathfinder, 1972).

Eysenck, H. (1964) *Sense and Nonsense in Psychology*. Harmondsworth: Penguin.

Fanon, F. (1965) *The Wretched of the Earth*. Harmondsworth: Penguin (New York: Grove-Weidenfeld, 1988).

Fawcett, E. (2015) *Liberalism: The Life of an Idea*. Princeton, NJ: Princeton University Press.

Festenstein, M. and Kenny, M. (eds) (2005) *Political Ideologies: A Reader and Guide*. Oxford and New York: Oxford University Press.

Figes, E. (1970) *Patriarchal Attitudes*. Greenwich, CT: Fawcett.

Fox, W. (1990) *Towards a Transpersonal Ecology: Developing the Foundations for Environmentalism*. Boston, MA: Shambhala.

Freeden, M. (2004) *Ideology: A Very Short Introduction*. Oxford and New York: Oxford University Press.

Freeden, M., Sargent, L. T. and Stears, M. (eds) (2015) *The Oxford Handbook of Political Ideologies*. Oxford: Oxford University Press.

Friedan, B. (1963) *The Feminine Mystique*. New York: Norton.

Friedan, B. (1983) *The Second Stage*. London: Abacus (New York: Summit, 1981).

Friedman, D. (1973) *The Machinery of Freedom: Guide to a Radical Capitalism*. New York: Harper & Row.

Fromm, E. (1979) *To Have or To Be*. London: Abacus.

Fukuyama, F. (1989) 'The End of History?' *National Interest*, Summer.

Fukuyama, F. (1992) *The End of History and the Last Man*. Harmondsworth: Penguin.

Galbraith, J. K. (1992) *The Culture of Contentment*. London: Sinclair Stevenson.

Gellner, E. (1983) *Nations and Nationalism*. Oxford: Blackwell.

Giddens, A. (1994) *Beyond Left and Right: The Future of Radical Politics*. Cambridge: Polity Press.

Giddens, A. (1998) *The Third Way: The Renewal of Social Democracy*. Cambridge: Polity Press.

Gilmour, I. (1978) *Inside Right: A Study of Conservatism*. London: Quartet Books.

Godwin, W. ([1793] 1971) *Enquiry Concerning Political Justice*, ed. K. C. Carter. Oxford: Oxford University Press.

Goldman, E. (1969) *Anarchism and Other Essays*. New York: Dover.

Goldsmith, E., Allen, R. et al. (eds) (1972) *Blueprint for Survival*. Harmondsworth: Penguin.

Goodhart, D. (2004) 'The Discomfort of Strangers', *Prospect*, February.

Goodin, R. E. (1992) *Green Political Theory*. Oxford: Polity Press.

Gray, J. (1995) *Liberalism*, 2nd edn. Milton Keynes: Open University Press.

Greer, G. (1970) *The Female Eunuch*. New York: McGraw-Hill.

Greer, G. (1999) *The Whole Woman*. London: Doubleday.

Hardin, G. (1968) 'The Tragedy of the Commons', *Science*, vol. 162, pp. 1243–8.

Hearn, J. (2006) *Rethinking Nationalism: A Critical Introduction*. Basingstoke and New York: Palgrave Macmillan.

Heywood, L. and Drake, J. (eds) (1997) *Third Wave Agenda: Being Feminist, Doing Feminism*. Minneapolis, MN: University of Minnesota Press.

Hitler, A. ([1925] 1969) *Mein Kampf*. London: Hutchinson (Boston, MA: Houghton Mifflin, 1973).

Hobbes, T. ([1651] 1968) *Leviathan*, ed. C. B. Macpherson. Harmondsworth: Penguin.

Hobsbawm, E. (1983) 'Inventing Tradition', in E. Hobsbawm and T. Ranger (eds), *The Invention of Tradition*. Cambridge: Cambridge University Press.

Honderich, T. (2005) *Conservatism: Burke, Nozick, Bush, Blair?* London and Ann Arbor, MI: Pluto Press.

Huntington, S. (1996) *The Clash of Civilizations and the Remaking of World Order*. New York: Simon & Schuster.

Jost, J., Kruglanski, A. and Sulloway, F. (2003) 'Political Conservatism as Motivated Social Cognition', *Psychological Bulletin*, p. 129.

Kelly, P. (2005) *Liberalism*. Malden, MA and Cambridge: Polity Press.

Keynes, J. M. ([1936] 1963) *The General Theory of Employment, Interest and Money*. London: Macmillan (San Diego, CA: Harcourt Brace Jovanovich, 1963).

Kinna, R. (2009) *Anarchism: A Beginner's Guide*. Oxford: Oneworld Publications.

Kropotkin, P. ([1902] 1914) *Mutual Aid*. Boston, MA: Porter Sargent.

Kymlicka, W. ([1995] 2000) *Multicultural Citizenship*. Oxford: Oxford University Press.

Laclau, E. and Mouffe, C. (2014) *Hegemony and Socialist Strategy*. London: Verso.

Layard, R. (2011) *Happiness: Lessons from a New Science*. Harmondsworth and New York: Penguin Books.

Lenin, V. I. (1964) *The State and Revolution*. Peking: People's Publishing House.

Lenin, V. I. ([1916] 1970) *Imperialism, the Highest Stage of Capitalism*. Moscow: Progress Publishers.

Leopold, A. ([1948] 1968) *A Sand County Almanac*. Oxford: Oxford University Press.

Locke, J. ([1690] 1962) *Two Treatises of Government*. Cambridge: Cambridge University Press.

Lyotard, J.-F. (1984) *The Postmodern Condition: The Power of Knowledge*. Minneapolis, MN: University of Minnesota Press.

MacIntyre, A. (1981) *After Virtue*. London: Duckworth.

Macmillan, H. ([1938] 1966) *The Middle Way*. London: Macmillan.

Macpherson, C. B. (1973) *Democratic Theory: Essays in Retrieval*. Oxford: Clarendon Press.

Maistre, J. de ([1817] 1971) *The Works of Joseph de Maistre*, trans. J. Lively. New York: Schocken.

Marshall, P. (1995) *Nature's Web: Rethinking Our Place on Earth*. London: Cassell.

Marshall, P. (2007) *Demanding the Impossible: A History of Anarchism*. London: Fontana.

Marx, K. and Engels, F. (1968) *Selected Works*. London: Lawrence & Wishart.

Marx, K. and Engels, F. ([1846] 1970) *The German Ideology*. London: Lawrence & Wishart.

McLellan, D. (1995) *Ideology*, 2nd edn. Milton Keynes: Open University Press.

McLellan, D. (2007) *Marxism after Marx*, 4th edn. Basingstoke: Palgrave Macmillan.

Meadows, D. H., Meadows, D. L., Randers, D. and Williams, W. (1972) *The Limits to Growth*. London: Pan (New York: New American Library, 1972).

Mill, J. S. ([1869] 1970) *On the Subjection of Women*. London: Dent.

Mill, J. S. ([1859] 1972) *Utilitarianism, On Liberty, and Consideration on Representative Government*. London: Dent.

Millett, K. (1970) *Sexual Politics*. New York: Doubleday.

Mitchell, J. (1971) *Women's Estate*. Harmondsworth: Penguin.

Modood, T. (2013) *Multiculturalism*, 2nd edn. Cambridge, and Malden, MA: Polity Press.

Montesquieu, C. de ([1748] 1969) *The Spirit of Laws*. Glencoe, IL: Free Press.

More, T. ([1516] 1965) *Utopia*. Harmondsworth: Penguin (New York: Norton, 1976).

Moschonas, G. (2002) *In the Name of Social Democracy – The Great Transformation: 1945 to the Present*. London and New York: Verso.

Murray, C. (1984) *Losing Ground: American Social Policy: 1950–1980*. New York: Basic Books.

Naess, A. (1973) 'The Shallow and the Deep, Long-range Ecology Movement: A Summary', Inquiry, vol. 16.

Naess, A. (1989) *Community and Lifestyle: Outline of an Ecosophy*. Cambridge: Cambridge University Press.

Nozick, R. (1974) *Anarchy, State and Utopia*. Oxford: Blackwell (New York: Basic Books, 1974).

Oakeshott, M. (1962) *Rationalism in Politics and Other Essays*. London: Methuen (New York: Routledge Chapman & Hall, 1981).

O'Hara, K. (2011) *Conservatism*. London: Reaktion Books.

O'Sullivan, N. (1976) *Conservatism*. London: Dent, and New York: St Martin's Press.

Özkirimli, U. (2017) *Theories of Nationalism: A Critical Introduction*, 3rd edn. Basingstoke and New York: Palgrave Macmillan.

Paglia, C. (1990) *Sex, Art and American Culture*. New Haven, CT: Yale University Press.

Parekh, B. (2005) *Rethinking Multiculturalism: Cultural Diversity and Political Theory*, 2nd edn. Basingstoke and New York: Palgrave Macmillan.

Pettit, P. (1999) *Republicanism: A Theory of Freedom and Government*. Oxford: Oxford University Press.

Plato (1955) *The Republic*, trans. H. D. Lee. Harmondsworth: Penguin (New York: Random House, 1983).

Proudhon, P.-J. ([1851] 1923) *General Idea of Revolution in the Nineteenth Century*, trans. J. B. Robinson. London: Freedom Press.

Proudhon, P.-J. ([1840] 1970) *What Is Property?* trans. B. R. Tucker. New York: Dover.

Purkis, J. and Bowen, J. (eds) (2004) *Changing Anarchism: Anarchist Theory and Practice in a Global Age*. Manchester: Manchester University Press.

Rand, A. ([1943] 2007) *The Fountainhead*. London and New York: Penguin.

Rawls, J. (1970) *A Theory of Justice*. Oxford: Oxford University Press (Cambridge, MA: Harvard University Press, 1971).

Rothbard, M. (1978) *For a New Liberty*. New York: Macmillan.

Rousseau, J.-J. (2012) *The Social Contract and Discourse*, ed. G. D. H. Cole. London: Dent (Glencoe, IL: Free Press, 1969).

Ruthven, M. (2007) *Fundamentalism: A Very Short Introduction*. Oxford and New York: Oxford University Press.

Said, E. ([1978] 2003) *Orientalism*. Harmondsworth: Penguin.

Sandel, M. (1982) *Liberalism and the Limits of Justice*. Cambridge: Cambridge University Press.

Sassoon, D. (2013) *One Hundred Years of Socialism*. London: Fontana.

Schneir, M. (1995) *The Vintage Book of Feminism: The Essential Writings of the Contemporary Women's Movement*. London: Vintage.

Schumacher, E. F. (1973) *Small Is Beautiful: A Study of Economics as if People Mattered*. London: Blond & Briggs (New York: Harper & Row, 1989).

Scott-Dixon, K. (ed.) (2006) *Trans/Forming Feminism: Transfeminist Voices Speak Out*. Toronto: Canadian Scholars' Press.

Scruton, R. (2001) *The Meaning of Conservatism*, 3rd edn. Basingstoke: Macmillan.

Sen, A. (2006) *Identity and Violence*. London: Penguin.

Singer, P. (1976) *Animal Liberation*. New York: Jonathan Cape.

Singer, P. (1993) *Practical Ethics*, 2nd edn. Cambridge: Cambridge University Press.

Smiles, S. ([1859] 1986) *Self-Help*. Harmondsworth: Penguin.

Smith, A. ([1776] 1976) *An Enquiry into the Nature and Causes of the Wealth of Nations*. Chicago, IL: University of Chicago Press.

Smith, A. D. (1986) *The Ethnic Origins of Nations*. Oxford: Blackwell.

Sorel, G. ([1908] 1950) *Reflections on Violence*, trans. T. E. Hulme and J. Roth. New York: Macmillan.

Spencer, H. ([1884] 1940) *The Man versus the State*. London: Watts.

Spencer, P. and Wollman, H. (2002) *Nationalism: A Critical Introduction*. London and Thousand Oaks, CA: Sage.

Stirner, M. ([1845] 1971) *The Ego and His Own*, ed. J. Carroll. London: Cape.

Tawney, R. H. (1921) *The Acquisitive Society*. London: Bell (San Diego, CA: Harcourt Brace Jovanovich, 1955).

Taylor, C. (1994) *Multiculturalism and 'The Politics of Recognition'*. Princeton, NJ: Princeton University Press.

Taylor, C. (ed.) (1995) *Multiculturalism: Examining the Politics of Recognition*. Princeton, NJ: Princeton University Press.

Thoreau, H. D. (1983) *Walden and 'Civil Disobedience'*. Harmondsworth: Penguin.

United Nations (1972). See Ward and Dubois (1972).

Waldron, J. (1995) 'Minority Cultures and the Cosmopolitan Alternative', in W. Kymlicka (ed.), *The Rights of Minority Cultures*. London and New York: Open University Press.

Walters, M. (2005) Feminism: A Very Short Introduction. Oxford and New York: Oxford University Press.

Ward, B. and Dubois, R. (1972) Only One Earth. Harmondsworth: Penguin.

Wolf, N. (1994) Fire with Fire: The New Female Power and How to Use It. New York: Fawcett.

Wolff, R. P. (1998) In Defence of Anarchism, 2nd edn. Berkeley, CA: University of California Press.

Wollstonecraft, M. ([1792] 1967) A Vindication of the Rights of Woman, ed. C. W. Hagelman. New York: Norton.

Wright, A. (1996) Socialisms: Theories and Practices. Oxford and New York: Oxford University Press.

Index

Location references in **bold type** refer to illustrative material and on-page definitions.